W9-BMM-869

LAUGHTER OF APHRODITE

Aphrodite Holding a Seashell. From Ephesus.

LAUGHTER OF APHRODITE

Reflections on a Journey to the Goddess

CAROL P. CHRIST

HarperSanFrancisco
A Division of HarperCollins*Publishers*

To my father, John Anthony Christ,
who always told me I could do anything well
if I tried hard enough,

and to my mother, Janet Claire Bergman Christ,
who taught me in her own way
to love being a woman,

this book is dedicated in love and gratitude.

FIRST HARPER & ROW PAPERBACK EDITION PUBLISHED IN 1988

Library of Congress Cataloging-in-Publication Data

Christ, Carol P.
Laughter of Aphrodite.

Bibliography: p.
Includes index.
1. Women and religion. 2. Feminism—Religious aspects.
3. Christ, Carol P. 4. Spiritual life. 5. Aphrodite (Greek deity) I. Title.
BL458.C48 1987 291.2'088042 86-42999
ISBN 0-06-250146-1—CLOTH
ISBN 0-06-25147-X—PAPER

---

93 94 95 CWI 12 11 10 9 8 7 6

Contents

ACKNOWLEDGMENTS

Permission is gratefully acknowledged to quote from "Virginity O/ my virginity! . . ." and "You know the place: then," Mary Barnard, translator, *Sappho: A New Translation,* University of California Press. Copyright © 1958, 1986 Mary Barnard; lines from "Diving into the Wreck," in *Diving into the Wreck, Poems 1971-1972,* by Adrienne Rich, by permission of the author and W. W. Norton & Company, Inc. Copyright © 1973; from "Natural Resources," from *The Dream of a Common Language, Poems 1974-1977,* by Adrienne Rich, by permission of the author and W. W. Norton & Company, Inc. Copyright © 1978 and from Darlene Clark Hine.

Portions of this book have appeared, sometimes in slightly different form, in the following publications, which granted reprint permission:
"Roundtable Discussion: What are the Sources of My Theology?" *Journal of Feminist Studies in Religion* 1, no. 1 (1985); "The Initiation of an American Woman Scholar into the Symbols and Rituals of the Ancient Goddesses," *Journal of Feminist Studies in Religion* 3, no. 1 (1987); "Heretics and Outsiders: The Struggle Over Female Power in Western Religion," *Soundings* 3, no. 61 (1978); "Feminist Liberation and Yahweh as Holy Warrior," *Women's Spirit Bonding*, ed. Janet Kalven and Mary I. Buckley. Copyright © 1984 The Pilgrim Press, used by permission; "Rituals with Demeter and Persephone," *WomanSpirit* 10, no. 40 (1984); "A Religion for Women," *WomanSpirit* 7, no. 25 (1980); "Another Response to Religion for Women," *WomanSpirit* 6, no. 24 (1980); "Expressing Anger at God," *Anima* 5, no. 1 (1978); "Rituals with Aphrodite," *Anima* 12, no. 1 (1985); "Why Women Need the Goddess," *Heresies* no. 5 (1978); also printed in *Womanspirit Rising*, Carol P. Christ and Judith Plaskow, eds. Copyright © 1979 by Harper & Row, Publishers, Inc.; "Women's Liberation and the Liberation of God," Elizabeth Koltun, ed., *The Jewish Woman*. Copyright © 1976 by Schocken Books, Inc. Reprinted by permission of Schocken Books; "Symbols of Goddess and God in Feminist Theology," from *The Book of the Goddess: Past and Present,* Carl Olson, ed. Copyright © 1983 reprinted by permission of Crossroad Publishing Co.; "Finitude, Death, and Reverence for Life," *Semeia* 40 (1987).

Permission for photographs is gratefully acknowledged for: "Aphrodite holding a Seashell" and "Artemis of the Ephesians," photographs by Carol P. Christ, used by permission of the Ephesus Museum, Turkey; "The Horns of Consecration," photograph by Roger C. Robinson, used by permission; "And God Created Woman in Her Own Image," copyright © Ann Grifalconi, used by permission; "Double Goddesses," from *Çatal Hüyük*, by James Mellaart, used by permission acquisitions #61-14-1316, The University Museum, University of Pennsylvania, Philadelphia, PA., photograph courtesy of the University Museum, used by permission; "Astarte Holding Sacred Flowers," "Classical Bird or Snake Goddess," and "Crowned Snake Goddess" from *The Goddesses and Gods of Old Europe 6500-3500 B.C.*, University of California Press, 1982, used by permission of Marija Gimbutas; "Demeter holding Persephone on her Lap," photograph courtesy of Eleusis Museum, Greece, used by permission; "Goddesses and Priestesses with Sacred Trees," photograph by Nicolas Platon, used by permission; "Aphrodite's Temple at Mesa," photograph by Alexis Masters, used by permission.

List of Illustrations

The Horns of Consecration. Palace of Knossos, Crete.

Introduction: Finding the Voices of Feminist Thealogy

The earth is the source and being of the people, and we are equally the being of the earth. The land is not really a place, separate from ourselves, where we act out the drama of our isolate destinies.

—PAULA GUNN ALLEN

My theology, or rather thealogy[1], reflections on the meaning of Goddess, is rooted in my experience. Two intuitions nourish this thealogy. The first is that the earth is holy and our true home. The second is that women's experience, like all human experience, is a source of insight about the divine.

I have known since I was very young that the earth is holy. I continue to intuit the connections of my spirit to the spirits of all living things. Though it is harder to feel a part of what we call "nature" in an urban setting than it was when people lived closer to the land in rhythm with the seasons, it is possible and essential. Our categories separate "man" from "nature," denying the truth that "we are nature."[2] While walking in my urban neighborhood, I sense the wonder of spring flowers: magnolias, daffodils, the first roses. I return to my center hiking in the woods, near California bay laurels, when a black-tailed deer stops to gaze at me, or when I am swimming in the embrace of the Aegean sea. For me spirituality is experiencing connectedness to the life force within all living things. The knowledge that this earth could be destroyed with the press of a button or gradually poisoned to death by pollution fills me alternately with a sense of futility and urgency about my work.

My feelings about the earth spring from mystical experiences, both ordinary and extraordinary, that I have had with nature.[3] There are moments when my connection to a bird, a tree, the sun, a stream, seems undeniable. I have always understood what the

Jewish theologian Martin Buber meant when he spoke of having an "I-Thou" relationship with a tree or a piece of mica.[4] One morning I got up early to hike in Sonoma County, California. After climbing up and down a steep trail at dawn, I found myself standing beneath one of the oldest redwoods in the park, a tree more than one thousand years old. It soared above me, and its gnarled trunk was many times too large to circle with my arms. I lay down beneath the tree and looked up. The sun began to stream through its branches, light filtering through the dark canopy. After some time, a hummingbird landed above my head. I knew myself to be between the most fragile and most persistent life forms. I was at peace with myself and the world, the energy of the life forces renewing me. Native Americans have similar feelings about the California land. We can learn much from them. I believe a sense of the sacredness of the ground on which we stand is crucial to our surviving on this earth.

The second focus of my thealogy is the interpretation and celebration of women's experiences. When I was a girl I sensed the contradiction between my father's admonition that I could do anything well if I set my mind to it and worked very hard, and the lack of support for women's intelligence and creativity in our culture. This was reflected in my parents' expectation that my education would be used primarily for finding a husband and raising children. In graduate school this contradiction intensified as I realized there was (in the late sixties and early seventies) very little encouragement for a women who wanted to be both sexual and a scholar. The women's movement has given me a language for interpreting my experience and has affirmed that I am not crazy to want more than women of my generation were taught to want. As I became aware of the importance of role models and of the power of language and images, I became increasingly estranged from the Christian tradition.

In my quest to articulate my spiritual intuitions, I was drawn to the writings of contemporary women, which helped me name my experiences of the sacred. I interpreted their works as illustrations of women's spiritual quest in my book *Diving Deep and Surfacing*. Naomi Goldenberg was right when she said that I was treating women's writings as sacred texts.[5] More recently, my thealogy has been inspired by ancient Goddesses. Though I write about women's experiences and Goddesses, I do not deny the validity of men's experiences (when they are not deformed by patriarchal assumptions), nor do I deny that Goddess/God may *also* be imaged as male. I write of women's experiences and Goddesses for the simple reason that I write what I know.

Goddess symbolism unites two themes in my work: she is woman and she is nature. I have been fortunate to be able to help create and participate in rituals at the sites of the temple of Demeter and Persephone at Eleusis, the temple of Artemis at Ephesus, the temple of Aphrodite in Mesa, Lesbos, and at the cave called *Minerva's* by local Greeks in Eressos, Lesbos, the alleged birthplace of Sappho. The presence of the Goddess in these rituals at ancient sites of worship, and in others celebrated closer to home, has created connections spiraling back through time. Ancient Goddess traditions function for me as *a* (not *the*) source for my thealogy. I believe that Goddess images arose in cultures where women were not subordinate.[6] Certainly Goddesses were also worshiped in cultures that were patriarchal. I sort through the evidence that remains—reminding myself that so much has been lost, so much has been destroyed—seeking a glimpse of Goddess who is source and reflection of the strength and creativity of women.

But Goddess traditions are not normative for me in the way that Scripture and tradition have been normative for Christian theology, *halakah* and Scripture for Jewish thought. I judge everything I learn from the past on the basis on my own experience as shaped, named, and confirmed by the voices of my sisters. Out of our intuition, experience, and research, Goddess traditions are being created anew. If I could appeal to Scripture and tradition to justify what I know and write, I would feel less alone and vulnerable. I gain courage to write through affirmations that what is true for me is also true for others.

In *In Memory of Her*, Elisabeth Schüssler Fiorenza wrote that it is "ahistorical" for those of us born into Christianity and Judaism to think that we can do theology out of a context other than that shaped by the biblical traditions.[7] Though she does not argue this point in her book, Schüssler Fiorenza is challenging those of us who claim to be working as post-Christian or post-Jewish thealogians.

There is a very important sense in which Elisabeth Schüssler Fiorenza is correct in saying that we cannot escape our histories. Those of us who create post-traditional thealogy cannot avoid being influenced by the categories and questions posed in Christian and Jewish theologies. I imagine, for example, that to someone looking at our work from the standpoint of less God-obsessed traditions such as Buddhism, Confucianism, Native American, or African traditional religions, there is something that looks very Western in all feminist writing about the Goddess. We assume that religion is about deity, for example. And we view the Goddess through our Western biblical and theological notions about God. Even if we heed Christine Downing's warning to speak of "Goddesses," not *the* Goddess—a point that is intended to jolt us out of the monotheistic frame of reference[8]—I doubt that we will ever be able to say "Goddess" or "Goddesses" in a way that is entirely free of assumptions from or reactions to Jewish and Christian images and ideas about God. However, and here is where I disagree with Schüssler Fiorenza, to acknowledge a kind of intellectual and conceptual debt to Western biblical traditions is not the same as to acknowledge loyalty to those traditions.

My father's family was German and Irish Roman Catholic; my mother's, Swedish, German, Scotch, and English Christian Scientist. I was raised Presbyterian. The question of being faithful to my history is complex. While both my grandmothers were Christian, the traditions they came from were dissimilar from each other and from the one in which I was brought up. Part of my heritage is a great-grandmother who rejected the more traditional Christianity of her father and mother in favor of a faith healing religion developed by a woman. But she also eventually left Christian Science to follow another woman religious leader, a "Mother Mae" who founded a community in the Simi Valley in California, according to my mother. In another century my great-grandmother might have been burned as a heretic or a witch. While it may be ahistorical for Elisabeth Schüssler Fiorenza to write as anything other than a Christian theologian, this is not true in the same way for me.

Feminist theologians and thealogians note that theology reflects the experience of those who write it, and assert that feminist theology and thealogy must begin with *women's* experience. We began by pointing out that when traditional theologians talked about "human nature" or even "God" from a purportedly universal perspective, they were usually talking about the experiences of males. As the feminist critique has developed, black, Hispanic, Native American, Asian, and other feminists have pointed out that feminist theology is subject to a similar criticism. Feminist theologians have often talked about women's experience as if it were a universal category. We now understand that neither women's experience nor men's experience are universal categories. It makes a difference if we are white, black, Chicana, or Asian, if we are poor or middle class or rich, if we are lesbian or heterosexual or celibate, if we are educated or uneducated, if our backgrounds are European, European-American, African-American, Mexican-American, Asian-American, Indian, African, Japanese, or Chinese, if our traditions are Native American, Christian, Jewish, Muslim, Hindu, or Buddhist. So what does it mean to say that "thealogy and theology begin in experience"?

This book is thealogy from the perspective of a white, middle-class, well-educated, California-born, feminist who has Catholic-Christian Science-Presbyterian, Northern European-American roots. But these terms can be misleading. They do not encompass the love for Judaism that is part of my history, nor my passion for Greece, Italy, and France. They tell you nothing of how I am moved by art, poetry, and ritual, nor of how I am transformed when I swim in the Aegean sea from the rocky shore of a small village in Lesbos, Sappho's island. They do not tell you whom I have loved or why. Nor do they tell you of the concern for peace and survival that motivates me and drives me to despair. As I look at my writing, I see that I have always been struggling to tell my story, to show the relation of the way I think to the way I live. Though I write poetry from time to time, I have no desire to give up my work as a thealogian. My struggle and my task is to integrate my life and my work. This is not easy. My education has taught me that if "one" does not write in an objective voice she is not a scholar. So I have often felt that I had to disguise or remain silent about the passions that inspire my work.

To create thealogy out of women's experience, to reveal connections between our own experiences and our thealogies, involves a critique of the scholarly and theological traditions in which we have been trained. We need to insist that the work we do is scholarship, even if it does not look like the scholarship we have read before. When I think about thealogy and experience, two books by feminist thealogians come to mind: *The Goddess* by Christine Downing and *The Journey is Home* by Nelle Morton. Neither of these books seems to be what we have been taught to recognize as theology, though they may remind us of theological classics like Augustine's *Confessions* and Pascal's *Pensées*. Both Downing and Morton took enormous risks in their books, incorporating much of their stories into their thealogical explorations. It is easy to dismiss their works as overly personal; it is more difficult to understand how they ask us to expand our notions of what scholarship is. The same will be true of this book.

We have come far enough in our work to know that one woman's experiences are not identical with the experiences of all other women. But we have only begun to plumb the resonances between our experiences and those of other women. Sometimes it is precisely in our particularities, in what seem to be our differences, that we hear each other to speech.[9] Recently, at a conference on transforming the curriculum in the humanities, while listening to a very particular story told by one of the other speakers, the black woman historian Darlene Clark Hine, I felt myself moved to tears. Though her story is not my story in a literal sense, in another and deeper sense, it is my story.

One Sunday evening I received a telephone call. The woman on the other end of the line said, "Are you Darlene Clark Hine, the historian?" I answered, "Yes." "Well, we have a book for you to write. It's on the history of black women in Indiana." I responded, "But I don't know anything about the history of black women in Indiana. I'm a historian. That's not how we do things." The woman continued, "We have the sources for you, we've spent over a year collecting them. You are going to write this book for us." "But I can't. It would take me years to research it. I have other projects. You don't understand how historians work." "I understand that you're going to write this book for us. You're the only black woman historian in Indiana. You're the only one who can write this book. Do you think you got to be a professor at Purdue on your own merits alone? No, you have the job because we went to jail. You're going to write this book for us." And I did.[10]

While listening to Darlene Clark Hine, many thoughts went

through my mind. One was that black women are more forthright than white women. I could not imagine my mother calling anyone up and asking to have her history written. And yet I recognized in that black woman's plea and Darlene Clark Hine's response the responsibility shared by all of us who work in women's studies. We all write for other women, for women who need to have their stories told, for women who will be empowered by the stories we tell. I was reminded of being confronted about my responsibility to my "spiritual daughters" at Eleusis, a story I tell later in this book and which I shared with Darlene Clark Hine that day.

As feminist thea- and theologians, we are challenged to name in more explicit ways that most of us have done the personal sources of our understandings of women's experiences and of our theo- and thealogical visions. Not only will this make our work richer and more interesting, but also more true to the insights from which feminist thealogy begins. If we are explicit about, and allow our readers to know, the personal sources of our work, then I think we will be less likely to make false and misleading generalizations. We can speak of the experience of Christian, Jewish, or post-traditional women, or of black, white, Hispanic, or Asian women, rather than writing simply of "women's" experience, as if it were a Platonic form. Thus we may avoid making the same kind of mistake traditional theologians have made when they discussed "man." If we are more clear about why we each think the way we do, we may be less likely to label or dismiss or misunderstand the work of other feminists whose work comes from different histories.

This presents a radical challenge to the myth of objectivity that shapes the norms of scholarship under which we often function and are judged. Though the notion that scholarship is objective has been criticized in continental critical and hermeneutical and other theories, much radical feminist scholarship continues to be dismissed as biased, polemical, limited, or confessional. This may be especially true in the field of religious studies, which has only recently established its academic legitimacy through appeal to the ideal of objectivity. I can hear choruses of criticism of this book saying "reductionistic," "self-indulgent," "narcissistic." Let me state very clearly that I do not propose to "reduce" thealogy to autobiography. I do not propose that we abandon historical research, philosophical reflection, literary analysis, or any of the other scholarly methods we have inherited. I ask only that we abandon the pretension to objectivity. Incorporating personal reflection into our work does not mean that our work becomes solipsistic. I propose that empathy, not objectivity, is the way out of solipsism. As scholars we should strive to constantly remember that we are grounded in particular experiences and histories, while seeking ever to expand the range of our empathy, our ability to imagine the perspectives of others.[11]

However, this may have radical consequences for the form of our work. We may begin, as I did in *Diving Deep and Surfacing*, by adding personal reflection as a preface to our work, or by moving back and forth between personal and impersonal voices as I do in this book, but I think that eventually the form of our work will have to change. I am reminded of a conversation that took place one summer at a taverna in Lesbos, the birthplace of Sappho, between a Greek-American woman poet who is doing historical research on Greek women's resistance to fascism, an Israeli woman professor of psychology who confessed to writing short stories under a pseudonym, and myself, who has found the boundaries between the scholarly, the personal, and the poetic breaking down in my work. The three of us spoke in different ways about what draws each of us to both scholarship and to more personal, poetic, and narrative forms. We spoke of our desires to integrate the two impulses in our work and of our fears that our scholarship would be discounted if we did not write in the "objective" voice. Through our conversation I became convinced that feminist scholars are moving toward the creation of new forms of writing. It may be frightening, but it is also exciting, for we all know how deadly much traditional scholarship has become.

I believe we must risk writing personally if we are to be true to what we know at the deepest levels of our being and to the insights with which we create feminist theology. This means that we will be drawn to write about our spirituality, our sexuality, our connections to each other and to the earth, our joy, our pain, our fears, our hopes, our dreams and longings, our visions.

I would like to thank my friends and colleagues, especially Naomi Goldenberg, Judith Plaskow, Mara Keller, Karen Brown, Alexis Masters, Carmen Torres, Christine Downing, Elisabeth

Schüssler Fiorenza, Susan Setta, Susan Brooks Thistlethwaite, Sallie McFague, Ellen Umansky, Anne Barstow, Ruby Rohrlich, Dorothy Austin, Starhawk, Charlene Spretnak, Hallie Iglehart, Z Budapest, Carol Lee Sanchez, Fanny Rinn, Arlene Jackson, Mardy Binter, Diane Schaffer, Lily Cincone, and Judy Mings, and my students at San Jose State University, the Graduate Theological Union, and the Aegean Women's Studies Institute, especially Caroll Blank and Rainbow, for their confidence in and support of my work. Thanks also to Roger Robinson for being there through so much of the writing of this book. Ellen Boneparth founded the Aegean Women's Studies Institute, which brought me to Greece and changed my life. My Greek and expatriate friends have made my times in Greece joyful. Marie Cantlon's imaginative and sensitive suggestions greatly improved the conception and final form of this book. Stacey Kabat miraçulously appeared in the fall of 1986 to offer much appreciated help with the final stages of preparation of the manuscript. A fellowship from the National Endowment for the Humanities in 1981–1982 and a sabbatical from San Jose State University in the spring of 1984 provided time for writing.

Carol P. Christ
Mithimna, Lesbos, Spring, 1986

NOTES

Epigraph: Paula Gunn Allen, *The Sacred Hoop: Recovering the Feminine in American Indian Tradition* (Boston: Beacon Press, 1986), 119.

1. From the Greek *thea*, meaning Goddess, a term coined by Naomi Goldenberg.
2. Susan Griffin, *Women and Nature: The Roaring Inside Her* (New York: Harper & Row, 1978), 226; also see chapter 12.
3. See Carol P. Christ, *Diving Deep and Surfacing: Women Writers on Spiritual Quest*, 2d ed. (Boston: Beacon Press, 1986), 19–23.
4. Martin Buber, *I and Thou*, trans. Walter Kaufman (New York: Charles Scribners Sons, 1970).
5. Naomi R. Goldenberg, *Changing of the Gods: Feminism and the End of Traditional Religions* (Boston: Beacon Press, 1979), 120.
6. See my article, "Toward a Paradigm Shift in the Academy and Religious Studies," in *The Impact of Feminist Research in the Academy*, ed. Christie Farnham (Bloomington: University of Indiana Press, 1987); also see chapter 10 of this book.
7. Elisabeth Schüssler Fiorenza, *In Memory of Her: A Feminist Theological Reconstruction of Christian Origins* (New York: Crossroad Press, 1983), xviii–xix.

8. Christine Downing, *The Goddess: Mythological Representations of the Feminine* (New York: Crossroad Press, 1984), 24.
9. See Nelle Morton, *The Journey Is Home* (Boston: Beacon Press, 1985), 16–18.
10. In a lecture at the symposium "Incorporating Women and Cultural Pluralism into the Curriculum," University of North Carolina at Charlotte, January 24–26, 1985. The title of the book is *When the Truth Is Told: A History of Black Women's Culture and Community in Indiana, 1875–1950* (Indianapolis: National Council of Negro Women, Indianapolis Section, 1985).
11. See "Toward a Paradigm Shift in the Academy and Religious Studies"; also see Evelyn Fox Keller, *Reflections on Gender and Science* (New Haven: Yale University Press, 1985).

I. DIALOGUES WITH GOD AND TRADITION

And God Created Woman in Her Own Image, by Ann Grifalconi.

Dialogues with God and Tradition

The shape of a cave, we say, the shape of a labyrinth. The way we came here was dark. Space seemed to close in on us. We thought we could not move forward. We had to shed our clothes.

—SUSAN GRIFFIN

The essays in this section were written during a time in which I moved from understanding myself as a Christian in dialogue with the God of Jewish and Christian traditions to becoming an active participant in the emerging Goddess movement. The reasons I left the church are complex.

When I was becoming a feminist and beginning to question the patriarchalism of the biblical traditions, I was also engaged in a struggle with the holocaust theology of Elie Wiesel. Wiesel's work spoke deeply to me because his understanding of God, like my own, was deeply shaped by the Hebrew Bible. Wiesel led me to question biblical theology's faith that God acts in history and forced me to acknowledge the roots of anti-Judaism in Christianity. I left the church not only because I concluded that patriarchy was deeply rooted in Christianity's core symbolism of God the Father and Son, but also because I could no longer believe that God acts in history, nor could I affiliate myself with a religious tradition containing the seeds of the anti-Judaism that resulted in the death of millions of Jews in the Nazi concentration camps. I share the story of my struggle with God and tradition on these issues not only because they are an important background to the essays in this section, but also because I believe that my struggles with the God of tradition reflect issues that cannot be ignored by anyone who thinks seriously about religion in the twentieth century.

In the spring in 1969 when I was a teaching assistant in a religion and literature class at Yale University, someone said to me, "Since you are interested in religion and literature, you really ought to read *The Gates of the Forest* by Elie Wiesel; it is a novel with religious themes." That summer, I picked up a copy of the book in the Harvard Coop. I was in no way prepared for Wiesel's story of Gregor, a young Jewish boy from Eastern Europe sent to the forest to hide from the Nazis, his struggle to understand the death of so many Jews, his anger at God, his determination to comprehend the laughter of Gavriel, the "angel" he met in the forest. Before I began reading *The Gates of the Forest,* I had never been told in a way I could understand about the Nazi death camps. I have a fleeting image of having seen a film on the concentration camps in freshman "civ," but it didn't affect me deeply. I had no illusions about the goodness of human nature or historical progress (having written papers on Conrad and Nietzsche in my freshman year), but I had little concept of the war towards the end of which I had been conceived. Reading *The Gates of the Forest* changed my life.

In college the focus of my studies had been the Hebrew Bible. My favorite theologians were Martin Buber, most of whose books I had read, and Abraham Heschel, who had spoken at Stanford when I was there. I loved studying the Hebrew texts, which, I felt, brought me closer to the God of Israel, the God of Exodus and the Hebrew prophets, whom I believed was the God of Christianity as well. The God whom Wiesel addressed and questioned in *The Gates of the Forest* was my God. Wiesel's struggle to understand God's relationship to the holocaust became my struggle. I understood Jews as well as Christians to be the special, the chosen, people of God. I believed the promises of God expressed in the Hebrew Bible in the covenantal formula, "I will take you for my people, and I will be your God" (Exod. 6:7).* For me the power of the Hebrew people's relation to God, which I believed to be extended but not superseded in the Christian covenant, was that it existed in this world, in history, in the daily and social lives of the people of Israel, and it was a personal relation of caring, concern, and mutual responsibility. In graduate school as I became deeply involved in the antiwar movement and the movements against poverty and racism, it seemed to me that the God of Israel and of Jesus was engaged in these struggles too. I understood these movements to be about establishing the justice of God in the world.

*This and subsequent biblical quotations, unless noted otherwise, are from the Revised Standard Version of the Bible. "Yahweh" is substituted for "the LORD" in most cases.

The Gates of the Forest begins with the laughter of Gavriel, a figure who comes to Gregor in the night in the cave where he is hiding, waiting for his father who never returns for him. Gavriel, whose name means "Angel of God" or "Man of God," is a mythic figure in the story. Gavriel exchanges names with Gregor, and Gregor's search for Gavriel, for the man, for his laughter, for the meaning of his name, becomes one of the threads of Wiesel's story.

Imagine a life-and-death struggle between two angels, the angel of love and the angel of wrath, the angel of promise and the angel of evil. Imagine that they both attain their ends, each one victorious. Imagine the laugh that would rise above their corpses as if to say, your death has given me birth; I am the soul of your conflict, its fulfillment as well.[1]

The day I read *The Gates of the Forest,* the laughter of Gavriel entered into my bones. I found myself laughing out loud and put the book down. I laughed for hours and hours. All my private, personal suffering during my first two years in graduate school flashed before my eyes and was dissolved in laughter. I saw myself in the office of the professor with whom I had come to study Hebrew Bible and heard him dismiss my interest in Hebrew poetry, saying, "Miss Christ, why did you come to this program, why didn't you go into Comp. Lit.?" And then I began to laugh, saying to myself, "And you cared what he said? And you thought you were no good just because he did not appreciate what you were saying?" I was engulfed in laughter again. "How silly you were," I said to myself laughing again. I pictured myself in my room sobbing over the man I had loved, who had abruptly broken off our relationship. And I said to myself, "And you sobbed for months about *that*?" I couldn't stop laughing. I realized that I had created much of my own suffering because I had given men, many of whom I did not even like, power over my life. I knew that my suffering was not Wiesel's suffering, but I felt closely bonded to him, and I knew I would read the rest of his books and write about his stories. When I finally stopped laughing because a friend was coming over, I felt transformed. I tried to explain to my friend what had happened, but he didn't understand.

Though I have never forgotten that day and have always viewed what happened as a kind of spiritual experience, I have not written about it before, because it seemed so personal, because people usually do not think of laughter as a spiritual experience. Recently, after writing about the laughter of Aphrodite, which I experienced in Lesbos, I began to think about the laughter of Gavriel again. I now understand that laughter can be the mediator of transformation. Gavriel's laughter, like Aphrodite's, enabled me to distance myself from pain, opening a new perspective on my life.

From the summer of 1969 to the spring of 1974 when I finished my Ph.D. thesis, "Elie Wiesel's Stories: Still the Dialogue," the question of God's relation to the holocaust was never far from my mind. Like others, I often found myself paralyzed, unable to write, wondering what I, who had never suffered as holocaust victims had suffered, could possibly have to say about Wiesel's work. Confronting the holocaust shattered the faith I had in the God of the Jewish and Christian people, the God of history. I agreed with Wiesel that if God had the power to act in history, then he should have acted during the holocaust. With Wiesel, I was angry with God for abandoning his promises to the Jewish people and, like Wiesel, I knew that anger is a form of relationship. I agreed with Wiesel that nothing the Jewish people might have done or not done could have justified the suffering and death they were forced to endure. The suffering of six million was different in magnitude than the suffering of one on a cross. I remember talking about my interest in Wiesel to one of my professors later that year. He invoked the cross and dismissed my questions by saying that he didn't think the holocaust raised any particular problems for Christian theology. I was appalled and for a time silenced. But with Wiesel, I continued to question the God whom I had been taught was both just and powerful. In the end I came to agree with Wiesel that either God is not just or he is not powerful. Wiesel's enigmatic statement at the end of *The Gates of the Forest* that when Gregor said the Kaddish, "He prayed for the soul of his father and also for that of God"[2] fascinated me. Wiesel seemed to be implying that human beings had the responsibility to redeem the soul of a God who had forgotten his promises to us.

My questions to God about the holocaust were intensified as I began to realize that if God were both powerful and just, then he also needed to be questioned about his role in the oppression of women throughout patriarchal history, a subject I have written about in the chapters that follow.

An even more serious challenge to my faith in the God of Jewish and Christian traditions came as I became aware of the role of Christian anti-Judaism in creating a climate in which in the holocaust could occur. In the second part of *The Gates of the Forest,* Wiesel's character Gregor is left alone in the forest after Gavriel gives himself up to the Nazi soldiers who are looking for Jews. He flees to the home of his family's former servant, Maria, a Christian, who shelters him, using the ruse that he is a deaf-mute to divert the suspicion that his Jewish accent might raise. The people in Maria's village imagine Gregor to be an innocent and, thinking that he can neither hear nor understand them, confess their sins to him. Unconsciously they make him their scapegoat, the repository of their sin and guilt, when they insist that he play the role of Judas, the betrayer of Christ, in their annual enactment of the passion play. Though the villagers do not know that Gregor is a Jew, Wiesel's point is clear: the villagers are doing what Christians have been doing for centuries, projecting their own feelings of sin and guilt, inspired by the figure of a crucified God, onto Judas and the Jewish people. As Wiesel writes, "[Judas] is the victim; not Jesus; he is the crucified; not Christ."[3] A crucified God and an imperfect humanity, Wiesel says, will inevitably lead to such projections, for humanity cannot bear the burden of responsibility for having crucified God. Wiesel makes it clear that the New Testament account of the passion of Christ contains the seeds of the persecution of the Jewish people that have been sown throughout Christian history.

In some ways Wiesel's indictment of Christianity for its role in the holocaust was more devasting to me than his indictment of God. Wiesel's indictment of God was a questioning that occurred within an ongoing relationship with the only God Wiesel or I knew. His indictment of Christianity was from the outside, and increasingly I felt estranged from Christianity. If God was powerless to act or for some reason chose not to act to save the Jewish people, God's person and his motives, like those of all persons, remained mysterious. Though I could never naively trust the biblical God again, I, like Wiesel, could still yearn for him to reveal his power and glory, or at least his presence. But if the Christian Scripture itself contained the seeds of the holocaust, how could I participate in the community that preached it? I began to read further about Christian anti-Judaism. Three of the many books I read during this time stand out in my memory: Richard Rubenstein's *After Auschwitz*,[4] Rosemary Radford Ruether's *Faith and Fratricide*,[5] and Gregory Baum's *Is the New Testament Anti-Semitic?*.[6] Ruether and Baum, both Catholic theologians, presented convincing evidence of the anti-Judaism within the New Testament. Ruether's argument that anti-Judaism is the "left hand" of Christology was frightening. The more Jesus is preached as Messiah, as Savior of all humanity, she argued, the more necessary it is to find fault with the Jews for not accepting him. On the whole, Ruether's book was more convincing to me than Baum's. For while Ruether admitted that anti-Judaism, both implicit and explicit, permeated the Christian preaching about Jesus in the New Testament and in later theology, Baum argued that anti-Judaism, though found in the New Testament, could be separated from the essential Christian message. Baum later came to agree with Ruether, as he wrote in the introduction to her book.[7] It became clear to me that the passion story, which is read during the Easter celebration, Christianity's most sacred ritual, could not be separated from condemnation of those who, given a chance, did not recognize the savior. Richard Rubenstein's account of his conversation with Dean Heinrich Grüber, a German Protestant who resisted the Nazis, provided a concrete example of the struggle and final inability of a good Christian to come to terms with the holocaust without attempting to justify it theologically.[8] The Christian Bible encourages justifications of Jewish suffering, and it seemed to me that unless Christians stopped reading from the Bible at Easter, they would continue to perpetuate its ideology. It did not seem likely to me that Christianity would give up the biblical passion stories and the symbolism embedded in them. I realized that I could no longer participate in Easter services, which with their powerful symbolism of life and death had once held great meaning for me.

Yet even confronting all this did not fully destroy my faith in the biblical God. The Hebrew Bible had always been more important for me than the New Testament as a revelation of God. I had often thought of myself as more Jewish than Christian, though I had never seriously considered converting to Judaism. Jesus had not figured strongly in my religious imagination. It would not have been easy, but I might have been able to give up Jesus as the Christ while still maintaining my dialogue with the God of the Hebrew Bible.

But reading further in *After Auschwitz,* I had to confront Richard Rubenstein's assertion that the notion of Christians as a chosen people redeemed in Christ (and all others as ignorant or guilty of rejecting Christ) was rooted in the Hebrew Bible's notion of Jews as a chosen people. If one was to reject the Christian version of particularism, which had proven murderous to the Jews, then one could not, Rubenstein argued, maintain the Jewish notion of a special relationship with God.[9] Though I had not thought of my understanding of God as negatively particularistic, I had to admit that I had always been drawn to the Hebrew Bible's notion of a special relationship with the God of the universe. I had understood this relationship to confer responsibilities on the people of God, ultimately issuing in the judgment of God against his people expressed in the prophetic writings. God expected his people to "do justice" as well as to walk "uprightly with their God." Rubenstein convinced me that not only the Christian but also the Jewish notion of choseness was pernicious. I was stunned.

At this time in my life I did not have an active relationship with a Christian community. While in New Haven I had continued to find solace in the Catholic Church and community among those who attended the Sunday evening folk mass, despite my growing estrangement from the patriarchal language of the Bible and liturgy. When I moved to New York in the summer of 1972, I did not seek out a church. Perhaps if I had been participating in a Christian community at the time I was working on my dissertation and entering deeply into questioning God and tradition, I would have found a way to ask my questions within the tradition. Instead, the questions I was asking seemed to make it more and more difficult for me to call myself a Christian. At the time I was struggling with these questions, Mary Daly's *Beyond God the Father* was published. Her argument that the Christian tradition was patriarchal at its very core, and that it was foolish to think that this core could change,[10] was convincing to me and paralleled my emerging views about the impossibility of overcoming Christian anti-Judaism. For me religion is constituted by the central symbols it evokes in prayer and ritual. Though I knew that there were Christians who shared my desire to change the anti-Judiac and patriarchal symbolism of Christianity, this was not sufficient for me. If I participated in Christian ritual (even while silently and through my writing dissenting from the implications of biblical stories and symbolism), it seemed to me that I was participating in the perpetuation of anti-Judaism and sexism.

When I was teaching at Columbia University, I heard about a special service of affirmation of several of the Episcopalian women priests who had been ordained by Bishops Robert L. DeWitt, Daniel Corrigan, and Edward Welles, despite their church's refusal to approve the ordination of women to the priesthood. Though I felt very much estranged from Christianity, I greatly admired the courage of the women priests and felt drawn to join them in affirmation of their victory over the patriarchal church in a service held at Riverside Church just down the street from where I was living. I went alone and sat near the back of the church. When the women priests walked in singing "A Mighty Fortress Is Our God," I could not raise my voice to join in their triumphal procession. Though I recognized this hymn written by Martin Luther as a sort of Protestant national anthem, its militarism and patriarchalism offended me. No attempt had been made to soften its language. When a male priest ascended the pulpit and began to speak about salvation through Christ, unconsciously affirming both the patriarchalism and anti-Judaism I had come to reject in Christianity, my body tensed with the anger I felt, the words I could not speak. Though I imagined that the women priests felt that their presence as priests alone was as much challenge as the church could take at the time, I could not join in affirming their ordination into such a church. I left the church and have not been back since.

"Women's Liberation and the Liberation of God" and "Expressing Anger at God" reflect my growing estrangement from traditional Christian worship and theology within the framework of an ongoing dialogue with the God of biblical tradition. Both are deeply embedded in biblical imagery and patterns and reflect the influence of Wiesel on my thinking and spirituality. They demonstrate my appropriation for feminist theology of the Jewish paradigm of expressing anger at God. As Irene Fine has noted, these essays are feminist *midrashim*, an attempt to find one's place in the history of one's people through a struggle with central themes and imagery, resulting in a new telling of its stories.[11]

These essays also reflect my understanding and appropriation of narrative or story theology as it was then emerging in the works of such thinkers as Stephen Crites and Michael Novak. According to this theory, religion is not primarily defined by theology, the statements we make about the great power or powers of the universe, but rather it is revealed in the stories we tell about our lives, in the way in which our stories reflect our orientation to the great power or powers that shape and bind our lives.[12] Though I no longer define my life through Jewish and Christian stories, I remain convinced of the validity of story theology. These essays, as well as my book *Diving Deep and Surfacing*, express my continuing effort to write thealogy out of the stories of our lives.

At the time I wrote those essays, I had no knowledge of the presence of the Goddess in contemporary women's spiritual quests, no understanding of the powerful history and prehistory of the Goddesses in the ancient world. My dissatisfaction with the tradition took the form of a dialogue with the only God I knew. Rereading the essays, I am struck by the powerful anger they express and by the transformative power the expression of my anger at God has had in my life. Expressing anger at anyone, let alone at God, has never been easy for me. It took me years of therapy to realize that unexpressed anger was paralyzing. My therapist encouraged me to express anger at others when I felt it rather than keeping it bottled up. The sisterhood of the women's movement gave me permission to express anger at the patriarchal society that had thwarted and crippled me. But without the influence of Elie Wiesel and Jewish tradition, I would have never thought of expressing my anger to God, nor have had the courage to confront him. It would have been simpler to blame patriarchal tradition, but not God, for my oppression, for the oppression of women. And yet the God I knew within biblical tradition was a living God, a God of history, a God who was passionately engaged in the lives of his people, both individually and collectively. If I had not confronted him directly, I might never have heard the still small voice that came to me in the night, when I discovered the female

God as a living presence in my life. In *From Housewife to Heretic*, Sonia Johnson described a similar experience of the liberating power that came from expressing her anger at God.[13]

Jewish and Christian feminist theologians sometimes blame the patriarchy within their religions on androcentric traditions, which have obscured the revelation of a God beyond gender who calls us to establish the full equality of women and men. I do not believe a God alleged to act in history and especially in the history of the people of God can be absolved of responsibility for participation in the patriarchal history of the synagogues, the churches, the world. I believe that women and men need to confront this God of patriarchal history and call this God to account. What will emerge for others from such a dialogue remains to be seen.

"Heretics and Outsiders" was written for a symposium on canon and tradition held at the University of Tennessee. In it, I had the opportunity to address the broad issue of canon as well as the specific issue of canon in Christian and Jewish traditions. When I wrote it, I was teaching in the humanities program at Columbia University where we read the "great books" of Western culture from Homer to Dostoevsky, all written by men. Like other good students of Western history (humanities had been my college major), I had assumed that the "great books" we studied were preserved and taught simply because they reflected the highest values of humanity. When I reread *The Iliad* in light of my feminist and antiwar convictions, I was appalled to discover that the "first" great work of Western culture celebrated rape and war. Though it is arguable that *The Iliad* questions the "honor" to be gained through these two endeavors, it does not clearly condemn them, nor does it suggest alternative conceptions of heroism.[14] This insight led me to question the notion that the canon reflects self-evidently "great" works of humankind. Were the great books preserved and taught because they were "great" by some abstract standard, or because they served the interests of a particular kind of society?

In "Heretics and Outsiders" I questioned the related notion that the Christian and Jewish canons contained the highest distillation of religious insight in the Western world. This essay was conceived shortly after my revelation that "God is a woman like yourself" had been confirmed through my participation in the emerging Goddess movement while on sabbatical in California. The power I found in the Goddess movement inspired me to begin to read about Goddess history and to look critically at the involvement of Judaism and Christianity in the suppression of Goddess symbolism and female religious leadership. Merlin Stone's *When God Was A Woman* opened my eyes to dimensions of the Bible and Christian history that I had never previously noticed or understood. Though I had written my senior thesis on "Nature Imagery in Hosea and Second Isaiah," translating the texts from the Hebrew and pondering them in depth, I had never read Hosea's polemic against "idolatry" as anything other than an abstract campaign against sinfulness. Stone's work enabled me to see that those who worshiped on every high hill and under every green tree might well have been worshiping Asherah, a Goddess often identified with trees, and that Hosea's wife, "wayward" Gomer, may not have been a prostitute but rather a priestess engaging in sacred rituals. This was a revelation, to me, because I had always naively assumed that the biblical canon, like the classical canon, reflected the highest values of humanity. In "Heretics and Outsiders," I argued that the process of canon formation in the religious traditions of the West was a political process in which some religious ideas and practices once considered orthodox or at least acceptable were deemed heresy or abomination. In this essay I focused on the suppression of Goddesses and female power within Jewish and Christian history. In so doing, I challenged the apologetic argument that the God of the Hebrew and Greek (Jewish and Christian) Bibles was imaged as male because there were no other models available in the cultures in which the biblical texts arose. I argued to the contrary that Goddess traditions were alive and well not only in the nonbiblical religious traditions of the ancient Near East and Hellenistic world, but also *within* the religion of Israel and Judah prior to the exile and *within* the early Christian religion. These traditions did not die a natural death because they no longer spoke to people. They were suppressed and their memory obliterated by self-proclaimed champions of what came to be known as orthodoxy.

To understand that our traditions have a history, and that the decisions made within those histories were not always in the best interests of women, gives us freedom with regard to the traditions we have inherited. For example, it might be argued that knowledge of Goddess worship in ancient Hebrew religion be used as a warrant to reintroduce Goddess worship and even polytheism into contemporary Jewish practice. Or that knowledge of Gnostic Christians' worship of God as Mother or Goddess and a trinity composed of Mother, Father, and Child, could justify similar images in contemporary Christian worship. But the issues raised in this essay are not easily resolved within Judaism or Christianity. It has been argued that the Bible and later Jewish tradition and not ancient Hebrew practice has formed and must continue to form the basis of Judaism.[15] Or that the church's gradual consensus against the so-called Gnostics and the orthodox doctrine of the trinity rule out Goddess symbolism within Christianity. On the other hand, as feminists begin to consider radical reconstructions of religious history, such as that proposed by Elisabeth Schüssler Fiorenza, the reclaiming the Goddess history within the traditions ought to be considered as well. There is no reason that Christian or Jewish feminists must accept the "orthodox consensus" on the Goddess any more than they have accepted the "orthodox consensus" on women's religious leadership. And if, as I suspect, these issues are related, it is not optional but imperative that Jewish and Christian feminists reflect upon the worship of Goddesses that occurred within the history of the traditions they claim.

"A Spirituality for Women," was written in response to two critiques of the Goddess movement published in Christian journals by feminist Christian theologian Rosemary Radford Ruether.[16] At the time I wrote this essay, I felt very much alone. As one of the few academic feminists who had openly embraced Goddess spirituality, I was aware that many of my good friends and most respected colleagues not only were reaffirming their commitment to work within their traditions, but also were finding the Goddess movement dangerous and disturbing. It was becoming clear that the churches and seminaries that control much of the hiring in the field of religious studies were not about to hire anyone who openly advocated the Goddess movement. This essay reflects the anger, the hurt, and the defensiveness I felt in being called upon to justify a spiritual tradition I had found enormously powerful but was only beginning to explore. That *Christianity and*

Crisis, after accepting my response to Ruether, eventually declined to publish it, increased the sense of isolation I felt.

In "A Spirituality for Women" I try to explain how an intelligent, theologically trained feminist could reject the Christian tradition in which she was raised in favor of an emerging Goddess spirituality movement claiming roots in ancient traditions. I point out that the reasons each of us has for continuing to work within inherited traditions or leaving them are complex and not reducible to intellectual, logical argument. I go on to discuss three areas that I see as problematic within Christian feminist theology.

The first is the publicly proclaimed male God symbolism of the Bible and liturgy. Though feminists continue to experiment with changing the language of the Bible and liturgy, the worship of God the Father and King still continues even in the most liberal congregations. Feminist ministers, rabbis, and theologians say that radical changes in language for God simply are not possible in most churches and synagogues, and that to insist upon this issue would alienate them from their congregations. Even *An Inclusive Language Lectionary,* which uses gender neutral and optional female language[17] has met with a great deal of resistance, demonstrating that for many Christians, male-genderized symbols of God as Father, Lord, and King are intrinsic to their faith.

Second, I begin to explain why I find the prophetic-messianic tradition that has been adopted by Ruether and liberation theologians, including feminist liberation theologians, inadequate for feminist theology. I find it ironic that feminist theologians have adopted the prophets, who were instrumental in extinguishing the worship of the Goddesses within Hebrew religion and were advocates of the exclusive form of monotheism that has led to violent suppression of opposing views in Jewish and Christian histories. I continue to develop my critique of the prophetic tradition in the next chapter in this section, "Yahweh as Holy Warrior."

In the following part of "A Spirituality for Women," I discuss Ruether's criticisms of the Goddess movement. Ruether continues to allege that ancient Goddess traditions, like the Jewish and Christian traditions, are patriarchal.[18] Though this is true for the Goddess traditions in the Near East and ancient Mediterranean world that Ruether continually cites, it is unlikely that this was true of the prehistoric Goddess traditions of these same areas. I develop my interpretation of Goddess history more fully in "Reclaiming Goddess History" in the next section of this book.

In the final section of this essay, I discuss the difficult issues of nature and culture and separatism in the Goddess movement. These issues are explored further in "Finitude, Death, and Reverence for Life" and "Reclaiming Goddess History." It is my view that the relation of nature and culture must be redefined in less dualistic ways. I do not believe it is the goal of the feminist spirituality movement to reject culture in favor of nature, but given the dualistic language we have inherited, it is difficult to conceptualize the relationship of nature and culture differently.

Ruether was certainly not wrong to notice separatist tendencies in the Goddess movement as in the women's movement generally in the late 1970s. The Goddess movement has been inspired by strong lesbian voices, such as that of Z Budapest, who advocates "Dianic" practice in groups for women only. But the Goddess movement as a whole has never been strictly separatist, any more than the women's movement has been. Just as women who continued to relate to men found the women-only space of the consciousness-raising group liberating, so too, many women who continue to relate to men as fathers, sons, brothers, and lovers have found that they could more freely express their spiritual insights and visions in groups for women only. This does not mean that we envision men as spiritually inadequate, nor that we imagine them only as sons of the Great Mother. It is interesting to note that as feminist Christian women begin to advocate Woman-Church[19] and "feminist base communities," and Jewish women meet in women's *minyans* and in experimental feminist communities like Cornwall[20] they face similar issues of separation and separatism.

"Yahweh as Holy Warrior" was written when, inspired by Helen Caldicott and others, I was devoting much of my energy to the antinuclear movement. With Karen Voss and Mara Keller I co-produced a slide show, "Genesis/Genocide: Women for Peace," which we showed to many educational feminist and antinuclear groups. This experience prompted me to reflect again on the relation of our images of God to the warrior image. Some years earlier when Mary Daly first proposed the Exodus as a positive image for feminist theology, I had experimented with translating some of my favorite passages from Exodus into the female gender.

Though I found it inspiring to think that a female God had compassion for the slaves who were in Egypt and thus might have compassion on women's bondage within patriarchy, I could not bring myself to affirm that "She is a Woman of War, Yahweh is Her name," an image of God inextricably bound up with the Exodus understanding of Yahweh's liberation of the Hebrew slaves. Similarly, though liberation theologians have focused on the prophetic critique of injustice within Israel, they have failed to note that throughout the prophetic books, the condemnation of those who, in Amos's words, "sell the righteous for silver, the needy for a pair of shoes" (2:7) is backed up by threat of violent destruction at the hands of Yahweh as warrior. In drawing upon the prophetic image of Yahweh as concerned for the poor, the "critical principle of liberation" cited by liberation theologians, one cannot avoid, I argue, reinforcing as well the image of Yahweh as warrior, an image I find unacceptable in the nuclear age. I argue that the critical principle of liberation can only be found in the prophetic tradition by abstracting certain elements of that tradition from their historical context.

"On Not Blaming Jews for the Death of the Goddess" was written for a session at the 1985 meetings of the Society of Biblical Literature titled "Jewish and Christian Feminist Hermeneutics: Confrontation or Co-operation?" The panel was a response to Judith Plaskow's "Christian Feminism and Anti-Judaism,"[21] in which she argued Christian anti-Semitic traditions are perpetuated in Christian feminist attempts to justify the vision of Jesus at the expense of his Jewish milieu. My contribution to the panel was a response to Annette Daum's "Blaming the Jews for the Death of the Goddess."[22] In it, I provide suggestions for discussing the roles that ancient Hebrew religion, Christianity, and Judiasm played in the development of patriarchy and the suppression of Goddess religions in ways that do not fuel anti-Judaism.

The final chapter in this section, "Daughters of the Father God," was written for a collection of essays on daughters and fathers. In it, I was given the opportunity to examine the issue of Father God symbolism in the context of the relationships of fathers and daughters in our culture. I chose to reflect upon my own relation to the Father God, to my father, and to father professors in hopes that my personal story would expose themes that appear in other women's lives as well. We need continually to remind ourselves of the damage done to women's psyches by enthrallment to the Father. The destructive impact of the Father God is not erased for us or for other women when some of us become feminists. As long as the Father continues to be invoked in churches and synagogues, the stage is being set for the continuation of pathological relationships to God and to the men in our lives. The God of the Bible, the God of liturgy and prayer, does not appear as a "Liberator" to many women. It is important that we not forget this.

These essays depicit and reflect upon my journey away from the God of the religious traditions I inherited and that once gave meaning to my life. I hope that the telling of my story will aid other women as they struggle with their histories. I hope that the questions I raise will be taken up by those who work to transform Judaism and Christianity. I am not optimistic that these questions can be resolved from within these traditions. For me, the discovery of alternative images and traditions has been empowering. But I continue to enter into dialogue with the tradition of my history and its God.

NOTES

Epigraph: Susan Griffin, *Woman and Nature: The Roaring Inside Her* (New York: Harper & Row, 1978), 159.

1. Elie Wiesel, *The Gates of the Forest*, trans. Frances Frenaye (New York: Schocken Books, 1982), 3.
2. Ibid., 226.
3. Ibid., 109.
4. Richard Rubenstein, *After Auschwitz* (New York: Bobbs-Merrill Co., Inc., 1966).
5. Rosemary Radford Ruether, *Faith and Fratricide* (New York: Seabury Press, 1974).
6. Gregory Baum, *Is the New Testament Anti-Semitic?* (Glen Rock: Paulist Press, 1965).
7. Baum, Introduction to *Faith and Fratricide*, 5.
8. Rubenstein, *After Auschwitz*, 48–56.
9. Ibid., 58. "Can we really blame the Christian community for viewing us through the prism of a mythology of history when we were the first to assert this history of ourselves?"
10. Mary Daly, *Beyond God the Father: Toward a Philosophy of Women's Liberation* (Boston: Beacon Press, 1973).
11. Irene Fine, *Educating the New Jewish Woman* (San Diego, CA: The Women's Institute for Continuing Jewish Education, 1985), 38–40.

12. See Stephen Crites, "The Narrative Quality of Experience," *Journal of the American Academy of Religion* 39, no. 3 (1971), 291–311; Michael Novak, *Ascent of the Mountain, Flight of the Dove* (New York: Harper & Row, 1971); and Carol P. Christ, *Diving Deep and Surfacing*, (Boston: Beacon Press, 1986), 1–12.
13. Sonia Johnson, *From Housewife to Heretic* (Garden City, NY: Doubleday, 1981), 112–14.
14. Simone Weil, *The "Iliad" or the Poem of Force*, trans. Mary McCarthy (Wallingford: Pendle Hill, 1956).
15. Ellen Umansky, "(Re)Imaging the Divine," *Response* 41–42 (1982): 110–19; and "Creating a Jewish Feminist Theology: Possibilities and Problems," *Anima* 10, no.2 (1984): 125–35.
16. Rosemary Radford Ruether, "A Religion for Women," *Christianity and Crisis* (December 10, 1979): 307–11; and "Goddesses and Witches," *The Christian Century* (September 10–17, 1980), 842–47.
17. See *An Inclusive Language Lectionary: Readings for Year A* (Atlanta, New York, Philadelphia: The Cooperative Publication Association, 1983).
18. Rosemary Radford Ruether, *Sexism and God-Talk: Toward a Feminist Theology* (Boston: Beacon Press, 1983), 39.
19. See Elisabeth Schüssler Fiorenza, *In Memory of Her: A Feminist Reconstruction of Christian Origins* (New York: Crossroad Press, 1983).
20. See Martha Ackelsberg, "Spirituality, Community, and Politics: B'not Esh and the Feminist Reconstruction of Judaism," *Journal of Feminist Studies in Religion* 2, no. 2 (1986): 109–120.
21. Judith Plaskow, "Christian Feminism and Anti-Judaism," *Cross Currents* 28 (1978): 306–09.
22. Annette Daum, "Blaming Jews for the Death of the Goddess," *Lilith* 7 (1980): 12–13.

1. Women's Liberation and the Liberation of God

In a story that concludes *The Town Beyond the Wall,* Elie Wiesel suggests that the liberation of God and the liberation of humans depend on the renewal of an ancient dialogue between them now charged with hatred, with remorse, and most of all, with infinite yearning. Wiesel's story gives form to the feelings[1] of resentment and betrayal many Jews direct toward God after the holocaust. His story also gives shape to the feelings of many women as they become conscious of their exclusion from the stories of God's relation to man.

Wiesel's story tells of a time in the distant past when God and man changed places. As I retell it, the story is of a time in the present when God and woman change places. I first told the story to express hatred and resentment of God, but the logic of the story led me to an insight about God's relation to woman that I had not imagined.

Wiesel tells the story in this way:

> Legend tells us that one day man spoke to God in this wise:
> "Let us change about. You be man, and I will be God. For only one second."
> God spoke gently and asked him, "Aren't you afraid?"
> "No. And You?"
> "Yes, I am," God said.
>
> Nevertheless he granted man's desire. He became a man, and the man took his place and immediately availed himself of his omnipotence; he refused to revert to his previous state. So neither God nor man was ever again what he seemed to be.
>
> Years passed, centuries, perhaps eternities. And suddenly the drama quickened. The past for one, and the present for the other, were too heavy to be borne.
>
> As the liberation of the one was bound to the liberation of the other, they renewed the ancient dialogue whose echoes come to us in the night,

charged with hatred, with remorse, and most of all, with infinite yearning.[2]

I tell it like this:

One day woman spoke to God in this way:

"Let us change places. You be woman, and I will be God. For only one second."

God smiled and asked her, "Are you afraid?"

"No, and you?"

"Yes, I am," God said.

But woman thought to herself bitterly, no matter. I want you to know how it feels to be me. I want you to know how much I have suffered because you let yourself be named in man's image as the God of the fathers, as the man of war, as king of the universe. I don't believe you'll know how I feel until you become woman. No, I am not afraid.

So woman becomes God and God becomes woman. But as woman takes the place of God she finds herself led to an insight she has not expected . . . As woman takes the place of God, she hears what she can only describe as a still, small voice saying, "in God is a woman like yourself. She shares your suffering. She, too, has had her power of naming stolen from her. First she was called an idol of the Canaanites, and then she ceased to exist as God." As woman becomes God, the God who had existed for her only as an alien ceases to be a stranger to her. In this moment, woman realizes the meaning of the concluding words of the story: the liberation of the one is bound to the liberation of the other, so they renew the ancient dialogue, whose echoes come to us in the night, charged with hatred, with remorse, and most of all, with infinite yearning.

According to the story, the liberation of both woman and God depends on their understanding what it means to stand in each other's place. Moreover, the liberation of both depends on their renewing an ancient dialogue. What does it mean to speak of God's liberation, and how is God's liberation related to the liberation of women?

In the story, woman wants to change places with God in order to force God to experience being a woman in a world shaped by God's covenant with man. She wants God to experience the suffering of women in a world where the mothers, the daughters, and the sisters do not exist—even for God. She hopes that after experiencing her suffering God will change the world he has created.

However, as she changes places with God, woman comes to recognize an essential kinship with God that had been hidden from her in the patriarchal stories of the God of the fathers. She learns that patriarchal history has led to a primoridial alienation within God. There once was a Goddess and stories of a Goddess, but she was called the idol of the pagans, her stories were forgotten, and she herself ceased to exist. In patriarchal culture, not only the human image of God, but the true God in her/his[3] primordial nature as both female and male, neither female nor male, is alienated from her/himself. The power of women to liberate themselves from a patriarchal history in which God is still chained makes women in some sense more powerful than God, as is suggested in the image of God and woman changing places.

According to the story, this new power of women over God is a power that may assist the very liberation of God. The concept of God's liberation is alien to theological traditions in which God is conceived as all-powerful, in which God is conceived as the initiator of all significant action, and in which the divine nature itself is sometimes conceived as totally unaffected by all human action. However, the notion of divine bondage and powerlessness is rooted in the Jewish mystical tradition with its symbol of the Messiah in chains. Kabbalistic and hasidic stories say that God needs humans to free him from bondage. The divine self-estrangement and the concomitant need for divine liberation[4] are familiar themes in Jewish mystical theology. They are expressed in the symbol of God's alienation from his female counterpart, the *Shekhinah*, who wanders the earth weeping over the suffering of the Jewish people. According to Jewish custom, the act of intercourse on the Sabbath reunites God with his *Shekhinah*. Women can perhaps reinterpret these symbols to counter the view that God is to be totally identified with the patriarchal image of God.[5]

The stories and the symbols insist that the alienation of God is not limited to the poverty of human symbolic expression but affects the very life of God. God, like humans, has been in bondage to patriarchal history. Thus, the story speaks of a divine liberation that is not simply a matter of human symbolic expression but has immense consequences for the divine life itself. The liberation of God spoken of here is not simply a matter of changing the way we talk about God. God himself and not just human language must be liberated. Divine bondage and potential liberation is also suggested in the Lilith story as told by Judith Plaskow. In the words of the story, God, so to speak, admits his bondage, saying, "I am who I am," and acknowledges that he must change, saying, "I must become who I will become,"[6] In both the Lilith story and the stories told here, God is held accountable for the patriarchal history in which he was enchained, *and let himself be enchained*. Yet in both stories, God, like women, may achieve liberation from that history. The notion that God be held accountable for the patriarchal history in which he has been known is essential if the biblical notion of a significant divine-human encounter in history is to be maintained. If God is totally unaffected by the history in which he has been known, or if our words about God are entirely a human projection, then the notion of God's accountability for patriarchal history is absurd. But if God really is involved in history, then God must be held at least partially responsible for that history and for the image of himself he allowed to be projected in it. Thus, renewal of a dialogue with the God of the patriarchal tradition will not only bring him out of his alienation from women, but also out of a primordial self-alienation.

The story says that this renewed dialogue with God will be charged with hatred and with remorse. Women's hatred and remorse stem from exclusion from the stories of God's covenant with man. Hearing the biblical stories, women must refuse to sit silent; they must charge God with his failures to them. Imagine the following scene. The Bible is read:

> And the people of Israel groaned under their bondage. . .
> And God heard their groaning, and God remembered his covenant
> with Abraham, with Isaac, and with Jacob. (Exod. 2:34ff)

> This is my God and I will praise him,
> My father's God and I will exalt him,
> The LORD is a man of war. . . (Exod. 15:2–3)

> And I will abolish the bow, the sword,
> and war from the land. (Hos. 2:18)

Hearing that God had compassion on the Hebrews in their time of slavery, a woman feels hopeful that her bondage, too, will be ended. But as she listens further, she hears that the covenantal promises were addressed to Abraham, Isaac, and Jacob, and she experiences her exclusion from the tradition that shaped her deepest longings for redemption. Instead of swallowing her anger, choking back the words forming in her throat, she rises and cries out, "What happened to the mothers, the daughters, and the sisters? How can we give allegiance to a tradition of fathers and sons? Where is the woman of God who could aid our quest? Where are the Goddesses? You, God, with the aid of your patriarchs and prophets, destroyed the powerful Goddesses of the ancient Near East as you continue to destroy us. By your very existence as male, you legitimatize the patriarchal order in which I cannot fully exist. How could you, God? You promise to abolish the bow, the sword and war from the land, but you yourself are called a man of war. How can you ever fulfill the promises you have made to us?"

The expression of such anger and bitterness may be offensive to some, but it may be essential to the achievement of both women's liberation and God's. Only through the expression of hatred and remorse will women bring to consciousness—their own, men's, and perhaps God's—the extent of God's alienation from them *and* the extent of God's alienation from her/his true selfhood. Just as in the women's movement expression of anger and resentment toward men precedes reconciliation, which can come only after anger has clarified the extent of mutual alienation, so, too, women's relation with God must proceed through anger to a possible reconciliation.

It should be noted that the indictment of God projected in the words of an imagined woman has biblical and traditional precedent. It is a woman's adaption of the covenant lawsuit form. The prophets made great use of this form; they presented God as indicting Israel for failing to live up to its side of the covenant and threatening to give up his promise to protect the people from their enemies. At times, representatives of the people have reversed this form and called God to account for failing to fulfill his side of the covenantal agreement. Rabbi Levi-Yitzak of Berditchev, tradition says, called God to account on Yom Kippur for ignoring the sufferings of his people. He was following Abraham, who questioned God's righteousness in destroying Sodom and Gomorrah, and Moses, who asked to be blotted out of the Lord's book if God utterly destroyed the people for worshiping the golden calf.

The story also suggests that the renewed dialogue with God will be charged with infinite yearning. Many women today reject the notion that they require the God of the patriarchal tradition for their liberation. That God is, they rightly say, part of the problem, and therefore, they conclude, could have nothing to do with its solution.[7] And yet, perhaps precisely because he is part of the problem, he must also be involved in its solution. Many women find that their feelings toward the God of the tradition are not indifference but are indeed, as the story says, hatred and remorse. To pretend indifference to the God of the tradition when anger and bitterness are one's true feelings is to deaden a part of oneself. This may be too high a price for women to pay. Furthermore, the God to whom those feelings of anger are directed is also the source, for many women, of their own hopes for liberation. It was, after all, from the Exodus story that many women learned that those who had been in bondage could achieve liberation. Thus women whose deepest identities were formed in religious traditions may find that to cut themselves off from the God of the tradition separates them from the root of the longing for liberation that has nourished their hopes in the women's movement. Even women who do not think themselves related to a religious tradition may find that their betrayal by all the liberation movements of patriarchal culture calls for metaphysical and ultimately religious expression.

Women, then, will perhaps move through expression of anger at God to a new relation with God. They will never again submit themselves to an all-powerful father figure. They will never forget—nor will they let God forget—that such a God is the symbol and source of their oppression. In renewing dialogue with a God who has betrayed them, women may follow the protagonist of Wiesel's *The Gates of the Forest* who hears a voice telling him, "He doesn't need your love, he can do without it; but you can't. It's not a question of him but of yourself. Your love, rather than his, could make the difference."[8] They will love the God who is the source of their yearning for redemption and whose loss diminishes them. Like Jacob with the angel, these women will struggle with God, and perhaps at the end of the night, both women and God will emerge with new names and the power of new being. At dawn women may hear a still, small voice speaking to them saying, "God is a woman like yourself; she, too, has suffered and ceased to exist through the long years of patriarchal history." With that sister God, and the sister earth she once represented, women will perhaps make a new covenant: promising to liberate her and the earth as they liberate themselves.[9]

NOTES

1. See Suzanne Langer, *Feeling and Form* (New York: Charles Scriber's Sons, 1953).
2. *The Town Beyond the Wall* trans. Stephen Becker, (New York: Avon Books, 1969), 190.
3. The use of pronouns is consistent in this essay. Masculine pronouns used of God refer to the God revealed in and known in patriarchal history. "She/He" did not lead us out of Egypt, for the God who led the Hebrew people out of Egypt is a male God, a "man of war." Dual pronouns used of God refer to the God who "somehow" lies beyond patriarchal religion.
4. These symbols are discussed in Gershom Scholem's *Major Trends in Jewish Mysticism* (New York: Schocken Books, 1969), 224–86 and in his *On the Kabbala and Its Symbolism*, trans. Ralph Manheim (New York: Schocken Books, 1970), esp. 109–17.
5. The idea that the doctrine of the *Shekhinah* might be reinterpreted as a resource for a feminist theology was suggested to me by Rita Gross. I recognize that to reinterpret these symbols from the perspective of women's alienation in patriarchal culture goes beyond the probable intent of their kabbalistic formulators, and that such an interpretation does not exhaust their significance.
6. Printed in *Religion and Sexism: Images of Women in the Jewish and Christian Traditions*, ed. Rosemary Ruether, (New York: Simon & Schuster, 1974), 341–44.
7. This case is powerfully presented in Mary Daly's *Beyond God the Father: Toward a Philosophy of Women's Liberation* (Boston: Beacon Press, 1973). I endorse her indictment of God the Father and the patriarchal tradition. However, as I suggest below, I read her indictment as a case against *God*, and I do not think the interchange between women and God is completed (at least for some women) with the presentation of the indictment. I realize that this position involves me in anthropomorphic theology (story theology cannot be of any other kind), but so be it.
8. Elie Wiesel, *The Gates of the Forest*, trans. Frances Frenaye (New York: Avon Books, 1967), 222.
9. I do not endorse traditional identifications of women and nature, which have served to exclude women from many scholarly and spiritual dimensions of religious life. However, I do believe that rethinking traditional views of women ought to lead to rethinking traditional views of nature as well.

2. Expressing Anger at God

This essay takes the form of story theology, theology as story and reflection on story. The biblical books of Job, Jeremiah, and Hosea provide intriguing models for the story theologian.[1] In each book the deep personal crisis of an individual (whether "real" or not) becomes a paradigm that illumines the community's relation to God. In each case, the probing of personal experience produces theological expressions which shock the pious and challenge the foundations of conventional faith. Despite the risks, I am convinced that by remaining faithful to the truth of our stories, no matter how difficult and isolating that truth seems at first, we will discover that our stories are shared. We may even find that they lead us, individually and communally, to a new relation with God.

Several years ago I met Caroline. One of the first women hired to teach at a major Eastern university, Caroline found her first years there difficult, frustrating, and painful. Our friendship developed as we discovered we shared many similar experiences, the same anger. We talked often about how our colleagues saw us as sexual beings yet did not take us seriously as scholars and thinkers. Caroline told me of her elation when one of her colleagues finally asked her to lunch to discuss her ideas, and her rage when he tried to seduce her. I told Caroline of my humiliation and rage on learning that the professor whose seminar I had actively participated in for a full year seemed to remember me simply as "the one with the long legs."

Through our friendship, and with the support of other women who shared our lives, Caroline and I began to learn together how to assert ourselves in a hostile academic environment without sacrificing ourselves as whole persons. For Caroline, the birth of her daughter Evelyn was a symbol of her power to be both a woman and a scholar. She felt her full self, her power, to be as new and as full of potential as her little daughter.

When Caroline asked me to become the godmother of her child, I knew she was asking me to affirm and help her daughter to grow into a full and vital woman. She hoped Evelyn would not know the bitter lonely struggle we had known. She wanted Evelyn to have me, her godmother, to help and guide her, to be the role model neither of us had known in our growing up. I also knew that Caroline's desire to baptize her daughter as a Christian expressed her trust that in some way the ground of our being and living supports and affirms the new becoming of women. Because I wanted to share in that affirmation, I agreed to become Evelyn's godmother, even though I was aware of my increasing estrangement from God the Father.

I knew I would feel discomfort at the baptismal service, but I was not prepared for the enormity of feeling that surfaced in me that day. Evelyn was the only child being baptized, and the young bearded minister, friend of the family, spoke only of the Christian and "his" baptism into the "fellowship" of Christian "men." I had expected to hear God referred to only as "Father," but I had not been prepared to hear this young girl's identity stolen from her by a man whose words were saying that she could not at one and the same time be a woman and a Christian. I remained silent during the service, but I felt a conflict growing within me. My shoulders tensed, my stomach knotted, my head ached. I did not want to spoil my goddaughter's baptismal day, but neither could I deny my feelings.

After the service, I walked up to the minister and told him I had not appreciated his sexist language. He angrily retorted that he was waiting for the day when women like me would not feel the need to impose their personal problems on the Christian liturgy, which transcended such petty problems. Because I was struggling to restrain the full power of my anger, I spoke in an offhand way to the minister, not revealing the depth of my feeling of betrayal. I had expected him to know without my saying it. This failure of communication underscores the need for anger to be expressed fully and directly.

The minister's response provoked me to tears, to the expression of more feeling. I became the center of attention at the gathering of friends and relatives after the baptism. First the mother, then the father, then the minister and others asked me about my tears and expressed their understanding of my pain. At the time, I was embarrassed and ashamed to divert attention from Evelyn on her baptismal day. Now I see that my anger and my tears were a gift to Evelyn. In speaking out about my sense of Evelyn's exclusion and my own from the service of her baptism, I expressed my commitment to her future.

Now I wish I'd had the courage to interrupt the service itself. The Christian tradition excludes and denies women's full selfhood. Recognizing this, women have three choices: to remain silent, to leave, or to confront. The third choice is the hardest. Some might suggest that this confrontation be kept out of the sanctuary, that women should meet with ministers and church members in order to convince them to change offensive language and the attitudes that give rise to it. Such struggles are important and useful. However, given the pervasive sexism of the tradition, simple elimination of the most offensive words from the liturgy will not suffice to bring about the kind of transformation of spirituality that is required. It may be that only the full and direct expression of women's feelings of anger and betrayal—before the community *and* before God—will create the situation in which genuine and creative healing can occur.

The suggestion that women's anger at God must be expressed both in solitude and in community provokes a deep resistance from both women and men. Will such rage destroy the community of faith? Ought women to feel it? And if they feel it, should they not keep it to themselves?

Let us imagine another scene. A woman sits in church and listens to the stories of the Exodus. Hearing of God's compassion on the Hebrew slaves, she takes hope that God will pity her in her bondage as well. But when she hears that the covenantal promises were not made to her or her mothers, but to her fathers, to Abraham, to Isaac, to Jacob, she experiences bodily her exclusion from the very tradition that shaped her longings for redemption. Imagine that instead of choking back her anger, she rises and cries out.

In the grip of powerful feelings and emotions, why does a woman swallow the words forming in her throat? Perhaps she thinks she is alone with her feelings. Perhaps she is afraid her feelings will not be approved by her sisters or brothers. Job was mocked by his friends, accused of impiety, when he called upon God to defend himself against accusations of injustice. How much more scorn would be heaped on the woman who expressed her anger at God, who called upon the Almighty to answer her charges! Surely the pious members of the congregation would accuse her of emotionalism, would wonder what was wrong with her that she forced her personal feelings on them, would accuse her of spoiling a beautiful service. How much easier to swallow her anger. How much easier to choke to death on it.

Still, there may be important religious reasons for expressing anger at God. While women sit silent, perhaps even unaware that they are deadening themselves in order to do so, others leave the churches and synagogues, cutting off their relation with the biblical God. In both cases, women who once had powerful feelings about the God of biblical tradition may be denying part of themselves. They may be deadening their religious sensibility altogether, suppressing powerful, conflicting feelings toward God that come to them, perhaps, "in the night, tinged with hatred, with remorse, but most of all with infinite yearning."[2] A woman who swallows her anger and bitterness at God may also cut off her longing for the God who provoked her to anger.

For many women, I suggest, it is far more true to speak of hatred for God than of indifference to God. This anger at God, like feminist anger at men, must be expressed. And, just as in some cases, the expression of anger at men precedes a reconciliation, so too, the expression of anger at God may precede a renewed relation.

There is also traditional precedent for expressing anger at God. The biblical notion of relation with a living God implies the notion of full presence. Martin Buber has suggested that the enigmatic name of God, usually translated as "I am who I am," might better be translated as "I will be there as I will be there," or even "I will be present (to you) as I will be present (to you).[3] God did not promise always to express loving feelings to the people but rather to be fully present with whatever God felt in response to the situation. Thus, God did not withhold anger when the people broke the covenant but was fully present with angry feelings. I suggest that God's ability to be present with whatever feelings God felt was the *sine qua non* of the possibility of a continuing relation. Had God repressed anger instead of expressing it, Israel would not have known the living God in the fullness of being. Like any other relation when anger is not expressed, the covenantal relation would have stagnated, gone dead.

In the Bible full presence also meant that the people could challenge God. Abraham and Moses questioned God's justice. Jeremiah, Jonah, and Job accused God of injustice.

In biblical religion the covenantal relation implied reciprocal obligations. When the people sinned God called them to court to present the case against them. The prophets often cast the relation between God and Israel into the form of the covenant lawsuit, as in Hosea 4:1, where God spoke to the people:

> Hear the words of the LORD, O people of Israel
> For the LORD has a case against the inhabitants of the land.
> There is no faithfulness or kindness
> And no knowledge of God in the land.[4]

God justified God's anger toward the people by pointing out what they had done to provoke it.

In the book of Job the covenant lawsuit form is turned around. Though not an Israelite, Job seemed to be familiar enough with the form to use it against God, as when he said:

> But I would speak to the Almighty
> And I desire to argue my case against God (13:3).[5]

I suggest that the covenant lawsuit form is one biblical precedent appropriate to women's relation to God today. Through the covenant lawsuit, women can appeal to God against God. They can use God's own words to indict God for failure to live up to the promises of covenantal relation. I suggest that the appropriate place for this in the liturgy would be either before or after the congregation's prayers of confession. At that time, a woman might rise and recite the "sins" of God, echoing the words of the people of Israel who said, "My God has passed over my rights" (Isa. 40:27). Women might begin to collect indictments against God from their own experiences and from literary sources, which could be used regularly or at set times in the liturgy. The words of the woman imagined above as crying out against God provide one example of such an indictment of God. The words of the black singer Nina Simone from her album "Emergency Ward," provide another example. The medley that she begins with George Harrison's song of passionate yearning, "I Really Want to See You Lord" and concludes with a terrible vision, "Who are you Lord? Today, today, today, You are a Killer"[6] would be powerful in a liturgical setting.

In proposing that women adopt covenant lawsuit to state their case against God, I am suggesting that women call on God to take responsibility for the patriarchal histories in which God has been known—biblical, Christian, and Jewish. When the question of God's responsibility for patriarchal history is asked, a theological objection is often raised, "But God himself is not male, it was only the patriarchal storytellers who imaged God as male." The problem, it is suggested, has nothing to do with God. I am suggesting that *for a storytelling theology*, this anwer will not do. In a storytelling theology the split between "God God's self" and the God revealed in the relation, in the story, cannot be allowed. In a storytelling theology, God "is" who God is in the story. It is equally true that in a storytelling theology, God may become who God may become.[7]

If the biblical tradition is viable, if Christians and Jews really experience a relation with God, then human dealings with God cannot be transacted simply on an intellectual level. The storytellers of the traditions have always known that. Nor need the community always express loving, humble feelings to God. Biblical tradition warrants the view that humans have a right and even a responsibility to question God, to wrestle with God, until the answers to human questions are revealed.

NOTES

1. The model of the prophets was suggested by Mary Wakeman in an article in *Beyond Androcentrism: New Essays on Women and Religion* ed. Rita Gross (Missoula, Mont.: AAR and Scholars Press, 1977).
2. Elie Wiesel, *The Town beyond the Wall*, trans. Steven Becker (New York: Avon Books, 1970), 190.
3. Martin Buber. *The Prophetic Faith*, trans. Carlyle Witton-Davies (New York: Harper & Row, 1960), 24–30.
4. My translation. The Hebrew word *'im* translated here as "against," carries the meaning "with" or "against."

5. See note 4.
6. Nina Simone, "Emergency Ward," side one, medley including "My Sweet Lord," by George Harrison and "Today Is a Killer," poem by David Nelson, music by Nina Simone (New York: RCA Records, 1972).
7. See Judith Plaskow, "The Coming of Lilith," in *Religion and Sexism*, ed. Rosemary Ruether (New York: Simon & Schuster, 1974), 341–43.

Artemis of the Ephesians. From Ephesus.

3. Heretics and Outsiders

I approach this topic as one who views herself as an outsider to the canons and traditions of the West. It is no secret that the "great works" of the Western tradition are written from a male-centered perspective in which the experiences specific to women are ignored, suppressed, or treated only in relation to the interests of men.

The *Iliad* is a case in point. Its major dramatic conflict between Achilles and Agamemnon generates Achilles' "metaphysical dilemma" of whether to seek honor and live a short but glorious life, or to refuse honor and live long but unmemorably. Critics rarely note that both the dramatic conflict and the metaphysical dilemma are generated by an argument between two men over one of the most precious spoils of war, the "spear captive" Briseis. Briseis is a raped woman, a victim of the wars of men, yet her tragedy is treated simply as the occasion for the conflicts of men. How can I find myself in such a tradition without losing my identity as a woman?

This sense of myself as outsider has led me to question many conventional pieties about canons and traditions, particularly the largely unexamined premise that the so-called "great works" have become central and authoritative primarily because they express the struggles and aspirations of humanity in a compelling and beautiful way.

Biblical scholar James Sanders, for example, expresses such a view when he says that his book *Torah and Canon* is a "quest for the essence of the power of life the Bible demonstrably has. This power is evident not only in the Bible's remarkable survival for over 2,500 years," he writes, "but in its function as the vehicle of survival to the communities whose identities and life-styles issue from their adherance to it."[1] Sanders apparently assumes that canonical works survive because of an intrinsic vision that commends itself to the hearts and minds of communities. Certainly the Bible has had a compelling power for some in the West; I only note that this view is deceptively one-sided. Sanders does not ask to what extent the survival of the Bible might also be due to political struggles, including slander and repression of rival traditions. Nor does he ask for whom biblical tradition is a power of life, and for whom, perhaps, a power of death.

It is precisely this mundane question that I wish to address here. My first point is simple, obvious, and often overlooked: the existence of a canon or a canonical tradition implies the existence of outsiders and heretics. Now the consequences of being outside a canonical tradition (in the West at least) are as follows: texts outside the canon are slandered, often suppressed, sometimes destroyed; groups existing outside canonical authority are often declared heretical; adherents of heretical groups are often persecuted, sometimes killed.

My second point is a hypothesis that I will explore through the discussion of three historic struggles between the proponents of the traditions that became canonical and those whom they declared to be outsiders and heretics. This hypothesis is as follows: myths suppressed by the canonical tradition often contained powerful female symbolism; the texts or traditions transmitting this symbolism may often have had a special appeal for women because they offered greater opportunities for the expression of female power; and the persons persecuted by the canonical tradition may have been disproportionately female.

I will explore this hypothesis by examining some intriguing evidence concerning the struggles between the proponents of views that became canonical and persons whom they identified as outsiders and heretics. Instances of such struggles will be drawn from ancient Hebrew religion, early Christianity, and the middle Christian period. The juxtaposition of these three periods presents a disturbing pattern of suppression of female symbolism and power by the traditions that became canonical in the West, challenging the apologetic argument stating that the male symbolisms and hierarchies of the Jewish and Christian religions were a spontaneous and natural development given their historical contexts. I will argue to the contrary that the Jewish and Christian traditions were not passive with regard to their environments. At crucial points proponents of the canonical traditions engaged in ideological struggles with competing religious traditions in the course of which female symbolism and female power were actively suppressed.

The historical arguments I make here are more difficult to document than the familiar charges of sexism in Western religion. Because histories of Western religion do not usually ask how Western religion came to be male-centered, there is no body of secondary scholarship to which to appeal. Moreover, the practioners of defeated religious traditions have been slandered as idol worshipers, whores, and worse in the official texts of the canonical tradition, and few scholars have been willing to challenge this official view. Finally, the texts of competing religious traditions were often destroyed by the canonical groups, for example, in the burning of the library at Alexandria and the book burnings of the middle Christian period. Because the evidence on which a clear picture of the outsiders and heretics in Western tradition could be constructed is too often nonexistent or not adequately interpreted by scholarship, the argument of this essay will have to be somewhat more hypothetical than I wish.

The interest of noncanonical groups in female power and female symbols is no longer hypothetical in the contemporary period, however. In the traditions being developed by some of today's most conspicious outsiders and heretics, the women in the women's spirituality movement and the feminist witches, there is a resurgence of interest in female power and female symbolism. In a final section of this essay I will briefly discuss this new development in contemporary religious consciousness, particularly as it bears on the relation of canon and anticanon.

According to a widely held view, the official religion of ancient Israel was largely a monotheistic worship of one God, Yahweh. The Hebrew people held to their monotheistic tradition against the temptations presented by the polytheistic traditions of neighboring peoples, because monotheism was ethically and religiously superior to polytheism. Only rarely did the people of Israel succumb to polytheistic practices, referred to as "Baalism," "fetishism" (often synonymous with Goddess worship), and "cult prostitution." The prophets criticized these "excesses" and "aberrations" of faith and returned the people to monotheism. Recent scholarship and archaeological discoveries have challenged this interpretive paradigm. Scholars have discovered that the religion of the Hebrew people was more pluralistic than the monotheistic paradigm indicates, and that the religion of the Canaanites was not mere fetishism and idolatry. Nonetheless, the paradigm of a dominant Yahwistic monotheism remains a major interpretive scheme through which the history of biblical religion is taught.[2]

In his book, *Palestinian Parties and Politics Which Shaped the Old Testament*,[3] Morton Smith questioned the standard paradigm of biblical religion. He argued that widespread adherance to monotheism in ancient Israel was a fiction created by ultimately victorious "Yahweh alone" groups that establish control of Israelite religion after the Babylonian exile. These Yahweh alone groups edited and rewrote the texts that became the biblical canon to make them conform to their view that the worship of Yahweh alone was the true religion of ancient Israel and Judah from the beginning and that worship of Gods and Goddesses other than Yahweh constituted heretical deviation. According to Smith the dominant groups in ancient Israel and Judah were polytheistic, worshiping several Gods and Goddesses, including Baal, Anath, Asherah, El, and others alongside Yahweh. The defining characteristic of ancient Hebrew religion was worship of Yahweh, but not worship of Yahweh only.

Mythologist Raphael Patai's *The Hebrew Goddess*[4] complements Smith's work. Patai also argues that Goddess worship was prevalent in the official religions of ancient Israel and Judah. He cites the books 1 and 2 Kings as one record of struggles between worshipers of Yahweh and worshipers of other Gods and Goddesses. Though these books were edited to slander the worshipers of Gods and Goddesses other than Yahweh as followers after "abomination," they acknowlege the widespread occurrence of polytheism and Goddess worship in the biblical period, not only among the populace, but in the official state religions. According to Patai's count the Goddess Asherah was worshiped in the temple of Solomon in Jerusalem for 236 of its 370 years of existence. In the Northern Kingdom Asherah was consistently worshiped in the capital city of Samaria from the time of Jezebel. Even if these precise figures are rendered problematic by the recognition that they may be the product of partisan editorship, as Smith suggests they are, the general picture of polytheistic worship in both kingdoms must be accepted. This picture is further supported by the discovery of female figures in archaeological digs at sites connected with worship in ancient Israel and Judah.

Based on the evidence brought forth by Smith and Patai, we might reverse the conventional notion of ancient Hebrew religion and speak instead of a dominant tradition of polytheism and Goddess worship in the official religion, which was broken only occasionally by the victories of Yahweh alone groups.

It should be stressed that the struggles between the Yahweh alone groups and the others were not mere ideological battles. They were political struggles in which force was often used. Exodus records that the Levites ordained themselves for the service of Yahweh by murdering 3000 worshippers of the golden calf (Exod. 32:25–29).[5] After Elijah's victory over Elisha 450 prophets of Baal were slain in the house of Baal in order to solidify his ascension to the throne following the slaying of Jezebel (2 Kings 10:18–30).[6]

Clearly, the struggles between the Yahweh alone groups and the other groups were not simple struggles between women worshipers of the Goddess and men worshipers of Yahweh. Men and women were involved in both the worship of Yahweh and the worship of Gods and Goddesses other than Yahweh. And the polytheistic groups were not exclusively devoted to the Goddess. Still, we may note that one consequence of the suppression of polytheism by the Yahweh alone groups was the elimination of Goddess worship. And we may ask whether women may have been particularly attracted to the worship of the Goddess as an expression of female power. There is some evidence to suggest that this may have been the case.

In the books of 1 and 2 Kings and 1 and 2 Chronicles the worship of the Goddess in Israel and Judah is often blamed on the influence of foreign queens, wives of the kings. Jezebel is the most notorious example. Now it is possible that the queens worshiped the Goddess because they were foreign, not because they were women. And it is also possible, though unlikely, that the misogynist biblical editors attributed everything they considered evil to the influence of women, but that women were not in fact central figures in the institution and defense of Goddess worship. Nonetheless, it is intriguing to speculate that foreign and native women, like the queens of Israel and Judah, were attracted to the worship of the Goddess as a symbol for female power. The murder of Jezebel (2 Kings 9:30–37) would then have been a political attack on the religion of the Goddess.[7] And the prohibitions at the time of the second Temple against Israelite men taking foreign wives would have been part of an attempt finally to suppress Goddess worship and polytheism, since women who had been reared in Goddess traditions would not easily give up the symbol of female power.

The book of Jeremiah offers further evidence in support of the view that women were especially devoted to the Goddess. In Jeremiah the following words are spoken by women:

> When we burned incense to the [Q]ueen of [H]eaven and poured out libations to her, was it without our husbands' approval that we made cakes for her bearing her image and poured out libations to her? (44:19)

Though the passage indicates that all the people participated in the worship of the Queen of Heaven, it also suggests that women performed many of the ritual acts and that women may have been viewed as the instigators or special devotees of Goddess worship.

Women's attraction to Goddess worship may not have been only a symbolic preference. In *When God Was A Woman* Merlin Stone brings together a great deal of evidence in support of her view that the status of women was higher in matrilineal Goddess worshiping cultures than it was in patrilineal Israel and Judah. In Egypt the woman was often head of the family, while in Babylon the wife could acquire property, take legal action, and make contracts.[8] In Israel and Judah these rights were curtailed.

These lines of evidence point to the conclusion that the Bible was shaped by politically victorious Yahweh alone groups whose victory had the effect (if not the intent) of slandering and prohibiting Goddess worship, declaring the religious inclinations of many women to be outside the tradition, and depriving women of many of the rights they had had in Goddess worshiping cultures. If this conclusion is correct, then we must ask whose "power of life" the biblical tradition expressed, and we must entertain the conclusion that it was not women's.

The victory of Christianity signaled the suppression of Goddess worship in the ancient world. The temples of the Goddess at Eleusis, Rome, Ephesus, Athens, and elsewhere were forcibly closed in the fourth and fifth centuries C.E. This was the end of public Goddess worship in the Christian West. However, it is not the struggle between Christianity and other religions over female symbolism and female power that I wish to consider here. Rather, I wish to consider a suppression of female symbolism and power that occurred *within* the Christian tradition in the struggles that led to the formation of the Christian canon.

A study of the religion of the Gnostic Christians suggests that the question of female symbolism and power was also a significant factor in their struggle with those who became orthodox Christians. In fact, if we are to believe the recent Vatican declaration denying the priesthood to women, the ordination of women by the Gnostics was one of the reasons the orthodox church suppressed them. "A few heretical sects in the first century, especially Gnostic ones, entrusted the priestly ministry to women," the Vatican statement reports, and "this innovation was immediately noted and condemned by the fathers."[9]

A common paradigm used to interpret early Christian history assumes that the early Christian communities that grew up after the death of Jesus were founded by Peter and Paul and the other male disciples, and that there was a fairly smooth transition between these groups and the early orthodox Church. If they are mentioned at all, the Gnostics are viewed as libertine heretics who denied the central Christian doctrine of the unity of the spirit and flesh, and whose factionalizing influence was rightly suppressed by the church fathers. So widespread is this view that "Gnosticism" has become a pejorative theological shorthand for any antinomian spiritualizing tendency.

As recent discoveries of Gnostic gospels have proved, this conventional view is more polemical than factual. Early Christianity seems to have been far more plural than is generally recognized. Both the Gnostic Christians and the groups that later declared themselves orthodox and canonical had their own gospels and claimed to be followers of the religion of Jesus Christ. Only after political struggles did some groups emerge victorious and declare the others heretical.

Elaine Pagels[10] offers convincing evidence that the Gnostic Christian groups provided more avenues for the expression of female symbolism and female power than did their orthodox Christian opponents. Gnostic Christian groups, as Pagels describes them, abounded in female imagery of God. The Valentinians, for example, imaged the divine as a dyad consisting of two elements, on the one hand, the Ineffable, the Source, the Primal Father, and on the other, the Silence, the Mother of All Things. Other Gnostics viewed the Holy Spirit as a divine Mother, and still others characterized the female elements in God as the Holy Wisdom, following Hebrew traditions of Wisdom as the companion of God.

Were the Gnostics declared heretical primarily because they employed female symbolism? Pagels rejects this conclusion as simplistic. However, among the "scandals" the victorious Christian groups claimed to find in the heretics, she notes the often-repeated charge that they allowed women authority in their communities. Gnostic works like the *Gospel of Mary* provide further evidence of a political struggle between female and male disciples of Jesus over the issue of female leadership. In the *Gospel of Mary* Peter objects to Mary's claim to have received a special revelation from Jesus, and he is rebuked by Levi, who says, "Peter you are always irascible. You object to the women as our enemies do. Surely the Lord knew her very well, and indeed loved her more than us. . . ." Mary is then allowed to speak with authority of the revelation Jesus entrusted to her.

From this evidence Pagels concludes that, whether or not it was the primary cause, one of the effects of the condemnation of the Gnostics by the canonical tradition was that female symbolism and leadership were suppressed.[11]

The evidence from the early Christian era suggests that the suppression of female symbolism and power was one of the results of the political struggles that led to the establishment of the Christian canon, a pattern similar to what apparently occurred in the establishment of the Hebrew canon. Again we must ask whose "power of life" the victorious tradition reflected. Perhaps women found themselves better represented by the traditions declared heretical.

The story of the suppression of female symbolism and female power by the canonical traditions of the West could be continued through a discussion of other "heretical" movements that surfaced within Christianity.[12] But I will instead focus on a conflict between the tradition and the outsiders in which the suppression of female power was carried out in particularly violent fashion, the witch persecution of the middle Christian period.

As with the Goddess worshipers and the Gnostics, the canonical view of the witches has impeded unbiased treatment of their practices and beliefs. It is commonly thought that witches worshiped the devil in bizaare rites in which children were sacrificed and that participants engaged in perverse sexual practices.

This view is the product of Christian polemic such as that found in *The Malleus Maleficarum*, but it has also influenced two standard paradigms used in scholarship concerning witchcraft. On the one side the "ultraconservative" scholars accept the charges of the persecutors that witchcraft was an anti-Christian rite inspired by the devil. On the other side the "liberal rationalists" view witchcraft as the creation of the witch persecutors and deny the historic reality of witch practice.[13] A third and different view is reflected in the much-disputed hypothesis of Margaret Murray that witchcraft was a survival of the pagan religions of Western Europe. Murray's work has been widely challenged by scholars, but her general theory has recently been defended by Mircea Eliade, a leading historian of religions.

Unfortunately, less is known about witch practice and belief than about the religions of the Goddess worshipers and the Gnostics. After the forced closing of their temples and the suppression of their priesthoods and priestesshoods in the early Christian period, European pagan traditions survived only in folk custom and in secret societies and were communicated orally. The major written documents concerning witch practice and belief are the trial documents and writings and decrees of Christian theologians and church councils, which are polemic. Thus the picture of witchcraft presented here will have to be somewhat hypothetical.

Though scholars disagree about what witchcraft was, except for the ultraconservatives, they agree that many of the charges against the witches were fabricated by their persecutors. It is further agreed by all that large numbers of people were killed as witches between the years 1400 and 1700 as a result of persecutions carried out in the name of the Catholic and Protestant faiths. Estimates of the numbers killed range from 100,000 to

1,000,000 or more,[14] staggering numbers considering the smaller population of Europe at the time. Though scholars also agree that women figured disproportionately among those persecuted as witches, few have asked why this was so.[15]

Often portrayed as resulting from peasant hysteria, the witch persecutions were in fact instigated by an educated elite who saw themselves as defenders of canonical tradition. In 1484 Pope Innocent issued a bull[16] making official the church's intention to persecute witches. Two Dominican theologians, Heinrich Kramer and James Sprenger, were the authors of *The Malleus Maleficarum*,[17] which became the classic text for witch "hammering." Kramer and Sprenger alleged that women are more attracted to witchcraft than men, providing arguments from Scripture and tradition to support their view. In answer to their question "Why is it that women are chiefly addicted to evil supersitions?" they asserted that women are more credulous and light-minded, more impressionable, and more given to gossip than men. But the most compelling reason "is that a woman is more carnal than a man, as is clear from her many carnal abominations." Or as they summed it up, "All witchcraft comes from carnal lust which in women is insatiable." The witch crimes that Kramer and Sprenger found most objectionable are related to women's alleged sexual nature, including copulating with devils, obstructing the act of generation, making the male organ disappear, and offering newborn children to the devil. Other crimes Sprenger and Kramer alleged against witches can be interpreted as species of folk magic, folk medicine, and folk psychology, including methods of preventing conception, procuring abortion, harming animals or crops, producing hail, and predicting the future through a variety of means.

The preoccupation of Sprenger and Kramer with crimes relating to female sexuality, female control over the birth process, and male impotence suggests that the witch persecutions were an attempt to suppress a form of female power that threatened the male authorities of church and state.

The question is, what sort of female power did witchcraft represent? Was it simply that female sexuality threatened the witch persecutors, or was witchcraft a competing religious system in which female symbolism and female power were recognized to a greater extent than they were in Christianity? A conclusive answer to this question cannot be obtained at present, but a number of lines of evidence suggest that the witch persecutions may fit into the pattern of suppression of female symbolism and female power that was hypothesized for the periods in which the Hebrew and Christian canons were formed.

One recent feminist interpretation, which falls into the liberal-rationalist camp, offers intriguing interpretations of the nature of the suppressed female power. Barbara Ehrenreich and Dierdre English, in their study *Witches, Nurses, and Midwives,*[18] suggest that many of those persecuted as witches were country doctors, midwives, and herbalists, women who delivered babies, cured the sick, and of course had patients who died. Ehrenreich and English argue that women healers were persecuted because their power over life and death challenged the church's claim that God and his male deputies, the priests, held all power over life and death. The hypothesis is supported by those portions of the *Malleus* that specifically accuse midwives of using witchcraft to control conception and produce abortion.

In 1921 Margaret Murray challenged both the Christian and the rationalist views of witchcraft and proposed the then startling thesis that witchcraft was a pagan religion and that the persecution of witches was part of a religious war. While many of the details of Murray's view of witch religion have been challenged, her basic hypothesis that witchcraft was a pagan survival has been supported by such scholars of religion as Mircea Eliade[19] and Rosemary Radford Ruether.[20]

Briefly, Murray's hypothesis, deduced from coherences she discovered in the testimony given at witch trials, is that witchcraft in Western Europe was an organized religion with a fairly uniform set of symbols, rituals, and social structures. The witches worshiped a deity who could be incarnate as a male figure (Janus or Dianus), a female figure (Diana), or an animal. The deity personified natural energy and was associated with fertility. Witches met in covens of thirteen and their major celebrations were on May Eve and November Eve. Women had access to leadership positions in the covens.

Rosemary Ruether disputes Murray's theory that witchcraft was an organized religion at the time of the persecutions. She believes that Christianity had already succeeded in destroying the official worship and priesthoods or priestesshoods of pagan religions by the middle Christian period. What survived, Ruether believes, was folk religion, that stratum of religion belonging to village daily life, the rituals of home and farming life that people carry on by themselves. It included group celebrations such as dances and festivals at planting and harvest times, folk magic, and folk superstition. Ruether believes that women were the primary cultivators of folk magic, of the use of charms, spells, and herbal remedies for curing illnesses. According to Ruether, those persecuted as witches were female charismatics, inheritors of traditions of folk religion and the power derived from it.[21]

In my opinion the theories of witches as midwives and healers should not be set over against the theories of witches as inheritors and transmitters of folk religion, for in these traditions, religion, medicine, and magic probably were not clearly distinguished. If the more spectacular charges of the witch persecutors (copulation with the devil, sacrifice of children) are discounted, a remarkably coherent picture of the practices of the witches can be suggested. Witches were wise and powerful women, practitioners of folk religion, magic, and medicine, whose knowledge of charms, spells, and herbal lore brought them to the bedside at times of birth, illness, and death. The wise woman was summoned at the crises of the life cycle *before* the priest; she delivered the baby, while the priest was called upon later to perform baptism. She was the first to be called upon to cure illness or treat the dying, while the priest was called in after all other remedies had failed, to administer the last rites. Moreover, if the wise woman had knowledge of herbs that could aid or prevent conception or cause abortion, she had a power over the life process that clearly was superior to that of the priest, and that according to official theology made her a rival of God himself. If, moreover, she appealed to pagan deities, some of them probably female, in the performance of divinations or blessings and spells used to promote healing and ward off evil, then it is not difficult to see why she was persecuted by an insecure and misogynist church that could not tolerate rival power, especially the power of women.

Though the evidence concerning witchcraft is inconclusive due to the lack of direct verification from the free testimony or written texts of witches, the lines of evidence cited here suggest that witch persecution followed the pattern of suppression of female symbolism and female power that seems to have occurred in the formative periods of Hebrew and Christian traditions.

This examination of three instances of conflict between the proponents of traditions that were or became canonical and the outsiders or heretics suggests that one of the issues at stake in the definition and defense of canonical tradition in the West was the suppression of female symbolism and power.

Given the persistence of this pattern in the history of the Western tradition, we must ask why scholarship has not been more vigorous in exploring it. The answer to this question seems to be that even the so-called objective traditions of scholarship in the university are not entirely free from certain biases of the canonical tradition. Specifically, the scholarly tradition has largely accepted three canonical views: (1) the ethical and religious superiority of monotheism over polytheism; (2) the inferiority of religious traditions in which sexuality and fertility are central concerns, and the equation of female symbolism with sexuality and fertility; and (3) the importance of maintaining order, and the interpretation of challenges to authorities as antinomian and therefore bad. In addition, the androcentrism of the scholarly tradition, which renders questions about women, female power, or female symbolism trivial and uninteresting because it accepts the subordinate status of women as a given, has blinded scholars to the fascinating history of the suppression of female power and symbolism by the traditions they study. But since an examination of androcentric and other biases in the *scholarly* tradition[22] could form the subject of another essay, I will not pursue it here.

The suppression of female symbolism and female power by the canonical traditions of the West is being reversed as modern women lay claim to their own forms of spirituality and power. If female symbolism was suppressed at least in part because it was viewed as an expression of female power, then it should not be surprising to discover that symbols of female sacrality are reemerging as women begin to reclaim their spiritual power.

The battles for the ordination of women in the major denominations of Protestantism and in the liberal wings of Judaism are only the most apparent manifestation of a widespread spiritual resurgence among women. A noninstitutionalized women's spirituality movement has become one of the major currents in the new wave of feminism. Susan Rennie and Kirsten Grimstad describe this current in their introduction to the spirituality section *The New Women's Survival Sourcebook*:

> We found that wherever there are feminist communities, women are exploring psychic and nonmaterial phenomena: reinterpreting astrology; creating and celebrating feminist rituals around birth, death, menstruation; reading the Tarot; studying pre-patriarchal forms of religion; reviving and exploring esoteric [G]oddess-centered belief systems such as wicca; developing and cultivating dream analysis, ESP, astral projection, precognition; learning psychic and homeopathic healing; rescuing the wholistic perspective of the right hemisphere of the brain from the contempt of left-brain linear mindedness. . . .[23]

Out of the key motifs of this spirituality movement is a new naming of ultimate power or powers. Many women are rediscovering that one of the oldest names for the fundamental energy—the energy of natural processes, the energy of life and death, the energy of sexual attraction and replusion, the energy concentrated in meditation and ritual, the energy felt vibrating in a room when people are really speaking to one another, the energy of psychic healing—is *Goddess*.

Barbry MyOwn described the experience of the Goddess as energy in a womanspirit circle called Ursa Maior. "We have not defined 'goddess' except in loose terms, 'woman-energy.' We hope to invoke a materialization of that woman energy, to love it, to play with it, exult in it. . . "Spiritually we see our bodies as divine manifestations of womanenergy." Barbry MyOwn and Hallie Iglehart created a menstruation ritual in which they named themselves sisters of the same mother and invoked "the Goddess whose blood, like our blood, flows with the cycles of the universe."[24] A combination of deep seriousness and playfulness is characteristic of a new attitude toward religion in these women's groups. Knowledge that they are invoking and connecting with fundamental power accounts for the deep seriousness of these women; but they dare to create new ritual forms because they do it playfully and only for themselves at a certain time and place—not for all times and places, not for other women whose experiences may be different.

WomanSpirit magazine[25] provided a space for women from around the country to name the sources of their power by sharing fantasies, rituals, poems, stories, drawings, and photographs on the themes of energy, healing, power, process, nature, wise women, the Goddess, and many more. Through *WomanSpirit* women discovered, created, chose their own religious identities. Though the Goddess was less freqently mentioned in the early issues, it is not surprising that her presence as a symbol for female power was increasingly felt.

The manifestations of the Goddess are manifold. A woman named Mountainspirit expressed her sense of the Goddess in the following way.

> I believe the [G]oddess is within and without. . . . Energy is within and without. Exterior and interior, all the dualities we function under lose their meaning when you go deep enough. But we are not all conscious of the [G]oddess within us.[26]

Gail Walker sought the Goddess through a study of the mythology associated with the moon and wrote

> The time seems ripe to explore the Moon as a spiritual reflection of the Goddess. . . . The moon's rhythm never misses a beat as her curved shape and arc path vary. The moon increases and decreases in crescents, bits of her own elemental form. . . . The moon is everchanging, reaching all of her points but rhymically and in due time.[27]

A third woman, Sarah Wisdom, wrote of encountering the Goddess in a dream:

> A wise woman
> sat there in the twilight
> "You must watch ahead," she said,
> "You must walk only on the edge of the sea.
> there is danger in the deep
> But in the sandy desert you will lose your way."
>
> So it is my sisters
> We are only empty shores
>
> uncreated spaces,
>
> filled with echoes of the primitive and the timeless
> and the mysteries of the deep.[28]

Wisdom's poem seems to me to express the situation of women who stand outside the canon on the "empty shores" but who sense their unique opportunity to reconnect with sources of wisdom deeper than those expressed in the canon.

Z Budapest, priestess of the Susan B. Anthony coven, has developed a feminist witchcraft tradition in which female power and female symbolism have a central place. Budapest believes that Western religion was developed to celebrate and legitimate male power and that women's liberation requires a secure grounding in women's religion. Budapest's Dianic tradition celebrates the female principle of the universe, the birthing power, as the ultimate sacred power and traces its heritage back to the Goddess worship of the ancient world and the witches of the middle Christian period.[29]

One might ask whether these developments in women's spirituality signal the creation of a new canon in which women will name the divine and define reality for themselves, claiming the power denied them in the canonical traditions of the West. This is an intriguing notion. However, it is not surprising to find that many women who stand outside the traditional canon object to the formation of a new canon.

Joan Mallonee states the view of many women in the women's spirituality movement when she says,

> I became reluctant to set down interpretations of the Goddess image in my dreams because of a sense that not only was I violating my own material but also in so doing the material would evolve into a dogma, a theology. I had a strong desire to speak about the images which were so strong and powerful, so individual and personal, but I had no desire to create the implication that She would be the same for others as She was for me.[30]

Mary Daly also has taken her stand against canonical traditions. In *Beyond God the Father* she speaks of "sisterhood" as "Anti-Church," a symbol that expresses women's position as outsiders in Western canonical tradition. For Daly, the essence of Anti-Church would be negated if women were to create a new authoritative tradition with official texts and liturgies. Daly envisions a "world without models" as the ideal and speaks of a feminist liturgy as a contradiction in terms, an "attempt to put new wine, women's awareness, into the old skins of forms that kill female self-affirmation and turn female consciousness against itself."[31] Jean Mountaingrove is even more explicit about the destructive potential of fixed feminist liturgies.

> I think it is important that we do not create new ways for women to fail, because we all have had so much failure. That's why I think it is important for rituals to be open and for each woman to feel her own way so that no one has to feel that they did it wrong. . . . We don't want to say that there is one way to be a feminist spiritual person and you are bad if you don't do it that way.[32]

Like Jean Mountaingrove, Daly sees a need for developing new rituals but asserts that they must remain open. "There is every reason for women to celebrate our history," Daly writes, "but in ever new ways, not encrusted in stagnant, repetitious ritual.[33]

Women who reject the idea of forming a new canon have a negative view of the canonical process as one that rigidly defines reality and declares certain texts, rituals, and experiences as authoritative while slandering and suppressing those reflecting alternate views of reality. They view canons as promoting conformity and authoritarian mind sets while denying individual experience and initiative. There is no question that canons function in this way, at least at some times and for some people, perhaps much of the time for women. But there is a second and more positive notion of canon. In this view of canon functions, as Sanders noted, as a "power of life" for a community, reflecting shared histories and shared perceptions of reality. Indeed there is a sense in which the possibility of communication and community requires implicit acceptance of a minimal canon. If canon is understood as the shared perceptions of reality that make communication possible, then a community that is totally anticanon is an impossibility. And certainly the women's spirituality movement is not without a canon in this second sense. Conversations about women's spirituality are deeper and more meaningful if those who participate have read Mary Daly, Starhawk, Z Budapest, and *WomanSpirit*.

Rather than rejecting the notion of canon, women might assume the responsibility for the creation of a new canon. It is important for women to celebrate their shared perceptions of ultimate reality and their power of life rituals. Women need a heritage and a tradition that will enable the expression of the vision of female power discovered outside the canons and traditions of patriarchy.

If the creation of a new canon is inevitable, then the question is whether a new canon can be created that will not also repeat the most destructive features of the old canon: the suppression of individual experience and the slander and destruction of rival traditions and their adherents. While it is probably not possible for a community to support and legitimate in the same degree the experiences of all of its members, it may be possible to create a tradition that is less oppressive than the ones we have known in the West. One sign of a vital tradition is the image the tradition holds of itself and its relation to the outsiders and heretics, the innovators on the periphery of the canon. The canonical traditions of Western religion do not fare well when judged by this criterion. Perhaps this is the reason many people, especially women, consider the traditional canons moribund. The challenge facing those who have deeply experienced exclusion as part of their own history is to create new traditions that do not exclude others.

NOTES

1. James Sanders, *Torah and Canon* (Philadelphia: Fortress Press, 1974), x.
2. Bernard W. Anderson's widely used text, *Understanding the Old Testament*, 2d ed. (Englewood Cliffs, N.J.: Prentice Hall, 1966) typifies the problem created when the new evidence about Canaanite religion is discussed within the old paradigm of dominant monotheism. Anderson takes account of the latest historical and archaeological evidence. However, the narrative structure of *Understanding the Old Testament* follows the Yahwistic narrative line, from Exodus, covenant with Yahweh at Sinai (chs. 1 and 2) to struggle between faith and culture (ch.4) to prophetic criticism (ch. 7) to renewal of covenant (chs. 12–14), etc. Within the chapter on Canaanite religion, Anderson improves on previous scholarship, "In many respects, this [the religion portrayed in the Ras Shamra texts] was a highly developed, sophisticated religion, far ahead of the belief in local fertility spirits which scholars once thought the religion of the Baals and Ashtarts to have been" (104). Yet Anderson's discussion of Canaanite religion is set within a chapter in which the narrative line stresses "the great dangers and temptations of life in Canaan" (100), a Yahwistic interpretation that Anderson adopts without acknowledging that he is presenting a Yahwistic viewpoint that may have been a minority opinion in Israel at the time of settlement in Canaan. A work on the religion of the Hebrew people not biased by the Yahwistic viewpoint would not speak of Canaanite religion as a "tempation," but rather as a plausible "solution" to the problems engendered by the settlement.
3. Morton Smith, *Palestinian Parties and Politics Which Shaped the Old Testament* (New York: Columbia University Press, 1971).

4. Raphael Patai, *The Hebrew Goddess* (New York: KTAV, 1967). See especially 42–43, 50, 58–61.
5. The "J" or Yahwistic source in Exodus, which records the political-religious murders of the worshipers of the golden calf in the presettlement period, may not be historically reliable. Still it reflects a pattern of murdering opponents of Yahwism which the "J" editors wished to legitimate by reading it back into the presettlement period.
6. The precise figures may not be historical but the pattern of suppression of competing religious groups through murder probably is. Also note that 1 Kings 18:19 mentions that Elijah called 450 prophets of Baal and 400 prophets of Asherah, but the test is waged only with the prophets of Baal for some reason that the text leaves unexplained.
7. See Merlin Stone, *When God Was A Woman* (New York: The Dial Press, 1976), 57–58.
8. Stone, esp. 30–61, and Roland de Vaux, *Ancient Israel*, Vol. 1, *Social Institutions* (New York: McGraw-Hill, 1965), 39–40.
9. "Excerpts from Vatican's Declaration Affirming Prohibition on Women Priests," *New York Times* (January 28, 1977): 8.
10. Elaine Pagels, "What Became of God the Mother? Conflicting Images of God in Early Christianity," *Signs*, 2, no. 2 (1976): 293–303, esp. 295, 299, 300–1.
11. Pagels, "What Became of God the Mother?" 300–1.
12. Gnosticism is not the only heretical movement that provided greater outlets for female power than canonical tradition. Elisabeth Schüssler Fiorenza notes that women had authority and leading positions in Montanism, Gnosticism, Manichaeism, Donatism, Priscillianism, Mesalianism, and Pelagianism, and that they were found among the bishops and priests of the Quintillians. "Feminist Theology as a Critical Theology of Liberation," *Theological Studies* 36, no. 4 (1975): 618. See also Robert E. Lerner, *The Heresy of the Free Spirit in the Later Middle Ages* (Berkeley and Los Angeles: University of California Press, 1972), 228–30, and Gottfried Koch, *Frauenfrage und Ketzertum in Mittelaiter* (Berlin, 1962), both cited by Anne Barstow Driver in "Materials Not Included in the Canon of Religious Studies: A Neolithic Goddess Cult," 6 (unpublished).
13. Mircea Eliade divides scholarship on witchcraft into the two groups discussed here. See his "Some Observations on European Witchcraft," *History of Religions* 14, no. 3 (1975): 150–151. He notes that the ultraconservative view is also held by some modern occultists and Luciferians.
14. Rosemary Radford Ruether, *New Woman/New Earth: Sexist Ideologies and Human Liberation* (New York: Seabury Press, 1975), 111.
15. See, for example, Margaret Murray, *The Witch-Cult in Western Europe* (Oxford: Oxford University Press, 1971), 225–70, and Ruether, *New Woman/New Earth*, 89.
16. See Heinrich Kramer and James Sprenger, *The Malleus Maleficarum*, trans. with introduction and notes by Montague Summers (New York: Dover Publications, 1971), xliii–xlv.
17. Ibid., esp. pp. 41, 44, 47, 54–61, 66, 80–82, 144–150.
18. Barbara Ehrenreich and Dierdre English, *Witches, Nurses, and Midwives: A History of Women Healers*, 2d. ed. (Old Westbury, NY: The Feminist Press, 1973).
19. Eliade, "Some Observations on European Witchcraft." Eliade discusses evidence that shows how pagan religious groups gradually came to incorporate practices they were accused of by their persecutors.
20. Ruether, *New Woman/New Earth*, 89–114.

21. Ibid.
22. See Rita Gross, "Methodological Remarks on the Study of Women and Religion: Review, Criticism, and Redefinition," in *Women and Religion*, ed. Judith Plaskow and Joan Arnold Romero (Missoula, Mont.: AAR and Scholars' Press, 1974), 153–65; also see Valerie Saiving, "Androcentrism in Religious Studies," *Journal of Religion* (April 1976): 177–96.
23. Susan Rennie and Kirsten Grimstad, *The New Women's Survival Sourcebook* (New York: Alfred A. Knopf, 1975), 191.
24. Barbry MyOwn and Hallie Mountainwing [Iglehart], "A Ritual Celebration," *WomanSpirit* (1975): 27, 25, 28.
25. Published quarterly, 1974-1984. Back issues available from 2000 KMT, Sunny Valley, OR 97497.
26. Mountainspirit, *WomanSpirit* 3, no. 9 (1976): 5.
27. Gail Walker, "Moon Change," *Lady-Unique* 1 (1976): 5.
28. Sarah Wisdom, "Sea Dream," *WomanSpirit* 3, no. 10 (1976): 30. Used with permission of the author.
29. See Z. Budapest, *The Feminist Book of Light and Shadows* (Los Angeles: Luna Publications, 1976).
30. Joan Mallonee, *Lady-Unique* 1 (Autumn 1976): 12.
31. Mary Daly, *Beyond God the Father* (Boston: Beacon Press, 1973), 145; also see 69ff, and 132ff.
32. Jean Mountaingrove, "What Is this Goddess Business," *WomanSpirit* 3, no. 9 (1976): 9.
33. Daly, *Beyond God the Father*, 146.

Double Goddesses. From Çatal Hüyük.

4. A Spirituality for Women

In an article titled "A Religion for Women," published in *Christianity and Crisis*, Rosemary Radford Ruether argued that feminists who do not use the biblical tradition as the basis for their spiritual vision have a tendency to "see the Bible through a screen of hostile caricature that ignores almost all of its actual content," that they sound like "ignorant bigots," and that some of them may have unresolved oedipal dependencies. In that article and elsewhere, Ruether stated that mature feminists can find a critical tradition in the Bible that can be used to form the basis of a religion for women. She implied that only immature feminists would not base their spiritual vision on this critical tradition.[1]

My first reaction to this article was surprised incredulity. As Judith Plaskow and I wrote in the introduction to *Womanspirit Rising*:

> We believe that the diversity within feminist theology and spirituality is its strength. Each of these feminist positions has a contribution to make to the transformation of patriarchal culture. The fundamental commitment that feminists in religion share to end male ascendency in religion is more important than their differences.[2]

I have been encouraged in this vision of mutual respect and interaction by a story Gail Graham Yates told about the course on feminist spirituality she taught at the University of Minnesota. At the beginning of the semester, class members asked to divide into three discussion groups, the "reformists," the "post-traditionalists," and the "seekers," those who hadn't made up their minds or who were just taking the course out of interest. Within weeks, the "seekers" group dissolved as their members joined the other groups. The two remaining groups continued to meet separately. Toward the end of the semester, the post-traditionalists decided to have a ritual, and they went outside, sat in a circle, and chanted to Goddess. Meanwhile, the reformers decided to have a ritual, and they sat in a circle, passed an apple, and asked the blessing of Mother God. The moral of the story according to Graham Yates was, "So much for the differences between the reformists and the post-traditionalists."[3]

The most obvious (though perhaps not the most significant) difference among feminists working in religion is the question of allegiance to biblical tradition. Some feminists work within biblical traditions to reform or transform them so that they will reflect a feminist vision of the equality of women. Their understanding is that traditions can change. They appeal to certain elements within their traditions as warrant for their visions of a transformed Judaism and Christianity. Other feminists do not consider themselves Christians or Jews and work to discover or create a spiritual vision that is not based on biblical tradition. I have used the word allegiance in describing this difference, because I think the question is one of loyalty and self-understanding. In the questions of loyalty or allegiance to a tradition a number of complex factors are involved, including matters of judgment or interpretation that cannot be definitively resolved one way or another. For example, feminists working in religion agree that much in the Jewish and Christian traditions is sexist. We agree on this (and disagree with some traditional apologists), because we begin with a common assumption that women and men ought to have access to the same religious and social roles. Once this assumption is accepted, the Bible and traditional Jewish and Christian teachings on the roles of women and men can be examined to see whether or not they envision equality. While there is room for some dispute about the intended meaning of some statements in the Bible or tradition, general agreement could probably be found among feminists about many passages in the Bible or in traditional texts and teaching.

For example, most would agree that Galatians 3:28, "There is neither Jew nor Greek, there is neither slave nor free, there is neither male nor female; for you are all one in Christ Jesus" is more positive toward women than 1 Corinthians 14:34, "The women should keep silence in churches. For they are not permitted to speak, but should be subordinate." But even here there is room for disagreement about whether Paul intended his statement in Galatians 3:28 to be taken as a justification for women's social and/or religious equality, or about whether Paul's alleged intention is relevant to the "meaning" of the text. The significant factor may be that this was a widely used baptismal formula.[4] But the interpretation of individual passages is not itself sufficient reason for making a decision about whether one will or will not understand oneself as a member of a tradition. A feminist who did not believe Paul in Galatians 3:28 ever intended that women should have social or religious equality could still be a Christian, and a feminist who believed that Paul intended to teach women's religious and social equality in Galatians 3:28 could still not find that sufficient warrant to be a Christian. The decision concerning allegiance to a tradition is based on complex questions of judgment, which include: Can I as an individual find more spiritual sustenance within or outside the church or synagogue? Can I have greater impact by working within or outside the church or synagogue? Are larger numbers of people hungering for a nonbiblical spiritual alternative? Or is it more pragmatic to work within an institution that still has many adherents? What is the potential for change within the church or synagogue? Does change occur faster through movements or through those working within institutions? Has the church or synagogue done more harm than good for women over the years or in the present? And finally, and most importantly, is the "essential core" of the Jewish and Christian faiths inalterably sexist, or can these faiths be interpreted or transformed to reflect nonsexist visions? The answers to some of these questions will vary from individual to individual, and the answers to others are matters of interpretation of history or the future for which reasons can be given, but which cannot be definitively resolved one way or another. Therefore, I do not think it is helpful to posit a need to "kill the father"[5] to explain the positions of those who reject biblical religion, any more than it is necessary to posit "continued dependence on the father" to explain the decision of others to work within the tradition. There are some matters about which reasonable women can disagree.

But if reasonable women can disagree, this does not mean we have no grounds for our disagreement. The reason I do not use the biblical tradition as the basis for my feminist vision is a judgment about the effect of the *core symbolism* of biblical tradition on the vast majority of Christians and Jews. I agree with Mary Daly that the biblical tradition is defined by a system of symbols centering around the images of God/He, God as Lord, King, Warrior, Father, and Son, which functions to teach and enforce the notion that legitimate power and authority in religion and society is appropriately held predominantly or exclusively by men.[6] Stated this simply, the argument might strike some as "extremely simplistic," or as "hostile caricature" (both phrases are Ruether's).[7] Yet anyone who has read Daly's work carefully knows that her argument is not simplistic. She acknowledges that theologians have always asserted that God is beyond sexuality, and she is aware that there are some passages in the Bible and tradition that indicate that some thinkers have seen beyond the image of God/Jesus as male. Daly's argument is not about the exceptions but about the rule. Her arguments are concerned with the effect of repeated symbolism on the conscious and unconscious mind and imagination. Ruether herself admits that the view of Naomi Goldenberg in *Changing of the Gods* (which is a restatement of Daly's) that Yahweh and Christ "were shaped by males principally to deify themselves and to sanctify the power of men over women in patriarchal societies" is one that she (Ruether) "would be disposed to take very seriously. Although I [Ruether] don't think it is the whole truth about these figures, it is much more deeply true about the way they have actually functioned culturally than most feminists, as well as most traditional theologians have been willing to grant."[8] On this point Ruether is in substantial agreement with nonbiblical feminists working in religion.

Where some of us disagree is on the importance of the argument about God symbolism. Ruether agrees with the feminist criticism of God symbolism stated above and acknowledges that she herself thinks of God as the "great Matrix [which] is neither male nor female" and prefers to think of "Her as She in personal prayer," though she would not want to dogmatize that preference as universal.[9] But attention to female symbolism for the divine was not a prominent theme in Ruether's work at the time she began to critique the Goddess movement. This suggests that Ruether might not have acknowledged the depth of the damage done to female and male psyches by the symbol of God as male. For Daly, Goldenberg, and myself, as well as for Starhawk, Z Budapest, and many other feminists, the symbolism of God as male in biblical traditions is crucially significant. The pervasive use of male genderized language for God is not the only objection I have to the biblical traditions, but it alone might warrant rejection of them. As I see it, specific instances of sexist opposition to women's full participation in religious and social roles found in Bible, tradition, and contemporary politics are a logical (according to the logic of symbols) outcome of the core symbolism of God/He. In this view, the fact that much of the well-organized opposition to women's rights in contemporary society—Catholic opposition to abortion and reproductive freedom, fundamentalist and Mormon opposition to E.R.A., nonsexist textbooks, and homosexual civil rights—comes from religious sources is disturbing but not surprising. There is much in biblical tradition that justifies patriarchal society. I do not believe the patriarchal attitudes of the vast majority of those whose religious faith is based on the Bible will be changed until the image of God is changed. To me, this means that coming to terms with the Goddess is a crucially important task for all feminists working within religion.

As part of her argument that mature feminists would reinterpret rather than reject biblical traditions, Rosemary Ruether has stated that there is a critical or liberating tradition in the Bible which can be useful for women despite the predominant male symbolism and language for God in the Bible. Ruether calls this the prophetic-messianic tradition. Of it she writes,

> Unlike most of Christian theology, the Bible for the most part, is not written from the standpoint of world power, but from the standpoint of people who take the side of the disadvantaged; the rural population against the landowners and urban rich; the small colonized nation against the mighty empires. In the New Testatment, this is continued. . . This inclines the Bible to a view of God as One who does not take the side of the powerful but who comes to vindicate the oppressed.[10]

It does not seem to me that matters are as simple as that. I do not believe the prophetic-messianic tradition can function as a basis for feminist theology—at least not without itself being criticized far more radically than Ruether and many other feminist liberation theologians have done.

Though it indeed appears that some of the prophets were from rural as opposed to urban backgrounds, and as such were representatives of the dispossessed, much of the Bible was written and/

or edited by a relatively comfortable, urban, (and it should be added misogynist) priestly class. Many of the priestly writings are concerned with excluding women from the central roles in religion. Thus I cannot agree with Ruether's statement that "*the Bible for the most part* [my italics] is not written from the standpoint of world power."[11] Though I too find some of the ethical injunctions of the prophets inspiring, I find them embedded in a patriarchal "Yahweh alone" theology, which I find problematic. For every prophetic injunction against those who "sell the righteous for silver, the needy for a pair of shoes" (Amos 2:6), there is a threat against those who worship "on every high hill and under every green tree" (Hos. 4:13). Surely many of the people who worshiped Gods and Goddesses in these rites were following ancient traditions of their peoples, and I have no doubt that many of them were from the rural poor group with which Ruether identifies. Surely many women as well as men from all classes found the notion of a Goddess who was connected to nature powerful (see Jeremiah 7:17–18 and 44:15–19). Moreover, the fact the Goddess religions in which women played key roles were among the religions condemned by the prophets certainly has contributed to the antipathy toward female leadership and Goddess symbolism in Judaism and Christianity.

I cannot embrace the prophetic tradition of the Hebrew Bible, which is vindictive against those who worship in other traditions. It seems to me that this prophetic tradition is also one of the key roots of religious intolerance in the West. I do not believe the attitude of intolerance toward other religions in the prophets is incidental to an otherwise liberating vision. I think it is fundamental to the particular shape that monotheism takes in both the Hebrew and the Christian scriptures.

In her article, Ruether also alludes briefly and positively to the God of Exodus who drowns the horsemen of the Pharaoh. As I read Exodus, the God who took the side of the oppressed Hebrew slaves is modeled on the holy warrior ideal. Yahweh proves himself the most powerful holy warrior by drowning Pharaoh's horsemen with their horses. This is not for me a liberating vision of divine power.

Even apart from these considerations, however, the fact that the judgment on the rich in favor of the poor in the prophetic tradition is delivered by a male God makes me question the validity of the "critical and liberating" potential of this tradition for women. For one of the messages conveyed to women by this tradition is that they must be judged, punished, and forgiven by a male authority figure (Yahweh and his representative, the male prophet) in order to be saved. This applies to what Ruether defines as the liberating potential of the New Testament as well. For, however much Jesus included women and the dispossessed in his community, the fact remains that the New Testament clearly portrays it as *his* community, and the message conveyed to women is that they must turn to a male to find salvation.

Ruether argues that this liberating prophetic-messianic tradition "can only be recovered by a thoroughgoing criticism of the way Christianity has generally functioned."[12] I would argue that even the traditions Ruether cites as liberating are themselves part of an oppressive patriarchal theology and not themselves adequate models for feminist theology and spirituality.

Rosemary Ruether criticizes "feminist Wicca" as described by Naomi Goldenberg in *Changing of the Gods* as an inadequate source for feminist theology. Though Ruether focuses her critique on feminist Wicca (and in this section of her article mentions only Goldenberg, Z Budapest, and others as advocates of the position she rejects), her comments have been taken as an indictment of feminist Goddess spirituality generally. Ruether's rejection of feminist Wicca is based on three objections: (1) that ancient Goddess religion was invented by men to celebrate male power; (2) that feminist Goddess spirituality imports nineteenth century romantic dualism into ancient patterns; and (3) that men do not have an adequate role in feminist Wicca.[13] I will respond to each of these objections from the perspective of the wider feminist Goddess movement, rather than feminist Wicca specifically.

Ruether alleges that "the cult [*sic*] of the Goddess and the King was not in fact shaped by women for women's liberation. It was shaped by men to make themselves 'kings of the world.' "[14] The interpretation of the roles of women and men in the various religions and cultures in which Goddesses were worshiped is not as clear as Ruether's statement implies. Much of the evidence concerning ancient Goddess religions has been lost through neglect or destroyed by superseding groups; adherants of biblical monotheism have been particularly vicious in destroying evidence for polytheistic religions in which Goddesses were worshiped. What evidence remains has been interpreted through the lens of patriarchal scholarship in which evidence of female power is often misinterpreted, ignored, or trivialized. For example, Goddess religions may be called "cults," Goddess images may be called "idols" or "fetishes," and female leadership may be ignored. Finally, much of the evidence suggesting that women may once have had a great deal of autonomy in religion comes from the period of prehistory, before written records. Evidence from prehistory is more difficult to interpret than evidence from historical periods, and therefore more subject to distortion by the biases of the interpreter than evidence from historical periods where written records are available.

Like many male scholars who dismiss the possibility that women may have had more prominent religious roles in pre- or nonbibilical religions, Rosemary Ruether apparently assumes that "history begins at Sumer" (the title of a book by Samuel N. Kramer) in about 3500 B.C.E.[15] This mistake is often made in discussions of Goddess symbolism and reflects our culture's bias toward written records and familiar patriarchal structures. If evidence from 3500 B.C.E. and later is all that is considered, then Ruether's conclusion that Goddess religions were shaped by men to assure male dominance may be correct. But as Merlin Stone has shown, drawing on the work of many other scholars, even after 3500 B.C.E. women may have had greater autonomy in matrilineal, polytheistic, Goddess worshiping cultures—the ability to buy, sell, and manage property in their own names, greater sexual freedom, and leadership roles in religion—than they did in the later patrilineal monotheistic God cultures of the Hebrews and Christians.[16] It surprises me that Ruether does not even mention this evidence.

More significant, however, is Ruether's failure to consider evidence of earlier Goddess cultures. Goddess religion did not begin at Sumer. Goddess images have been dated to 32,000 B.C.E., or even earlier. Considerable evidence exists to suggest that Goddess religion flowered in horticultural and early agricultural societies that developed at the end of the last ice age in the period scholars call Neolithic. These societies existed several thousand years before Sumer.

It is the hypothesis of many feminist (and some other) scholars that the religion of the Goddess and the King was preceded by millennia of Goddess religion in which Goddesses were not subordinate to Gods and women had social and religious power. Autumn Stanley has argued that women had a great deal of power in "horticultural" societies (an anthropological term denoting agricultural societies without the animal-drawn plough). She argued that in the horticultural period agriculture was controlled by women in many societies, that women shared control of it with men in others, while in only a few societies was it controlled by men. This ratio shifts in favor of men in agricultural societies with the animal-drawn plough, the societies to which scholars refer when they claim that men control agriculture. Based on the assumption that the worker invents the tools, Stanley hypothesized that women in the horticultural period were responsible for many inventions, including the domestication of plants and selective breeding and propagation techniques; the development of cultivating tools, including the hoe, spade or shovel, and early plough; the creation of improved food-gathering tools, including basketry; improved food-processing techniques; the development of early irrigation methods; and the domestication of animals. She hypothesized that women's power was gradually eroded in developed agricultural societies where a number of factors—including the ability to feed more children led to women's more numerous pregnancies and more frequent involvement in the care of young children—made them increasingly dependent on men at the same time that men's control of the animal drawn plough gave them greater social power.[17]

In ancient horticultural and earliest agricultural societies Goddesses were not subordinated to Gods. Goddess worship was not initially "shaped by men to make themselves kings of the world." Indeed, it is highly unlikely that kingship even existed in horticultural and early agricultural societies.

Anne Barstow's interpretation of Çatal Hüyük, a Neolithic society that existed in Anatolia (now Turkey) about 6500 to 5700 B.C.E., provides compelling confirmation of Stanley's view. Interpreting the archaeological finds of James Mellaart, Barstow finds "no evidence for either centralized power or for an antinature, antiwoman mentality." Instead, she finds "a town of possibly

6000 persons, containing hundreds of shrines and the earliest wall paintings, the earliest textiles, and the earliest pottery yet found. . . shrines dominated by bulls' horns representing the god, by scenes of hunting celebrations, and by the [G]oddess represented anthropomorphically in plaster relief and in clay or stone cult [*sic*] statues." With Mellaart, Barstow concludes that in Çatal Hüyük "the family centered around the woman, was matrilocal and probably matrilineal . . . [and] that women exercised certain kinds of power at Çatal Hüyük, because its chief source of wealth was agriculture *and women were in charge of its development.* They controlled the home and the economy, and eventually they molded the religion . . . [which was] a celebration of fecundity and rebirth, and of the beauty and strength of textiles, animals, and women."[18] If Barstow is correct, then the religion at Çatal Hüyük was a far cry from Ruether's depiction of the religion of the Goddess and the King.

Whatever the historical evidence may reveal, contemporary feminist Wicca, which is but one branch of a much larger feminist Goddess movement, is not a simple revival of the religion of the Goddess and the King. Feminist Goddess spirituality is a syncretistic combination of elements of pre-Christian religion with contemporary ideas and experiences.

Like Rosemary Ruether, I "am not opposed to the adoption of images from Goddess religion as a valid source of spirituality."[19] But while Ruether seems uneasy about this development, I am excited about it. Like many contemporary women, I am sensitive to the psychic damage done to women by the male God imagery of the biblical traditions. When I first said the word *Goddess,* I experienced my own being in the image of God(dess) in a new way. The word *Goddess* was for me an important affirmation of the legitimacy and beneficence of female power, of the goodness and beauty of women's bodies and their connection to nature, of the validity of the female will, and of the importance of female-female bonds. Like Ruether, I am willing to acknowledge that Goddess symbolism comes *to me* (but not necessarily to other feminists) through the lens of my own Christian background and through Tillich's symbol of the Ground of Being. But I would also note that Tillich's Ground of Being was an abstract symbol for me until Goddess as the life, death, and transformation power gave it content.

I must also acknowledge that *for me* the symbol of Goddess is different than anything I ever found in the Christian tradition. My relationship to Yahweh was a dynamic one and one filled with the biblical symbolism of chosenness, demand, judgment, rejection, and ultimate acceptance. Like Ruether, I was particularly moved by the prophets' concern for social justice and harmony with nature. For me the biblical God was "beyond sexuality" as theological tradition asserts, but "he" retained a certain aura of masculine presence and authority. It wasn't until I said *Goddess* that I realized how significant that remaining aura of masculinity was in my image God. Not until I said *Goddess* did I realize that I had never felt fully included in the fullness of my being as *woman* in masculine or neuterized imagery for divinity.

Moreover, I found in Goddess spirituality an image that affirmed my own experience of the holiness of nature as a significant element in the divine reality. I do not view Goddess's (or my own) relation to nature through the lens of "nature-culture dualism of nineteenth-century romanticism" as Ruether says is the case in contemporary feminist Goddess religion.[20] To me, Goddess is a symbol of the waxing and waning, life-and-death powers that are reflected in nature and in all human activities. To me, Goddess is a symbol for the integration of nature *and* culture, a symbol both for my connection to nature and for my creative processes that lead to cultural activity, such as the creation of this essay. I certainly do not advocate a simplistic back-to-nature movement, much less an identification of women solely with the irrational, the inarticulate, or the capacity to give birth to physical children.

But if nature-culture dualism is not reflected in contemporary feminist Goddess symbolism, another duality does appear, which may have led to Ruether's confusion. It is a duality between an overmasculinized, overtechnologized, overmilitarized, patriarchal society that threatens to destroy the possibility of life on this earth with nuclear power, and the vision of a more wholistic culture in which women and all beings are valued, and in which the grounding of human life in nature is recognized as the basis of all cultural activities. In modern Western culture men are socialized to become part of the overtechnologized male-dominated society. Men are socialized to be rational, aggressive, assertive, and never to show their emotions or let feeling influence thinking. And they are taught to subdue or control the irrational, nature, and women. Women, on the other hand, are socialized to be sensitive to emotions and relationships, and are said to be closer to nature than men. Within traditional patriarchal culture, women's emotionality and closeness to nature is kept separate from the spheres of culture and politics: women create a haven for men in home and garden, which compensates for the alienation men experience in the male world. The cultural association of men with the rational and the cultural and women with the irrational and nature is deeply rooted in Western culture, as Ruether has argued.[21]

Spiritual feminism, of which the feminist Goddess and feminist Wicca movement are a part, criticizes *patriarchal* culture and male roles in it, celebrates women's (and the human) connection to nature, and encourages women to develop a form of thinking that includes feeling and to develop "nonrational" capacities such as intuition and psychic power while moving toward achieving cultural power. This apparently is what leads Ruether to conclude that feminist Goddess symbolism imports "the female-male, nature-culture dualism" of nineteenth-century romanticism into ancient religious patterns. However, nineteenth-century romanticism (like its twentieth-century offspring, Jungianism) was a celebration of nature and women by men in which women were encouraged to remain natural and intuitive (and thereby dependent on men) at the expense of developing their full human capacities and freedom. It was a new version of "barefoot and pregnant." Feminist women are not about to celebrate our connections to nature within a dualistic framework that leaves us socially and culturally powerless. But women need not accept male notions of what society and culture are or should be. In feminist spirituality Goddess is a symbol both for female power and for the integration of culture and nature. Feminist spirituality, like the larger feminist movement, is concerned to help all women achieve psychological, personal, social, cultural, political, *and* spiritual power.

Ruether's final criticism of the feminist Wicca movement is that it makes women the overwhelmingly dominant partners. The males present are reduced to son-lovers of the Great Mother.[22] The question of men is indeed problematic in feminist Goddess spirituality. While some men have been involved in some feminist Goddess groups, many, and probably the majority of feminist Goddess and women's spirituality groups have been women's groups.

Most feminist Wicca, Goddess, and women's spirituality groups have evolved out of the wider feminist movement in which the small group of women is a predominant form. In small groups women share experiences and stories. As Judith Plaskow has noted, "The Yeah-Yeah experience," in which women recognize that others share similar feelings, similar hopes, similar oppressions, is the central theme of women's groups. Men are traditionally excluded from women's small groups because it is felt that the presence of men would inhibit most women from expressing our own views freely and fully.[23] In feminist spirituality groups women meet to share spiritual experience and to discover common patterns in our stories. The desire to give a female name to the divine power and to celebrate women's connections to nature are two prominent themes in most feminist spirituality, feminist Goddess, and feminist Wicca groups. Coming out of a culture in which women's experience and women's spiritual visions are not valued, women's first concern has been to give voice to our own spiritual longings. Obviously, figuring out how men fit into women's spirituality groups has not been a first priority for most women.

Though Rosemary Ruether states that in feminist Wicca groups "males present are reduced to son-lovers of the Great Mother," it is my experience that men are rarely present at all in feminist spirituality groups and are spoken of very little. I personally believe that as the feminist spirituality develops further from spiritual consciousness-raising and ritual groups into a cultural alternative, the role of men and male symbolism in feminist religion will need to be more carefully considered. As women become more confident in articulating spiritual vision, many will want to celebrate with men. In such a situation, a religion of the Goddess only could be oppressive to men.

But it is important to remember that feminists in the spirituality movement, like feminists generally, do not have a single view on any question, and certainly not on the question of men. Positions or attitudes that may be held by some individuals or groups within the larger movement should not be attributed to the movement as a whole. Also, in discussing the role of men in a *feminist* spirituality, Goddess, or Wicca movement, it must be remembered that the number of men who are strongly committed to feminism in general and feminist spirituality in particular, while growing, is not large. It is premature to condemn a feminist movement for its failure to include men when in fact very few men are interested in having a part in it.

The issue of the role of men in the feminist spirituality movement is related to the issues of *separation* and *separatism* in the feminist movement generally. In the feminist small group, women separate from men in order to get in touch with their own experience. As long as patriarchal culture continues to exist, women will still need to find spaces where we can be somewhat free of patriarchal attitudes. Whether we like it or not, it remains true that in mixed groups men will often try to dominate or diffuse women's creative energy. Separatism as a total world view must be distinguished from instances of separation. Separatists argue that if some separation from men is powerful, then complete separation from men would be ideal. Separatists believe that women can become emotionally, financially, sexually, culturally, spiritually, and in all ways independent of men. A common separatist ideal is to live self-sufficiently in a commune of women in the country; another is to open a small business such as a bookstore or restaurant that employs and serves women exclusively. Separatist visions of free and independent women can be empowering even to women who are not separatists. While many feminists have espoused complete separation from men, and some have, as Ruether notes, excluded men from large feminist gatherings, most feminists are not separatists, and in practice, few separatists are completely consistent. On the other hand, most women who are feminists have participated in at least one group for women only, and male feminists organize groups for men only.

Few feminists would deny the validity of women forming groups in which women can share and articulate our spiritual visions with other women. On the other hand, I believe most women in the spirituality movement would be uncomfortable with a *purportedly universal* religion that excluded men or gave them only a subordinate role.

While I disagree with many elements of Ruether's critique of

Goddess spirituality, I agree with her that the issues of men and male symbolism will eventually need further attention by feminists. Starhawk has discussed the role of men and male symbolism in feminist Wicca in *The Spiral Dance*, and though I do not find her image of the Horned God entirely adequate, I applaud her attempt to develop male symbolism and male roles in feminist Goddess worship.[24] My suspicion, however, is that a more satisfying resolution of this problem awaits the time when large numbers of men become deeply committed to feminism and feminist spirituality. In the meantime, it is clear to me that the image of Goddess within the feminist spirituality movement is profoundly important for women.

NOTES

1. Rosemary Ruether, "A Religion for Women," *Christianity and Crisis* (December 10, 1979): 307–11, esp. 308; "Goddesses and Witches: Liberation and Countercultural Feminism," *Christian Century* (September 10–17, 1980): 842–47. But for another view, see Ruether, "Moving Beyond Who Killed the Goddess: Female Symbols, Values, and Context, *Christianity and Crisis* (January 12, 1987): 460–64; and my response, "Dialogue, Accuracy, and Ambiguity," *Christianity and Crisis* (February 16, 1987): 55–56.
2. Carol P. Christ and Judith Plaskow, eds., *Womanspirit Rising* (New York: Harper & Row, 1979), 15.
3. Gail Graham Yates at a conference on Women and Religion sponsored by University of Minnesota and the College of St. Catherine, Minneapolis, Minnesota, October 19, 1979.
4. Elisabeth Schüssler Fiorenza, *In Memory of Her: A Feminist Theological Reconstruction of Christian Origins* (New York: Crossroad Press, 1983), 108.
5. Ruether, "A Religion for Women," 309.
6. Mary Daly, *Beyond God the Father: Toward a Philosophy of Women's Liberation* (Boston: Beacon Press, 1973).
7. Ruether, "A Religion for Women," 309.
8. Ibid., 308.
9. Ibid. 310.
10. Ibid.
11. Ibid, 309.
12. Ibid., 310.
13. Ibid.
14. Ibid.
15. Samuel Noah Kramer, *History Begins at Sumer* (New York: Doubleday, 1959).
16. Merlin Stone, *When God Was a Woman* (New York: Dial Press, 1976).
17. Autumn Stanley, "Daughter of Isis, Daughter of Ceres: Women Inventors of Agriculture," presented to the 1980 meetings of the National Women's Studies Association in Bloomington, Indiana.
18. Anne Barstow, "The Uses of Archaeology for Women's History: James Mellaart's Work on the Neolithic," 4, no. 3 (1978): 8, 15.

19. Ruether, "A Religion for Women," 310.
20. Ibid.
21. Ruether, "Motherearth and the Megamachine," in *Womanspirit Rising* (New York: Harper & Row, 1979), 43–52.
22. Ruether, "A Religion for Women," 310.
23. Judith Plaskow, "Toward a Coming of Lilith," *Womanspirit Rising*, 198–207.

5. Yahweh as Holy Warrior

As I have noted, it has been alleged by some feminist Christian liberation theologians that a liberating vision can be found in the Exodus liberation of the Hebrew slaves, in the prophetic call for social justice, and in Jesus' preaching to the poor and outcasts of his society.[1] The image of Yahweh as warrior in Exodus and the prophets needs to be examined more directly than it has been by feminist theologians. Though I focus my criticism on the Exodus and prophetic traditions because I know them better than I know the Jesus traditions, the apocalyptic traditions of the New Testament are a continuation of the Yahweh war tradition. Moreover, when Christianity became accepted as the official religion of the Roman Empire through Constantine's alleged vision of a flaming cross in the sky, inscribed with the words "In this sign shalt thou conquer," the holy warrior tradition was continued in Christian history.

It is true that the Exodus tradition of liberation from oppression and the prophetic call for social justice have inspired social liberation movements. Clearly, these traditions have provided hope to Jews in diaspora, to blacks in slavery and in racist America, to Latin Americans in poverty and destitution, and also to feminists in both the nineteenth and twentieth centuries. Nevertheless, as a feminist concerned with social justice and peace issues, I cannot find in these traditions adequate expressions of my spiritual and social vision.

My understanding of the potential scope of feminist theology was shaped in the late 1960s and early 1970s. I became convinced of the wrongness of the Vietnam war some time before I consciously became a feminist. Adrienne Rich's poem "The Phenomenology of Anger" expressed my understanding of the close relationship between patriarchy and war, feminism and my concern for peace:

I suddenly see the world
as no longer viable:
you are out there burning the crops
with some new sublimate
This morning you left the bed
we still share
and went out to spread impotence
upon the world

I hate you.
I hate the mask you wear. . .

Last night, in this room, weeping
I asked you: *what are you feeling?*
do you feel anything?
Now in the torsion of your body
as you defoliate the fields we lived from
I have your answer.[2]

I believe that many of the attitudes and behaviors associated with the male image and role are at the root of the threat of global destruction. Human survival depends in part on our examining the relationship between power and violence in the male psyche. My feminist work has focused on women's experience with the hope that it contained a web of values with which we could reconstitute the world: a world without war, without violence as we know it today in patriarchy.

I do not attribute war to the male nature, nor do I argue that women are incapable of warlike action, but I do believe that as feminists we must examine the equation of "manhood" and power with war that has been the legacy of patriarchal cultures. In his brilliant book *The Male Machine*, Marc Feigan Fasteau has shown that boys in our culture must learn to test their manhood through violence in sports and fighting, and he has shown the devastating consequences of the rhetoric of masculinity in shaping U.S. foreign policy with regard to the war in Vietnam. We cannot afford to ignore his message.[3]

My rejection of the image of Yahweh as warrior in Exodus and the prophets is further shaped—but not dependent on—a historical hypothesis about the relationship between patriarchy and war: patriarchy and large-scale warfare arose together, *although not by simple cause and effect.* Warfare is not a major part of life in preagricultural and early agricultural societies. It is widely accepted by classical scholars that settled matrilineal and relatively peaceful societies in Greece and the Mediterranean area were conquered by and/or assimilated with patrilineal, patriarchal, and warlike invaders during the fourth, third, and second millennia B.C.E. The warlike Zeus was the God of these patriarchal peoples.[4] I do not believe that the warrior Gods or Goddesses of this era should be models for feminist theology.

The God of Exodus and the prophets is a warrior God.[5] My rejection of this God as a liberating image for feminist theology is based on my understanding of the symbolic function of a warrior God in cultures where warfare is glorified as a symbol of manhood and power. My primary concern here is with the function of symbolism, not with the historical truth of the Exodus stories, with questions of how many slaves may or may not have been freed, nor by what means, nor with questions of the different traditions that may have been woven together to shape the biblical stories. Since liberation theology is fundamentally concerned with the use of biblical symbolism in shaping contemporary reality and the understanding of the divine ground, this method is appropriate here. In a world threatened by total nuclear annihilation, we cannot afford a warlike image of God. The image of Yahweh as liberator of the oppressed in the exodus and as concerned for social justice in the prophets cannot be extricated from the image of Yahweh as warrior.

In Exodus Yahweh is imaged as concerned for the oppressed Israelites. Exodus 3:7–8 is a good example. "Then Yahweh said, 'I have seen the affliction of my people who are in Egypt, and have heard their cry because of their taskmasters; I know their sufferings, and I have come down to deliver them out of the hand of the Egyptians.'" People in oppressed circumstances and liberation theologians find passages like this inspiring. I too have been profoundly moved by the image of a God who takes compassion on suffering, but this passage has a conclusion I cannot accept. The passage continues "and to bring them up out of that land to a good and broad land, a land flowing with milk and honey, to the place of the Canaanites, the Hittites, the Amorites, the Perizzites, the Hivites, and the Jebusites." Here Yahweh promises "his people" a land that is inhabited by other peoples. In order to justify this action by Yahweh, the inhabitants of the land are portrayed in other parts of the Bible as evil or idolators (a term that itself bears further examination). More recently liberation theologians have portrayed these other peoples as ruling-class opponents of the poor peasant and working-class Hebrews. However that may be, the clear implication of the passage is that Yahweh intends to dispossess the peoples from the lands they inhabit.

In the so-called Song of Moses in Exodus 15:1–18 (which many scholars believe is very ancient), Yahweh is celebrated as a warrior.

> I will sing to Yahweh, for he has triumphed gloriously;
> the horse and his rider he has thrown into the sea.
> Yahweh is my strength and my song,
> and he has become my salvation;
> this is my God, and I will praise him,
> my father's God, and I will exalt him.
> Yahweh is a man of war;
> Yahweh is his name. . . .
>
> Who is like thee, O Yahweh, among the gods?
> Who is like thee, majestic in holiness,
> terrible in glorious deeds, doing wonders?
> Thou didst stretch out thy right hand,
> the earth swallowed them.
> —Exodus 15:1–3, 11–12

This passage is a celebration of Yahweh as the most powerful warrior imaginable, more powerful even than the legendary Pharaoh and his armies. Yahweh accomplishes the liberation of his people through a magnificent act of war, made all the more magnificent, if we are to believe the story as it is told, by Yahweh's clever act of setting up the Pharaoh not to negotiate peacefully with Moses by "hardening his heart" (see Exod. 4:21 and *passim*). In Exodus 15:3, Yahweh is explicitly called "a man of war," a line paralleled by "Yahweh is his name." The poem details Yahweh's killing of Pharaoh's chariots and armies and continues with a prophecy of his victories over the inhabitants of Philistia and Canaan, the chiefs of Edom and Moab.

Clearly the image of military victory over one's foes is attractive to oppressed peoples. I myself have sometimes fantasized violent ends for certain selected patriarchs. Still I must say: this is not my

God. This God of war stands for far too much that I stand against.[6]

A second tradition that feminist liberation theology has put forward as an example of the liberating vision of the Bible is the prophets' concern for social justice. This vision of social justice, however, is also embedded in the tradition of Yahweh war that was present in Exodus; further, it is intertwined with a tradition of religious intolerance that has been the source of a great deal of suffering. The prophetic vision of social justice is well expressed in Amos 2:6–7.

> Thus says Yahweh:
> "For three transgressions of Israel,
> and for four, I will not revoke the punishment;
> because they sell the righteous for silver,
> and the needy for a pair of shoes—
> they that trample the head of the poor into the dust of the earth,
> and turn aside the way of the afflicted."

This is an eloquent vision of divine concern for the poor and the needy. There was a time when I considered it both the finest poetry and the highest moral ideal. The passage portrays Yahweh as prepared to punish his own beloved people because they have not upheld social justice within their own community. It reflects a social or corporate rather than an individual notion of salvation, which is attractive because it holds all responsible for the ills of the social body.

On closer examination, however, even this vision must be seen as embedded within the larger structure of a theology rooted in the image of Yahweh as warrior. With great irony, the two chapters of the book of Amos in which this passage is embedded build up to Yahweh's judgment of Israel. In the earlier verses Yahweh tells how he has punished or will punish Damascus, Gaza, Tyre, Edom, the Ammonites, Moab, and Judah. Yahweh says that just as he has punished or will punish other peoples for their transgressions, so will he punish Israel. Yahweh's method of punishment is fire, mentioned seven times (Amos 1:4, 7, 10, 12, 14; 2:2, 5); exile, mentioned twice (Amos 1:5, 15); and slaying, mentioned twice (Amos 1:8, 2:3). These are typical images of warfare. This passage can be interpreted as an example of the covenant lawsuit in which

Yahweh declares his mighty acts, in this case his acts against the other peoples, and his act of deliverance of the Hebrews from Egypt, which is mentioned in Amos 2:10–11. The prophetic call for justice within Israel is not simply a moral injunction presented by a kind and just God; it is a threat that the warlike nature of Yahweh will be unleashed against his own people as it has been unleashed against other people. While I admire the ethical statement that a people is a social unit within which social justice is to be maintained, I do not find the threatening warrior God who makes the ethical statement a liberating vision of the divine power.

I have a second quarrel with the prophetic vision. This passage in Amos contains an example of the pervasive prophetic intolerance toward other religions that has produced, among other horrors, a climate in which witches could be put to death in Europe, in which the genocide of Native Americans could be attempted by Europeans, and in which genocide of Jews could be attempted by the Nazis.

The passage immediately following Amos's castigation of the Israelites for selling the needy for a pair of shoes reads:

> A man and his father go in to the same maiden,
> so that my holy name is profaned:
> they lay themselves down beside every altar
> upon garments taken in pledge.
> —Amos 2:7–8

This is Amos's version of the charge of idolatry, which is sprinkled even more liberally throughout most of the other prophetic books, for example, Hosea.

> My people inquire of a thing of wood,
> and their staff gives them oracles.
> For a spirit of harlotry has led them astray,
> and they have left their God to play the harlot.
> They sacrifice on the tops of mountains,
> and make offerings upon the hills.
> —Hosea 4:12–13

Several years ago, as a Christian brought up with little knowledge of other religions and rituals, I could read passages like this and think, "What could be worse than turning away from God?" It never crossed my mind that the people inquiring of wood might be addressing the Goddess Asherah symbolized as a wooden pole or living tree, or that the rites celebrated on mountain tops and hills could have been celebrations of the divine manifest in nature. Now I am troubled by a spirit of religious intolerance that condemns the followers of other faiths as idolaters and labels their rituals abomination.

I find the intolerant form that monotheism so often takes in the West—whether preached by extremists like Jerry Falwell or the Ayatollah Khomeini or by "cultured" theologians who insist that salvation is only in Christ—utterly unconscionable. I find that spirit of intolerance implicit in Exodus and vividly expressed in the prophets. This recognition became yet more devastating when as a feminist I began to understand that the prophetic criticism of idolatry was in part an attempt to solidify patriarchy, patrilineage, and the exclusively male priesthood through the elimination of female images of the divine. My reasons for rejecting the patriarchal God of the Bible are not limited to his sex, or even his warlike nature, but include as well my rejection of a form of monotheism that spawns religious intolerance and a climate in which destruction of peoples who practice other religions can be countenanced.

I would like to examine the implications of my contention that the image of Yahweh as liberator in Exodus and in the prophets is part of an image of Yahweh as divine warrior that I as a feminist and peace activist reject. Some feminists have appropriated the image of warrior reflected in figures like the Amazon or Maxine Hong Kingston's Woman Warrior. While respecting my sisters who make this choice, I ally myself instead with the long tradition of feminist peace activism represented by the Women's International League for Peace and Freedom, Women's Strike for Peace, and recently for Women's Party for Survival.

I have also been asked whether my views on violence and war stem from my powerless position as a woman and from my privileged position as a white American. Perhaps my valuing of peace does stem from a heritage of female powerlessness, a heritage in which I was not taught that I had to test my "womanhood" through fighting, hitting, kicking, football, or boot camp. But if that is so, I affirm the power of women as peacemakers and my own power as a woman and a peacemaker. At the same time, I disaffirm the tradition of female powerlessness that has led women to say, "War is men's business; I don't know anything about it. If they say it has to be, then I guess it has to be." I also reject the image of the divine warrior as female. To change Exodus 15:3 to read: "She is a woman of war; Yahweh is her name" would mean that women had adopted the patriarchal equation of power and violence. I also reject Goddesses of war such as Ishtar and Athena. I do not believe that the images of warrior Goddesses grew out of experiences, values, and cultures created by women. But even if they did, I would not view them as liberating images for us today.

A second response to my rejection of Yahweh as warrior is to assert that my revulsion for war images arises out of my privileged class and national position. The argument here is that if I were a starving peasant woman in Latin America, I would realize the necessity of revolutionary war—of fighting back against the violence initiated by oppressive governments and military regimes. I do not know what I would think if I were a poor woman living under an oppressive regime. I do believe that the horror of war, especially from the point of view of a woman who is likely to be raped by soldiers, is much greater than I can imagine. I am certain that oppressed women have a wide variety of feelings and views about the destruction wrought by war and whether or not their situations can be improved by violent revolution. As a woman and as a feminist, I am wary of adopting a prowar position—even a pro-revolutionary war position. I am suspicious of any man who says violence and war are the solutions to any problem, because I know that almost every man in almost every culture has grown up learning to associate manhood with violence, fighting, and war. I am also suspicious of women who advocate revolutionary war because women in patriarchal cultures are not immune from equating power with war.

I do not know whether my stand for peace against war is relative or absolute, because I do not know how I would react if I were in a different historical and social situation. But if I cannot urge all feminists absolutely to reject war and warrior God/Goddess images, perhaps I can at least encourage those who find the symbol of Yahweh in Exodus and the prophets liberating to examine the roots of that image in the God of war and to acknowledge that the liberating God of Exodus and the prophets acts through war. Instead of referring to that God only as the Liberator of the oppressed; I urge them to think about how they feel about referring to him as a "Man of War" and perhaps even to "her" as a "Woman of War." I hope they will also carefully examine the implications of the symbol of a warrior God/Goddess in a nuclear age. I cannot find that God liberating. I choose to "cast my lot with those who age after age, perversely, with no extraordinary power, reconstitute the world."[6]

NOTES

1. See Rosemary Radford Ruether, "A Religion for Women: Sources and Strategies," *Christianity and Crisis* (December 10, 1979): 307–11.
2. Adrienne Rich, "The Phenomenology of Anger," in *Diving into the Wreck, Poems 1971–1972* (New York: W. W. Norton, 1973), 29. Used by permission.
3. Marc Feigan Fasteau, *The Male Machine* (New York: McGraw Hill, 1974).
4. Marija Gimbutas, "Women and Culture in Goddess-Oriented Old Europe," in *The Politics of Women's Spirituality*, ed. Charlene Spretnak (Garden City, N.Y.: Anchor Books, 1982), 22–31.
5. See for example George Ernest Wright, *The Old Testament and Theology* (New York: Harper & Row, 1969), especially chapter 5, "God the Warrior," 121–50; Patrick D. Miller, Jr., *The Divine Warrior in Early Israel* (Cambridge: Harvard University Press, 1973); Rudolf Smend, *Yahweh War and Tribal Confederation: Reflections upon Israel's Earliest History*, trans. Max Grey Rodgers (Nashville: Abingdon, 1970).
6. Adrienne Rich, "Natural Resources," in *The Dream of a Common Language, Poems 1974–77* (New York: W. W. Norton, 1978), 67. Used by permission.

Astarte Holding Sacred Flowers. From Beth Shemesh, Israel. Circa 1200-900 B.C.E.

6. On Not Blaming Jews for the Death of the Goddess

The feminist reconstruction of the history of religion and society in the ancient Near East and Mediteranean is fraught with difficulty. The evidence has been obscured not only by androcentric traditions that have destroyed or distorted the history of women, but also by antipagan and anti-Judaic biases that have obscured both the histories of nonbiblical religions and the history of the religions of ancient Israel and Judah. While feminist scholars have attempted to correct for androcentric bias, their work has sometimes repeated or unconsciously reinforced the anti-Judaic and antipagan biases that are both implicit and explicit in the historical traditions we have inherited. In this essay I shall address the question of anti-Judaic biases expressed in the work of some scholars from both Jewish and Christian backgrounds as they address the question of the reconstruction of Goddess history from a feminist perspective. The question of antipagan biases in the reconstruction of biblical and Jewish and Christian histories is implicit in this essay but is not its focus.

Negative evaluations of Judaism and other non-Christian religions are implicit, I believe, in all attempts to proclaim the life and death of Jesus Christ as a universal salvation event. For how can Christ be proclaimed as universal savior apart from negative evaluations of other religions in relation to Christianity? Other religions may be portrayed as idolatry or even devil worship, or more subtly as requiring completion through recognition of the salvation that is alleged to be accomplished through the life and death of Jesus Christ. Judaism is often treated differently from other religions in such discussions. On the one hand positively because the Jewish people are heirs to the revelation in the history of Israel which Christians have appropriated as their own, and thus according to Christians, Jews stand in a special relation to

God. And on the other negatively because the Jewish people did not recognize Jesus as the Messiah, and thus are alleged to have failed to recognize a salvation that was offered first to them. Anti-Judaism in Christianity is rooted in the New Testament's comparisons of Christianity and Judaism using the paradigm of the "law and the gospel," in which Judaism is negatively compared to Christianity, in theological depictions of the God of Jesus as a God of love in contrast to the God of Israel who is depicted as a God of judgment only, and in the New Testament writers' attempts to blame the death of Christ on a disciple named Judas and on the Jews.

As Judith Plaskow has shown, the traditions of Christian anti-Judaism have been reproduced in some Christian feminist attempts to argue for the feminism of Jesus and his God at the expense of Judaism.[1] This is not surprising given that anti-Judaism is deeply rooted in Christian theology and in Christian traditions of biblical interpretation. This subject has begun to be addressed by Christian feminist theologians and interpreters of the Bible,[2] but it is not the subject of this essay.

Anti-Judaism can also affect scholarship on the history and pre-history of the Goddesses.[3] This too is not surprising, given the endemic nature of anti-Judaism in Western culture. Another factor is also operative. Those of us who grew up thinking of the Bible as a source of revelation about the nature of God and truth, and who have now discovered the Goddesses who were suppressed in the histories of biblical religions, cannot fail to be outraged when we discover that the "idols" castigated by the prophets of Israel and Judah and by other biblical writers may have included the Goddesses whose histories and images we seek to reclaim. It is often overlooked that the New Testament and early Christian writers display similar prejudices. Those raised in Christian and Jewish traditions are likely to feel especially betrayed by the knowledge that "our God" and "our Bible" participated in the denial of female power represented by the symbol of the Goddess. Because the God and Bibles of Judaism and Christianity still have a strong hold on the psyches of many people in our cultures, many feminist writers have stronger feelings about the suppression of the Goddess within the Bible than about the suppression of the Goddesses within other traditions such as those of Greece or of

Sumer. Unfortunately, such strong feelings can easily be attached to traditions of anti-Judaism, which are readily available. For example, works that focus on the role of the prophets of Israel in the suppression of the Goddess may express or reinforce pervasive cultural patterns in which Judaism is denigrated.

Some feminist works on the Goddesses have been read as blaming "the Jews" for the death of the Goddess. If any one group is to be "blamed" for the suppression of the Goddess in Western culture, "the Christians" seem to me to be a more likely candidate, given that it was the Christian emperor Theodosius I (known as "the Great") whose edicts at the end of the fourth century C.E. led to the closing and officially sanctioned mob destruction of the so-called "pagan" temples. In truth, the story is far more complex than this, for the suppression of the power of the Goddesses is found within all the cultures of the Near East and Mediterranean during the period in which patriarchal, militaristic, slave-based state societies emerged from more egalitarian and peaceful clan-based Neolithic agricultural societies in the fourth millenium B.C.E. The transformations of religion and society that took place in this era did not occur overnight. The powers of the Goddess Creatress and the priestesses and queens who reflected her power were gradually transformed. In Sumer, for example, Innana of the date palm and communal storehouse was turned into a Goddess of war and sexuality and subordinated to male Gods, and her priestesses were separated from the economic and political power that once was theirs as guardians of the agricultural wealth of their communities.[4] But this process took thousands of years; and at various periods within the history of Sumer, the images of the Goddesses and the religious and social powers of women were not identical.[5] Careful historical scholarship is required to understand which manifestations of the Goddesses were being confronted at various stages in the history of Israel, Judah, and early Christianity.

As a post-Christian feminist who is sensitive to the anti-Judaism in the religion of my history, I have struggled with the question of how to understand the role of biblical religions in the suppression of Goddess religion and female power in the West without "blaming Jews." I have found several methodological principles useful in this task.

First, it is important to distinguish the religions of Israel and Judah from the religions we know as Christianity and Judaism. The religion represented in the Hebrew Bible, as it is known to Jews, who do not consider it an "Old Testament," is not identical with the religion known today as Judaism. This is obvious to the historian of religion. However, in Christian culture Judaism is often identified with the "Old Testament." Jewish tradition has a long history of interpretation separating it from the religion of the Bible. Rabbinic Judaism is a first-century C.E. development, a reaction to the destruction of the second temple. Conservative, Reform, and Reconstructionist Judaism are more recent developments of the modern period. Christians and others need to familiarize themselves with the history of Judaism in order to avoid identifying elements of the Bible uncritically with contemporary Judaism. I suggest as a beginning that feminist interpreters avoid using the Christian-based term *Old Testament* in referring to the Hebrew Bible. Also, in referring to the religions represented in the Hebrew Bible, the terms *Judaism* and *Jews* should not be used. One can speak of the religion of the Hebrews, the religions of ancient Israel and Judah, or use more precise terms such as the religion of the monarchy or of the prophets. It is important to be aware that the Hebrew Bible reflects several thousand years of history, that it contains various types of materials—legal, liturgical, mytho-historical, and so forth—and that it was edited from a partisan point of view after the building of the second temple.[6] The Greek Bible,[7] known as the Christian New Testament, represents a much shorter period of time.

The Bible should not be used as the sole basis for making comparisons between Judaism and Christianity. As Judith Plaskow has noted, Jesus might better be compared with other rabbis of his era whose stories are preserved in the Talmud, and the legal material of the Hebrew Bible might better be compared with the writings of the Church Fathers. Another term to be avoided is *the Judeo-Christian tradition*, which implies that the religions known as Judaism and Christianity represent one unbroken tradition, with Christianity implicitly understood as superseding Judaism. Jews do not consider the "Judeo-Christian tradition" to be theirs.[8] When referring to values shared by Jews and Christians, I prefer to refer to the "Jewish and Christian religions" or to the values expressed in "biblical religions."

Second, it is crucial to strive for evenhanded treatment of Judaism and Christianity in regard to the suppression of the Goddesses. It is true that the prophets of Israel and Judah railed against "idolatry," and that this view is reflected in the so-called "Yahweh only" strain in the Hebrew Bible, which was the view of its final editors. It is also true that Christian culture waged its own campaign against "paganism" and "heresy" in which the suppression of female symbolism for the divine was a factor. Paul actively missionized in the Hellenistic world where religions of the Goddesses (as historically transformed in patriarchal societies) remained powerful. The book of Acts records that Paul's preaching in Ephesus, the site of the Temple of Artemis, which was known as one of the seven wonders of the ancient world, was greeted by the cry, "Great is Artemis of the Ephesians," and that a crowd attempted to harm Paul's companions (Acts 19:28–41.) As mentioned above, it was later Christian emperors who passed laws allowing for the destruction of pagan temples, including Goddess temples in the Christian empire. Though ancient Hebrew religion and Judaism played a role in the suppression of the Goddess, they were hardly alone in this matter. However, all discussions of the role ancient Hebrew religion in the suppression of the religions of the Goddesses should not be read as anti-Judaism.[9]

Third, it is useful to set the biblical suppression of the Goddess in the context of the prebiblical rise of patriarchy. Though Christianity and Judaism can both fairly be defined as patriarchal religions in my opinion, and though both played a role in the consolidation of patriarchal power, neither Judaism nor Christianity nor the religions of ancient Israel and Judah were the originators of patriarchy. Feminist and other scholars are beginning to develop a picture of the rise and development of patriarchy in the Near East and Mediterranean worlds in the fourth, third, and second millenia B.C.E. I can only allude briefly to the conclusions of such research here. Archaeologists Marija Gimbutas, who has done extensive excavation in southern and eastern Europe, and James Mellaart, whose work centered in Anatolia in the Near East, believe that the Neolithic (c. 7000–3500 B.C.E.) societies of Old Europe and the Near East were Goddess-centered, peaceful, and matrifocal. They find no evidence that women were subordinate in either religion or society. Archaeological evidence indicates that women played important, perhaps central, roles in Neolithic religion. The anthropological theory that women invented agriculture, weaving, and pottery in the Neolithic period suggests that women held important social and economic as well as religious roles in these societies. That there is no evidence of chronic warfare, highly centralized social organization, or slavery in this period adds weight to the hypothesis that these societies did not reflect the subordination of women. Goddess images predominate in Neolithic religion, with Goddesses symbolizing not only the powers of birth, death, and regeneration, but also the mysteries of transforming seed into grain into bread, flax and wool into thread into cloth, and earth into clay into pot. Goddesses were symbols not only of women's power to give birth, but they also reflected women's social and economic roles as inventors of agriculture, weaving, and pottery. Gimbutas and Mellaart agree that Neolithic societies began to be transformed into patriarchal, militaristic, class-stratified, slave-holding state societies around 3500 B.C.E.

Patriarchy is not a single factor in the transformation of societies in the fourth, third, and second millenia B.C.E. The rise of chronic warfare, the centralization of society in the hands of the warrior king, the accumulation of wealth in the hands of an elite, and the creation of slave classes out of conquered peoples, especially women, along with institutionalization of the patriarchal family, were all factors in the rise of the kinds of societies we call "civilization." As Ruby Rohrlich has written, "institutionalization of the patriarchal family, economic stratification, militarization, and the consolidation of the state in the hands of a male elite"[10] can all be documented in Sumer during the fourth millennium B.C.E. It is during this period that male Gods begin to rise in prominence over the female Goddesses, often through murder, as is reflected in the story of Marduk's slaying of his Grandmother Tiamat in the Babylonian myth the *Enuma Elish* (first millenium C.E.). In considering the transformations of religion and society that occurred over several millenia, it is important to remember that this process was gradual and that women retained important religious and social powers, perhaps especially important religious powers, even as their spheres of influence were curtailed.[11] We know that women had certain property rights in Sumer,[12] and it appears that priestesses retained certain degrees of autonomy, even in Babylon.[13] Thus, generalizations about the degrees of power women held in the societies that were confronted and challenged within the histories of the religions of Israel and Judah and within the histories of Judaism and Christianity must be made with careful consideration of the historical evidence concerning the development of patriarchy. While is is clearly false to allege that the religion of Israel represented a moral advance in all respects over the religions of its neighbors, it is equally false to allege that religions of its neighbors represented a Goddess utopia. Patriarchal, militarized, class-based, slave-holding societies had already flourished in the Near East before the times of Abraham and Moses.

When the rise and development of patriarchal societies and religions is more clearly understood, we can be more specific in the questions we ask about the roles of the religions of ancient Israel and Judah, and of Judaism and Christianity, in the suppression of Goddess symbolism and female religious and social power.

Finally, we need to place the biblical suppression of the Goddess in the context of centuries' long struggles between polytheism and monotheism *within* the histories of Israel and Judah. According to the book of Kings, Solomon, also known as the wisest king in Israel, worshiped on the high places and built altars to Astarte, Milcolm, and Chemosh as well as to Yahweh. The book of Kings records an often violent struggle between the prophets of Yahweh, such as Elijah, who insisted that the Hebrew people worship only Yahweh, and the kings, queens, and people of Israel, many of whom thought otherwise. Most of the data concerning the Hebrew people's worship of Goddesses and Gods other than Yahweh has been destroyed. But the book of Jeremiah preserves one remarkable passage that demonstrates not only the Hebrew people's devotion to the Queen of Heaven, but also their resistance to Jeremiah's "Yahweh alone" theology that became normative in the final editing of the Hebrew Bible:

> Then all the men who knew that their wives had offered incense to the other [G]ods, and all the women who stood by, a great assembly, all the people who dwelt in Pathros in the land of Egypt, answered Jeremiah: "As for the word which you have spoken to us in the name of Yahweh, we will not listen to you. But we will do everything that we have vowed, burn incense to the [Q]ueen of [H]eaven and pour out libations to her, as we

did, both we and our fathers, our kings and our princes, in the cities of Judah and in the streets of Jerusalem, for then we had plenty of food, and prospered, and saw no evil. But since we left off burning incense to the [Q]ueen of [H]eaven and pouring out libations to her, we have lacked everything and have been consumed by the sword and by famine." And the women said, "When we burned incense to the [Q]ueen of [H]eaven and poured out libations to her, was it without our husbands' approval that we made cakes for her bearing her image and poured out libations to her?" (Jeremiah 44:15–19)

Though the Bible portrays this struggle as one between idolatry and true religion, this is clearly a partisan view.[14] In my opinion, the word *idolatry* with its value-laden connotations and historical association with the worship of nonbiblical Goddess and Gods ought to be dropped from the vocabulary of feminist historians, theologians and thealogians.

In *The Hebrew Goddess* Raphael Patai has reconstructed this period of ancient history, arguing that the worship in Yahweh and the Hebrew Goddess was the dominant thread in ancient Hebrew religion from the time of the establishment of the monarchy until the Babylonian exile. Patai argues that "the Hebrew Goddess" has always been worshiped both in ancient Hebrew religion and in later Jewish developments.[15] His work has obvious feminist implications, which he does not spell out. Steve Davies is surely correct in pointing out, in response to Patai, that the Hebrew people were polytheistic in the period of the monarchy, worshiping not only Yahweh and the Hebrew Goddess, but Yahweh, Asherah, Astarte, Milcolm, Chemosh, Baal, and many other deities.[16] Davies's argument with Patai seems directed at discouraging feminist attempts to appropriate the Hebrew Goddess. Though I believe Davies is correct in asserting that the Hebrew people were polytheistic in the period of the monarchy, his argument that this polytheism within the history of Israel and Judah should not be called "Hebrew" religion is tautological. He defines "Hebrew" religion as the worship of Yahweh only and thus excludes worship of Goddesses and Gods other than Yahweh from his definition.[17] Feminist scholars need to engage in a reconstruction of this historical period of Israel and Judah in the context of ancient Near Eastern religion. We need to piece together evidence with which we can gain access to the roles of women and priestesses in ancient

Hebrew religion and the effects of the suppression of polytheism and the images of the Goddesses on the lives of Hebrew women.

Jewish and Christian feminist theologians have generally shied away from the radical implications of Patai's reconstruction of ancient Hebrew religion. Ellen Umansky, for example, has argued that Jewish feminists may not appeal to pre-exilic polytheism as a positive resource, because to do so would set them apart from the "voice of Israel" reflected in the final editing of the Hebrew Bible, in the rabbinic consensus, and in later Jewish history, which have defined *Judaism* as a monotheistic religion.[18] But Judith Plaskow has argued that the word *Goddess* must be spoken again in Judaism.[19] I submit that more positive attention to this period in ancient Hebrew history (whatever theological or thealogical conclusions may or may not be drawn from it) would be helpful in the feminist dialogue about the suppression of the Goddess.

NOTES

1. Judith Plaskow, "Christian Feminism and Anti-Judaism," *Cross Currents* 28 (1978): 306–9, reprinted as "Blaming Jews for Inventing Patriarchy," *Lilith* 7 (1980): 12-14.
2. See for example, Elisabeth Schüssler Fiorenza, *In Memory of Her: A Feminist Theological Reconstruction of Christian Origins* (New York: Crossroad Press, 1983), 106–10.
3. See Annette Daum, "Blaming Jews for the Death of the Goddess," *Lilith* 7 (1980): 12–13; and "Feminists and Faith: A Discussion with Judith Plaskow and Annette Daum," *Lilith* 7 (1980): 14–17.
4. See Ruby Rohrlich, "State Formation in Sumer and the Subjugation of Women," *Feminist Studies* 6, no. 1 (1980): 86, 91.
5. See Rohrlich; and Gerda Lerner, *The Creation of Patriarchy* (New York: Oxford University Press, 1986).
6. See for example, Morton Smith, *Palestinian Parties and Politics Which Shaped the Old Testament* (New York: Columbia University Press, 1971).
7. This term was suggested by Esther Fuchs in the discussion that followed the panel "Jewish and Christian Feminist Hermeneutics: Confrontation or Cooperation?" at the 1985 meetings of the Society of Biblical Literature at which this paper was originally presented.
8. See Plaskow, "Christian Feminism and Anti-Judaism."
9. This is the tendency of Daum's comments in "Blaming Jews."
10. Rohrlich, "State Formation," 84.
11. See Savina J. Teubal, *Sarah the Priestess* (Athens, Ohio: Swallow Press, 1984).
12. Rohrlich, "State Formation," 89–90.
13. See Ulla Jeyes, "The Naditu Women of Babylon," in *Images of Women in Antiquity*, ed. Averil Cameron and Amelie Kuhrt (Detroit: Wayne State University Press, 1983), 260–72.

14. See Morton Smith; *Palestinian Parties*, and Merlin Stone, *When God Was a Woman* (New York: Dial Press, 1976).
15. Raphael Patai, *The Hebrew Goddess* (New York: KTAV, 1967), esp. chs. 1 and 2.
16. Steve Davies, "The Canaanite-Hebrew Goddess," in *The Book of the Goddess*, ed. Carl Olson (New York: Crossroad Press, 1983), 74.
17. Davies, "The Canaanite-Hebrew Goddess," 74.
18. Ellen Umansky, "(Re)Imaging the Divine," *Response* 41–42 (1982): 110–9; and "Creating a Jewish Feminist Theology: Possibilities and Problems," *Anima* 10, no. 2 (1984): 125–35.
19. Judith Plaskow, "The Right Question Is Theological," in *On Being a Jewish Feminist*, ed. Susannah Heschel (New York: Schocken Books, 1983), 221–233, esp. 230.

7. A Daughter of the Father God

To know ourselves as daughters of a Father God who claims to be the only parent is to be involved in a pathologically dependent relationship in which our strength and power as women can never be fully affirmed. I will explore this thesis through reflection on my own story as a daughter of the Father God. In so doing I will reveal some of the pathology in my own relationship to the Father and fathers. I take this risk because I am convinced that none of our stories are ours alone. We are all products of our culture. All of our stories are shared. I am also convinced that reflecting on the truths of our lives is part of the process that leads to personal and cultural renewal. I do not claim that what I share here is the whole story of my relation to the Father. Nor do I imagine that the kind of relationship I had with him is shared by all women. Some women have focused more on Jesus than God; some approach God through the mystical traditions; and some had no relation to God. Their stories also need to be told and reflected upon. I share my story because I think it is typical of one kind of relationship women have had to the Father God, a relationship that reflects major themes in religious and cultural traditions.

When I was a girl I went to Protestant churches in which the Lord's Prayer (or Our Father) and the Gloria were part of each Sunday's services. Though I might have said, if I had been asked, that I knew God was not really a man, nonetheless the images that I had of "him" were male. What were the messages that I must have unwittingly received each Sunday as I participated in worship?

"Our Father. . ." It was always a male minister who began this prayer for us, and I imagine I made the connection that God and the minister had something in common. I don't believe it ever crossed my mind to ask why God was never called "Mother," or why the clergy was never female. It was clear to me that my father had the last word when it came to major decisions in our home.

The words "ask your father," and "wait till your father gets home" were familiar to me. My father, like God the Father, was the one whose permission I had to ask, the one who set limits on my behavior.

"Who are in heaven. . ." God was unlike my father in that he had no body and his power was both invisible and unlimited. If I sometimes intuited my own father's limitations, I could imagine that there was a more perfect Father whose judgment never failed, whose love was unceasing, and whose wisdom was unbounded. As I grew older, I found it easy to transfer my adoration for my father to spiritual fathers, my male professors, who like God, I thought, were powerful, paternal, and concerned with the higher realms.

"Hallowed be Thy name. . ." In naming the Father holy, did I understand that his name was a masculine one? Did I make an intuitive connection with my mother's often repeated declaration that the happiest day of her life was the day she took my father's name? Did I understand that to be female was to have a name that was not holy? Did I suspect that to be female was to live in a world where men—but not women—had the power to name the world, to define "reality" as they saw it or wanted it to be?

"Thy will be done. . ." Did I realize that as a good daughter, my role was to fulfill the will of my father, later my boyfriend, finally my husband? Did I realize that my will was not meant to be done in my family or my society?

"On earth as it is in heaven. . ." Did I realize that I was participating in the legitimation of a world where all publicly acknowledged power is in the hands of men?

"Give us this day our daily bread. . ." This must not have made a very big impact upon me; I left these words out in several drafts of this essay. Did I intuit the hollowness of these words in a society in which mother, not father, prepares and serves us our food? Is that perhaps why I also resisted saying "grace" to the Father before meals? And why I find it appropriate now to thank the Mother or Earth for the food I eat?

"Forgive us our debts (trespasses). . ." I didn't know what "trespass" meant, and "debt" was a relatively abstract concept for me, but I think I grasped the message that before the Father we are all guilty. Did I somehow understand that my sin was being born female in a society where fathers and sons were preferred? Did I comprehend that I could be forgiven the original sin of femaleness[1] by gaining the approval of men?

"As we forgive our debtors (those who tresspass against us). . ." Did I understand that I was to forgive the sins of the fathers and sons? "Your father is so tired—he doesn't mean what he is saying." "Your brother can't control his temper. When he hits you, it doesn't mean he hates you." And that in exchange for my forgiveness of their trespasses on my body and soul, I would be forgiven the original sin of being born female?

"For Thine is the kingdom, and the power, and the glory forever. Amen." It couldn't have been made more clear. And yet somehow I persisted in thinking that God was fair and that I too would have a share in the *king*-dom, the power, and the glory, if only I could figure out how to please him.

When praying to a Father God, a girl or woman can imagine that he loves his sons and daughters equally. But what can have been the effect of singing the Gloria each Sunday:

> Glory be to the Father
> and to the Son
> and to the Holy Ghost
> as it was in the beginning
> is now and ever shall be
> world without end. Amen.

When singing to the Father and Son, a girl must hear her exclusion. She must begin to recognize that the power and the glory are not to be hers. Did I understand the parallels between my family's focus on the male rituals of competitive sports—Little League and high school and college basketball, starring my brothers—and the worship of the Son? Did the rituals of religion help me to accept my exclusion from the teams my brothers played on, my father coached, and my mother and I could only watch? Did I somehow know that no matter what I did, I would never be the beloved Son?

Thus far I have described the pathology of exclusion in which a girl or woman implicitly learns of her inferiority while listening to or participating in a liturgy in which her existence is not acknowledged. Now I wish to discuss a related, but more destructive, message which a girl or woman may derive from biblical religion.

Psychologists who have named some of the distorted patterns

of relationship to fathers in our culture can help us to understand how these distorted patterns affect our relationship to the Father God. Arthur and Libby Colman describe a typical pattern in American father-child relationships when they write:

> Many of our most treasured memories [of our fathers] are of unexpected tender moments with them. We respected their hard work. . . Yet we also resented their aloofness, their distance, the scarcity of those memorable intimate moments. Thus our feelings toward them contain. . . the mixture. . . [of] admiration and idealization, resentment and anger; the dream of a reconciliation. . . which never quite comes.[2]

Colman and Colman describe a relationship doomed to frustration because the traditional father is not present, unable to be emotionally close with his children in a sustained way. What they do not point out is that ordinarily the father will spend even less time with his daughters than with his sons, so that for the daughter this pathological pattern of relationship is intensified. Linda Schierse Leonard depicts the particular wounding of daughters by such fathers: "From [other daughters] I learned that fathers who were strict and authoritarian might give their daughters stability, structure, and discipline, but often gave them little in the way of love, emotional support, validation of the feminine.[3]

To attempt to derive one's sense of worth and value from a distant and demanding father is problematic because he is incapable of fulfilling our needs for love and affirmation. Through the relationship with such a father, we learn to confuse love with the absence or even the negation of love. And, as daughters who identify with such fathers, we participate in the denial of our female selves which our culture encourages. I believe such a pattern often exists in our relationships to the Father God. This is illustrated in the relationship I had with Yahweh during the time I was planning to become a scholar of the Hebrew Bible. I fell in love with Yahweh, the God of the Hebrew Bible narratives and prophecies. For me Yahweh was a passionately choosing, rejecting, and redeeming figure. He chose Israel even though they were a stiff-necked people. (Didn't I know myself to be the stubborn child of a sometimes capricious father?) He gave his chosen people a set of commandments, which they failed to fulfill. He judged and punished them for their failures. (Did I sense my unacceptability in the house of the fathers?) But in the end God's love overcame his stern judgment. Yahweh realized he could not utterly condemn Israel. (Didn't I hope for ultimate acceptance in the world of the fathers?) This was one of my favorite passages from the prophets:

> How can I give you up, O Ephraim!
> How can I hand you over, O Israel!
>
> My heart recoils within me,
> my compassion grows warm and tender.
> I will not execute my fierce anger.
> I will not again destroy Ephraim. (Hos. 11:8–9)

In this passage God's love is contrasted with his judgment. His right to destroy Ephraim is unquestioned. God had earlier declared: "Ephraim must lead forth his sons to slaughter" (Hos. 9:13); "I will slay their beloved children" (Hos. 9:16); and:

> Therefore the tumult of war shall arise among your people
> and all your fortresses shall be destroyed
> as Shalman destroyed Betharbel on the day of battle
> mothers were dashed in pieces with their children. (Hos. 10:14)

The prophet affirms God's right, power, and intention to utterly destroy but affirms also that God's destructive power is the other face of his love. For me this passionate drama of choosing and being chosen, failing and being rejected, yet being ultimately accepted and loved, was very powerful.

In the years I studied the Hebrew Bible, I sought and found approval in the eyes of my male professors, while at the same time incurring my father's anger for wasting the money he was spending on my education by studying religion. Like the God of the Bible, my father chose, rejected, and (I hoped) would ultimately forgive me. I think I knew that on some level I would always be a stiff-necked daughter, and that the love he felt for me would be in spite of my not doing what he wanted me to do. The unpredictable and emotional nature of the Father God mirrored my experience of my father. And the promise that God would not ultimately reject me gave me hope.

Throughout this time I read myself sidewise into the stories of fathers and sons in the Bible. I assumed that I could be the favored child of the Father if I figure out how to please him. It never occured to me to question whether daughters could ever find an equal place in the house of the Father. Despite the pathological elements in my relationships with fathers, I did gain confidence in my own intelligence and abilities through their support. I gained a degree of freedom from traditional female roles by imagining a core of self that transcended femaleness. I assumed that the God whose words I would study transcended the genderized language of the Bible. I thought I could become like my male professors because we shared a common humanity, defined by our love for the intellectual life, our interest in religious questions. Like many women I felt flattered to be told that I thought like a man, and I felt contempt for women who were satisfied to live out traditional women's roles. I understood myself to be an exception, a favored daughter.

But this abstracted modeling of myself on the fathers did not give me any help with the crucial task of my life: the integration of my femaleness (including my sexuality) with my intelligence. I had assumed that I could combine career and family like my professors. As I grew older, I realized that I could never be like them because I would never have a wife. Their whole lives were made possible by women. Their wives bore and reared their children for them, kept them away from Daddy while he was writing, edited and typed their manuscripts, washed their socks, and ironed their shirts.[4] If I wanted to be sexual as well as intellectual, did I sleep with the father or with one of the sons? And if I did so, would I lose my status as favored, exceptional, and become an ordinary women in their eyes? What would become of my career if I became pregnant and had a child? Who would keep my children fed, clothed, and out of my study while I was writing? And was it possible to be a scholar without that kind of support from someone? Moreover, this modeling of myself on the Father, the fathers, gave me not a clue as to what it might mean to think like a women with a female body, in identification with women, and in recognition of my position as a woman in a patriarchal society.[5]

In graduate school my relationship to the fathers changed. This was in part because I moved from a coeducational university in the west to an eastern men's school. But it was also because I was no longer a promising undergraduate but a potential colleague in training. And because I began to try to visualize my future in more realistic ways. In graduate school I found that I was viewed first as a woman by the men with whom I studied. Their nonacceptance of me as a colleague was the catalyst that made me begin to question whether or not daughters could ever be accepted in the house of the fathers. In turn, since I was studying theology, this led me to question the role of the Father God in legitimating the world of fathers and sons that I experienced as excluding me.

I began to see that language is a powerful shaper of reality and that the sex of God does matter. I began to ask myself what the religious experience of women would be like if we defined it ourselves out of our own experience rather than accepting the words of men. The Father God, my male professors, and my father could not help me answer these questions. I needed female role models who could provide me with images of female strength, sexuality, and intelligence, not the understanding nor the approval of the Father. I needed to find the source of my strength, my sexuality, and my intelligence within myself. I needed to learn that I was not dependent on any Father or father for my sense of my own value as a person, as a woman, as a scholar, as a teacher.

Though I began to become aware of the failure of the fathers to nurture my growth, it took me a bit longer to become aware of the failure of the Father.

The pathology in women's relationships to the Father God I have described is reflected in a pattern of choosing/commanding, rejecting/destroying, and loving/redeeming. This pattern is found in the Yahweh narratives and prophecies in the Hebrew Bible and is codified and intensified in the New Testament/Christian ideas of original sin and redemption through the suffering and death of Christ. In these paradigms, daughters and sons find themselves relating to a God who is said to create, choose, and love them, who judges their responses to his demands inadequate, declares them unworthy of his love, but who ultimately reverses his judgment with love and redemption. The Father God I experienced was not unlike the fathers described by Arthur and Libby Colman and Linda Schierse Leonard, not unlike my own father. He represented the extremes of love and judgment. Though affirmed as loving creator and redeemer, he was also known as destroyer of his own special people (in the Hebrew Bible) and as justified in condemning everyone to hell (in Christian theology). Like my father, God was loving, judgmental, and unpredictable, yet because of his superior authority, he provided a sense of order in my life. Like the father described by the Colmans, he had his moments of tenderness, which I valued above all. I expected love to be combined with stern judgment in my relationship with the Father God because that was the way I experienced love from my father, and vice versa. I do not believe I am the only woman who has had such a relationship with the Father or fathers.

Susan Brooks Thistlethwaite has described her work with battered women whose interpretation of Christian Scripture made them view leaving their battering husbands as contrary to the will of God.[6] Though I have not been physically battered, raped, tortured, or molested, I know something of the pathology that allows women to accept such victimization. When our model of the ultimate power is a male God whose judgment issues or can issue in violence or death, when we understand the love of God within the framework, then we lose the capacity to distinguish love, hate, and indifference. ("Even though he can never say it/he hits you/he appears indifferent/your father loves you.") When I loved the God of Hosea, whose love was defined against a backdrop of the slaughter of sons and the dashing of mothers with their children into pieces, was I not accepting brutal punishment as one of the faces of love? And when I loved a God who required the sacrifice of his beloved son, didn't I fail to distinguish between love and death? Isn't it this sort of confusion that has kept so many of us bound to relationships with men who destroy our bodies and souls?

Men too many find themselves is this kind of relationship to the Father, or fathers. But men also have the option of identifying with Father, of seeing themselves not only as the recipients of, but the dispensers of judgments, not only as dependent, but as powerful, even omnipotent (of course this too is pathology). But women more commonly find ourselves stuck on the dependent side of this mutal relationship, continually seeking validation of our worth in the eyes of men.

Merlin Stone has written, "At the very dawn of religion, God was a woman. Do you remember?"[7] The night when I expressed my anger at God and heard a still, small voice saying "in God is a woman like yourself" was the beginning of my remembering, which was also a re-membering,[8] enabling me to claim my female being and my female body in a new way. This process did not happen in a vacuum. At this time I was becoming a part of the emerging feminist movement and learning to value women as colleagues and friends. In consciousness raising, I was discovering that the affirmations of women as we "hear each other into speech"[9] are empowering. I was beginning to see that as women value each other, we are valuing that female part of ourselves which we share with other women.

About that time I found a poster in a woman's bookstore, which reinforced my vision: Ann Grifalconi's redrawing of Michelangelo's famous fresco, "The Creation of Man" from the Sistine Chapel. In Grifalconi's drawing, God is a black woman reaching out to create Eve. Since that time I have discovered in the history and prehistory of the Goddesses images and symbols that have taken the place of the Father God in my imagination. The images of the female God/Goddesses and the power of women in my life enabled me to begin to overcome my dependence on the Father and fathers.

For me, recognizing the pathology in my relationship to the Father God and fathers combined with my awareness that there are religious traditions I can draw upon that do not contain the same patterns has meant that I no longer choose to define myself within the Christian symbol system. I believe it is important for women who have known dependence on the Father or fathers to name the great powers within and without as Goddess. Certainly this naming can help us to overcome our dependence on the judgment and approval of Fathers. But it is necessary as well to remind ourselves that there are many names for the powers we call divine. These names may be male, female, or not genderized. The problem comes when we do not recognize power within ourselves as well as within others and when we do not recognize our connection to all beings within the circle of life.

NOTES

1. See Mary Daly, *Beyond God the Father* (Boston: Beacon Press, 1973), 44–50.
2. Arthur Colman and Libby Colman, *Earth Father/Sky Father* (Englewood Cliffs, N.J.: Prentice Hall, 1981), 184.
3. Linda Schierse Leonard, *The Wounded Woman* (Boulder and London: Shambhala, 1983), xvii.
4. See Carol P. Christ and Judith Plaskow Goldenberg, "Against My Wife: A Form Critical Study in the Art of Acknowledgement," *Bulletin/CSR* (June 1972): 10–14.
5. For a different kind of vision of the scholar at work, see "Introduction: Black

Feminist Process" in *Black Feminist Criticism*, ed. Barbara Christian (New York: Pergamon Press, 1985), xi–xv.

6. See Susan Brooks Thistlethwaite, "Every Two Minutes: Battered Women and Feminist Interpretation," in *Feminist Interpretation of the Bible*, ed. Letty M. Russell (Philadelphia: Westminster, 1985), 96–107. Thistlethwaite provides an alternative hermeneutic for interpreting the Scripture.
7. Merlin Stone, *When God Was a Woman* (New York: Dial Press, 1976), 1.
8. See Christine Downing, *The Goddess: Mythological Representations of the Feminine* (New York: Crossroad, 1981), 5.
9. The phase was coined by Nelle Morton; see her *The Journey Is Home* (Boston: Beacon Press, 1985).

II. JOURNEY TO THE GODDESS

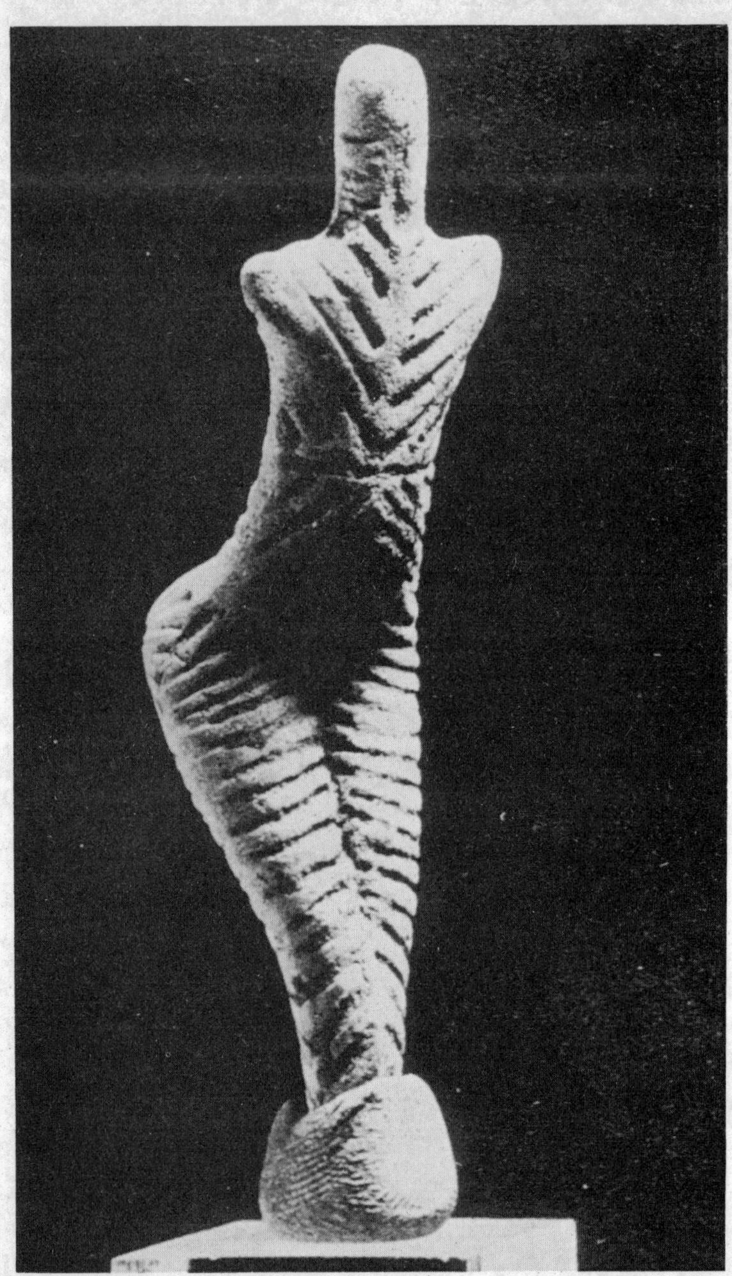

Bird or Snake Goddess. From Old Europe.

Journey to the Goddess

"There are no excuses for anything," Agnes once told me. "You change things or you don't. Excuses rob you of power and introduce apathy."

—LYNN V. ANDREWS

The essays in this section express my growing realization of the power of Goddess, reflection on the meaning of contemporary Goddess symbolism, my research on Goddess history, and my participation in Goddess rituals. As I have understood more deeply that "in God is a woman like yourself," I have gained confidence in my own power, which is the power of earth, of life, death, and rebirth, the power symbolized by the Goddesses. No longer do I stand in the shadow of male Gods who are defined in opposition to the powers of earth, nature, myself. This power is not power over, but a deeply relational power, which comes from understanding the connection of my power of being to that of all other life.

From the time I became a feminist, I became convinced that our language for God had to be a changed if women were to see ourselves as being fully in the image of God. In 1971 at the first Conference of Women Theologians in Alverno College, two other women and I stayed up late into the night writing a tract on female God language, after our arguments that God must be addressed as "She" and as "Mother" were dismissed. At this conference my suggestion that God might be found in nature, "as in Martin Buber's I-Thou relation with the tree," fell on deaf ears.

When I first began teaching and writing about women and religion, I sought sources that might reflect, as Anne Barstow later put it, "a religion created at least in part by women."[1] None of my academic training had introduced me to Goddesses, and the images of Goddesses that I found in the obvious sources, such as the

Homeric Hymns and Jungian writings seemed to reflect androcentric imagination. But I discovered that *The Four-Gated City* by Doris Lessing and other works of fiction and poetry by women writers seemed to my students as they did to me to reflect women's spiritual quest. Contemporary women's writings sustained me as my alienation from the Bible and the church grew. The writing I did during that period on the works of Doris Lessing, Margaret Atwood, Kate Chopin, Adrienne Rich, and Ntozake Shange has been incorporated into my book *Diving Deep and Surfacing*. These women's writings with their vision of the spirit found within the body and nature prepared me for the Goddesses.

In 1975 my friend Naomi Goldenberg raved about a conference called "Through the Looking Glass" held in Boston at which Z Budapest, a feminist witch, had presented a slide show on the Goddesses. It was the most exciting thing she had seen, Naomi said. While on leave in my native California, I was introduced to *WomanSpirit* magazine by my friend Kit Havice, who encouraged me to take a workshop with her on women's spirituality from Hallie Iglehart. This was my first introduction to the women's spirituality movement. Many of my thoughts and feelings about the spirit and nature were confirmed in Iglehart's group. Later that year Naomi Goldenberg and I took an alternative university class from Starhawk on witchcraft. From that first night in Starhawk's class, as I heard my own spiritual quest articulated, I felt myself powerfully drawn to the Goddess and to the raising of energy in circles. My longing for a female name for a God who was more of nature than history was confirmed in Starhawk's naming of Goddess. I was elated that women in California, my birthplace and home for many years, shared my feelings that the divine could be found within nature. And excited to learn that these women were naming a God I had always known with a very female name, "Goddess." At the end of Starhawk's first class, she lit a candle and invited us to participate in the raising of energy through nonverbal chanting. Her ritual did not seem strange to me because I had learned to work with energy in gestalt and bioenergetic therapy. That night I found a spiritual tradition in which I felt very much at home.

During the next year I participated in several rituals with Starhawk and when I returned to New York, I began to experiment with creating rituals. At a class party one evening, my students spontaneously began chanting the name of a woman in our class who had gone home to be with her dying mother. As we chanted her name and called out to her mother, we felt their presence. Months later when I ran into this student, we talked about that evening. She said that when she had arrived at the hospital, her mother had already slipped into what was described as a final coma. But during the night her mother had awakened and they had been able to talk. Though she had not known that we had chanted, she said she felt we brought her mother back to say good-bye. I felt chills run through my body.

Many of my colleagues in the New York Feminist Scholars in Religion, a group of academic feminist women, many of whom were close friends, seemed disturbed by what I told them about the Goddess movement in California and my involvement. Naively I thought that we were all moving in similar directions. Instead I met harsh criticism. The Goddess was "dangerous," I was told. And Goddess religion lacked a "critical principle of justice." It became clear that not only were my colleagues not coming with me into the Goddess movement, but they felt a need to distance themselves from it.

At the same time, reading Merlin Stone's *When God Was a Woman*, which was published that year, I began to learn about the millenia of Goddess history that had never been mentioned in my years of academic study. I began to feel my loyalties were with those castigated by my tradition as idolaters.

I knew I could not turn back from the path that had led me to the Goddess. But I felt alone, confused, and frightened. Many long telephone calls to Naomi Goldenberg and a trip to visit her in Central Michigan when Z Budapest came to speak convinced me that the "Goddess is alive, magic is afoot,"[2] that I was part of a movement that might transform our culture. Just before I left New York I decided to offer a workshop on the Goddess modeled on the classes I had taken from Starhawk. The twenty women who took this workshop were enormously receptive. Sometime during that year I knew that I had left the church for good. However, I hesitated to state this publicly, because I knew that most of the jobs for feminist theologians were in seminaries.

Naomi Goldenberg and I invited Starhawk to present a paper

on a panel with us at the 1977 meeting of the American Academy of Religion. When Naomi and I met to prepare our papers for the session with Starhawk, we were apprehensive. We did not know how academically trained feminists would respond to the Goddess, and I feared that to speak about the Goddess would harm our careers. I remember the difficulty I had writing "Why Women Need the Goddess," which subsequently has become the most published and republished of my works. I read Naomi every paragraph of that paper as I wrote it, prefaced by comments like, "I don't dare say this," or "Everyone knows this." She assured me that I could say it, and that everyone didn't know it. I gave her similar encouragement on her paper, which eventually became part of her chapter on the Goddess and witchcraft in her book *Changing of the Gods*. The session with Starhawk went very well, though I will never forget the shocked look on the face of a former student as I spoke of the Goddess. "But Carol," she said to me, "you loved Wiesel, Buber, the Hebrew Bible, how can you abandon all that?"

In the spring I presented "Why Women Need the Goddess" as the keynote address to the Great Goddess Re-Emerging Conference at the University of California at Santa Cruz. As I heard my speech interrupted by stunning applause from the audience of over five hundred, I knew that I had voiced many women's thoughts and feelings.

The next year four of us started a women's ritual group meeting on full moons and the seasonal holidays to celebrate our connections to the earth, to the Goddess, and to each other. Though its membership has changed over the years, and I have become a less active member since I moved, this group continues to thrive. When we initiated ourselves as Rising Moon at Candlemas in the group's second year, Carmen Torres and I were affirmed as priestesses. Today we almost all call ourselves priestesses. For us becoming a priestess means developing skill in creating ritual and taking responsibility for the survival of the group. This women's circle has been very important in strengthening my knowledge of ritual and of the Goddess. Celebrating the cycles of the moon and the seasons of the year affirms of my connection to the earth, to finitude, to change, to death, to rebirth. Raising power in a circle of women reminds each of us of our abilities to shape our lives and to heal each other and the earth. Ritual participation is essential to me. Ritual connects us to each other and to the earth; ritual is physical and nonverbal as well as verbal, and it thus opens channels of understanding that could not be reached through study alone. In ritual our understandings are challenged, grounded, and expanded by the participation of others. Our group has been inspired by the writings of Starhawk, Z Budapest, and others, but we have also drawn on our own intuition, creativity, and knowledge, finding our own way.

When I began to go to Greece with the Aegean Women's Studies Institute in 1981, I had the opportunity to create and participate in rituals at the ancient sites of Eleusis, sacred to Demeter and Persephone; Ephesus, sacred to Artemis; and Mesa, Lesbos, sacred to Aphrodite. I have also visited many other sacred sites and sacred caves. The Goddesses are palpably present at the sites of their ancient worship. I have often sensed enormous energy stored in those places, waiting to be tapped. Celebrating rituals to the Goddesses at the sacred spaces of the past has been enormously powerful.

In Greece, the Goddesses who have moved me most profoundly are Gaia, Demeter and Persephone, and Aphrodite. Gaia is Earth, oldest of the Goddesses and Gods, whose rocky presence reminds me of the constancy that undergirds the change I experience daily. I have felt Gaia's presence most strongly in the caves of Greece, which once were known as her womb, the place of emergence and return, the place of communion with her deepest mysteries. Demeter and Persephone pulled me long before I went to Greece, their ancient mysteries promising to unlock the pain of separation and joy of reunion with my mother, and to communicate the secret of life, death, and rebirth. Aphrodite initially drew me because of her temple on Lesbos which has become my spiritual home. In my dedication to her as priestess, I recognize that the transforming power of sexuality is a mystery, never to be understood or rationally controlled, only to be experienced again and again in its cycles of joyous communion and separation. I have come to understand, as Sappho also did, that the powers evoked in sexuality open the deepest source of my creativity as a writer, a poet.

I do not believe we need to go to Greece to meet the Goddesses.

There are sacred spaces and female presences in every land, as the ritual our group created in Alum Rock Park in San Jose, California, reminds us. It is crucial that European-Americans whose ties with the lands of their origins have been severed discover the sacred places in the land where we live. In Europe the sacred places are still known, if unconsciously, because churches were often built at the sites of earlier worship, at the places where springs or the sea or the outcropping of rock were called holy because they offer vivid intuition of ties to an earth more ancient than ourselves. The Europeans who came to America with a religion of promise and history unwittingly broke their spiritual links to earth, which our ancestors in Europe retained. We Americans, who are not fully rooted in the land that we have claimed as our home, must learn to trust our deepest intuitions of connection to our particular part of the earth. We also have much to learn from Native American Indians about the sacred places in our land.

The rituals I share here reflect pieces of my spiritual journey. They by no means encompass the variety of rituals I have created or participated in, nor do they reflect the whole of my understanding of the Goddesses. Gaia and Aphrodite, Demeter and Persephone are not the only Goddesses, though they are the Goddesses whose names have been most important to me. Underlying each of these differentiated Goddesses is Earth, the pulsing energy of life, death, and rebirth, which I experienced most profoundly in the cave at Eressos and have felt at other times as well. This energy is symbolized by the stones and shells I have on my altar, by the image of the Minoan snake Goddess who watches over my home, and by the snake jewelery I wear.

For me this power is both Goddess and Goddesses and Earth itself. It can be invoked through female, male, or nonpersonal imagery. I sense an underlying unity as well as a multiplicity of life forms. I address her in personal language, and I recognize her in the sea, in trees, in stones and shells, in me, in you, in all life, and in death. Though my theological training tells me I must know whether Goddess is one or many, personal or impersonal, whether she is nature or more than nature, I am not certain that these questions can be answered. The answers do not seem to be required for participation in ritual.

Most of the Goddess rituals I have participated in have been with and for women. I believe that it is crucial for women to claim separate spaces where we can give free rein to our imaginations and our spiritual longings and lay claim to our power to create ritual apart from the critical voices of male authorities. However, this is not to say that all feminist worship is for women only. The women's ritual group to which I belong has begun to open several of the seasonal holidays to men and boys, with great success. For those of us who understand our human community to include men this is a necessary development. When men are included in our rituals, we invoke both Goddesses and God, not wishing to perpetuate the exclusion we have felt in rituals where our sex was not affirmed as the image of divinity.

"Why Women Need the Goddess" raises issues that remain important as we think about the transformation of religion from the perspective of feminism and women's experience. The most important point in that essay is that Goddesses are about female power. Probably that is why Goddesses have been suppressed in Western religion. This power is so threatening to the status quo that the word *Goddess* still remains unspeakable even to many of the most radical Christian and Jewish theologians. Yet Goddess is a name that must be spoken if female power is to be acknowledged as legitimate. Goddesses also celebrate the female body, remind us of our connections to nature, and encourage us to celebrate the bonds we share as women. Occasionally "Why Women Need the Goddess" has been read as a separatist statement. Though it is strongly rooted in women's experience, "Why Women Need the Goddess" was not intended to exclude men. I believe that men also need the Goddess, and I hope they will write more about their experience.

In "Symbolism of Goddess and God in Feminist Theology," I analyzed feminist writing on God/Goddess language. In thinking about the different solutions we were considering, it seemed to me that feminist work on God/Goddess language did not fall on a simple line from conservative to radical. Rather, some feminists whose theologies could be called conservative were radical on the question of God/Goddess language, and vice versa. In this essay, I also argued that the affirmatively female language of God/She, God the Mother, and Goddess must be used if female power is to be fully acknowledged within religious traditions.

This analysis remains relevant. Even in the most liberal churches and synagogues, including many led by women, God the Father, Lord, and King continues to be invoked in prayer, liturgy, and scripture readings. Many of the most important feminist theologians have remained remarkably silent on this issue. Though Rosemary Radford Ruether uses the word "God/ess" in *Sexism and God–Talk*,[3] she states that this word cannot be pronounced, implicitly denying its relevence to worship. Elisabeth Schüssler Fiorenza argues in *In Memory of Her* that God the Father as understood by Jesus is not a patriarchal image.[4] She argues that the patriarchal texts of the Bible should not be made inclusive but should be left as part of the androcentric record; she does not offer alternative imagery for liturgy. *An Inclusive Language Lectionary*,[5] a path-breaking attempt to provide a nonsexist version of the Bible for use in liturgy produced under the sponsorship of the National Council of Churches, has been denounced by conservative and fundamentalist denominations and many within the so-called liberal churches. The vehemence of the attacks on the lectionary demonstrate that it has seemed to many to challenge their image of God as male. According to Susan Brooks Thistlewaite, whose name was used in the press release announcing the lectionary, the major theme of the many hate letters she received was that "God really is male, and he will condemn you to hell for changing his word."[6] The lectionary's solution to the problem of God language falls primarily into the gender neutral category. It has eliminated the most obviously genderized language for God: *Lord* becomes the *Sovereign*, *Son of Man* becomes *the Human One*, and the references to God as *he* or *him* are eliminated by repetition of the word *God*. The lectionary also takes the more radical step of offering the possibility of praying to God as *Father [and Mother]*. Here it moves beyond the gender neutral solution and opens the door for more radical transformation of our images of God. However, this possibility is limited by the committee's recognition that to call God "our Father and Mother" cannot be understood as translation of the original text; therefore the words *and Mother* are put in brackets and marked as optional. Even as optional, however, they represent a radical departure from the traditional imagery of Christian worship. And it must be noted that in those congregations where the words *and Mother* are read, the brackets are not. Such steps must continue to be taken if the patriarchal bias of biblical religions is to be transformed. The authors of *An Inclusive Language Lectionary* are to be commended for the important and risky work they have done. Yet from the point of view of my article, the lectionary fails to eliminate completely the image of the male God from the Christian imagination. Hearers of the Word as preached from *An Inclusive Language Lectionary* are deprived of the comfort of (or shielded from the blatant offense of) traditional patriarchal language, but they may not forced to give up their traditional images of God as a male presence. Given almost two thousand years of patriarchal imagery, I suspect that many who hear gender neutral inclusive language continue to think of God as abstractly male. Unless affirmatively female language of God/She, God the Mother, and Goddess is used, I argue, female power will not be unequivocably affirmed as being equally as valuable as male power.

"Reclaiming Goddess History" attempts a partial reconstruction of the history of the Goddesses in the Old Europe, the Near East, and the Mediterranean. Androcentric interpretations of the Goddesses in the primary sources, including the earliest written records, and in much of the scholarly tradition up to the present, have presented us with images of the Goddesses as subordinate to Gods. Contemporary women who advocate Goddess symbolism are often told that Goddess symbolism does not provide us with images of female power. Goddesses, it is commonly argued, come from patriarchal societies, and their symbolism has been used to support patriarchal power. Thus, it is said, there is no reason to believe that the reemergence of Goddess symbolism today will advance the cause of women. Even if Goddess symbolism in the past supported male power, it does not have to do so today. However, such an argument is contrary to the intuition many women have, which archaeological research is beginning to confirm, that ancient Goddess images do reflect female power.

In order to reconstruct the history and prehistory (before written records) of the Goddesses, we must first critically reflect upon patriarchal history. We must question the patriarchal assumption that men have always and everywhere held power, and we must question the reliability of patriarchal history, both the primary sources that come down to us from the past, and the secondary sources of contemporary scholarship. We must entertain the hypothesis that men may not have held power always and everywhere, and we must search the androcentric traditions for clues to a history that can empower women. In this question, the evidence of prehistory, the time before written records, must be given weight. A plausible case can be made that writing and patriarchy arose together, at the time (between 4000 and 3000 B.C.E.) when constant warfare led to the consolidation of power in the hands of warrior kings. Centralized governments required writing to control the flow of goods and eventually to create a standardized mythos that could legitimate and justify the power of the king. In my essay "Reclaiming Goddess History," I suggest that the prehistoric Goddess reflected the power of women in societies where women were not subordinate, socially or religiously. The emergence of the Virgin Goddess, on the other hand, reflects the patriarchal attempt to control women by controlling our sexuality and by separating our sexual power from our other creative powers. This essay reflects my attempt to use a feminist critical method to recover the prehistory and history of the Goddess.

An invitation to participate on a panel on "Initiation" at the American Academy of Religion led me to name my experiences of Goddess as an initiation in my essay "Laughter of Aphrodite." I feel grateful for this opportunity to reflect upon some of the various ways the Goddesses have revealed the unexpected, grounded and supported my quest to understand my life and place in the world. To speak of these experiences and rituals at a scholarly conference and to publish them is to risk having my scholarship dismissed as confession, for it is contrary to the canons of scholarly objectivity to reveal personal experiences that inspire and undergird scholarly research. Yet I remain convinced that the inclusion of this and other very personal reflections in this volume is neither incidental nor self-indulgent but rather reflects the fundamental feminist insight that scholarship begins in experience and must continually be tested by it.

NOTES

Epigraph: Agnes Whistling Elk quoted in Lynn V. Andrews, *Jaguar Woman* (San Francisco: Harper & Row, 1985), xii.

1. Anne Barstow, "The Prehistoric Goddess," in *The Book of the Goddess*, ed. Carl

Olson (New York: Crossroad, 1983), 8.

2. These are the words to a chant Z Budapest shared that weekend.
3. Rosemary Radford Ruether, *Sexism and God-Talk* (Boston: Beacon Press, 1983), 46.
4. Elisabeth Schüssler Fiorenza, *In Memory of Her* (New York: Crossroad Press, 1983), 130–40.
5. *An Inclusive Language Lectionary: Readings for Year A* (Atlanta, New York, Philadelphia: The Cooperative Publication Association, 1983), esp. the appendix.
6. In a paper delivered at the 1983 meetings of the American Academy of Religion. Also see her "Opening the Mail that Did Not Tick," *Review of Books in Religion* 12, no. 2 (May 1984): 6–8.

Demeter Holding Persephone on Her Lap. From Eleusis.

8. Why Women Need the Goddess

At the close of Ntosake Shange's stupendously successful Broadway play *for colored girls who have considered suicide when the rainbow is enuf*, a tall beautiful black woman rises from despair to cry out, "I found God in myself and I loved her fiercely."[1] Her discovery is echoed by women around the country who meet spontaneously in small groups on full moons, solstices, and equinoxes to celebrate the Goddess as symbol of life and death powers and waxing and waning energies in the universe and in themselves.[2]

It is the night of the full moon. Nine women stand in a circle, on a rocky hill about the city. The western sky is rosy with the setting sun; in the east the moon's face begins to peer above the horizon. . . The woman pours out a cup of wine onto the earth, refills it and raises it high. "Hail, Tana, Mother of mothers!" she cries. "Awaken from your long sleep, and return to your children again!"[3]

What are the political and psychological effects of this fierce new love of the divine in themselves for women whose spiritual experience has been focused by the male God of Judaism and Christianity? Is the spiritual dimension of feminism a passing diversion, an escape from difficult but necessary political work? Or does the emergence of the symbol of Goddess among women have significant political and psychological ramifications for the feminist movement?

To answer this question, we must first understand the importance of religious symbols and rituals in human life and consider the effect of male symbolism of God on women. According to anthropologist Clifford Geertz, religious symbols shape a cultural ethos, defining the deepest values of a society and the persons in it. "Religion," Geertz writes, " is a system of symbols which act to produce powerful, pervasive, and long-lasting moods and motivations"[4] in the people of a given culture. A "mood" for Geertz is a psychological attitude such as awe, trust, and respect, while a "motivation" is the social and political trajectory created by a mood that transforms mythos into ethos, symbol system into social and political reality. Symbols have both psychological and political effects, because they create their inner conditions (deep-seated attitudes and feelings) that lead people to feel comfortable with or to accept social and political arrangements that correspond to the symbol system.

Because religion has such a compelling hold on the deep psyches of so many people, feminists cannot afford to leave it in the hands of the fathers. Even people who no longer "believe in God" or participate in the institutional structure of patriarchal religion still may not be free of the power of the symbolism of God the Father. A symbol's effect does not depend on rational assent, for a symbol also functions on levels of the psyche other than the rational. Religion fulfills deep psychic needs by providing symbols and rituals that enable people to cope with crisis situations[5] in human life (death, evil, suffering) and to pass through life's important transitions (birth, sexuality, death). Even people who consider themselves completely secularized will often find themselves sitting in a church or synagogue when a friend or relative gets married or when a parent or friend has died. The symbols associated with these important rituals cannot fail to affect the deep or unconscious structures of the mind of even a person who has rejected these symbolisms on a conscious level—especially if a person is under stress. The reason for the continuing effects of religious symbols is that the mind abhors a vacuum. Symbol systems cannot simply be rejected; they must be replaced. Where there is no replacement, the mind will revert to familiar structures at times of crisis, bafflement, or defeat.

Religions centered on the worship of a male God create "moods" and "motivations" that keep women in a state of psychological dependence on men and male authority, while at the same legitimating the political and social authority of fathers and sons in the institutions of society.

Religious symbol systems focused around exclusively male images of divinity create the impression that female power can never be fully legitimate or wholly beneficent. This message need never be explicitly stated (as, for example, it is in the story of Eve) for its effect to be felt. A woman completely ignorant of the myths of female evil in biblical religion nonetheless acknowledges the anomaly of female power when she prays exclusively to a male God. She may see herself as like God (created in the image of God) only by denying her own sexual identity and affirming God's transcendence of sexual identity. But she can never have the experience that is freely available to every man and boy in her culture, of having her full sexual identity affirmed as being in the image and likeness of God. In Geertz's terms, her "mood" is one of trust in male power as salvific and distrust of female power in herself and other women as inferior or dangerous. Such a powerful, pervasive, and long-lasting "mood" cannot fail to become a "motivation" that translates into social and political reality.

In *Beyond God the Father*, feminist theologian Mary Daly detailed the psychological and political ramifications of father religion for women.

> If God in "his" heaven is a father ruling his people, then it is the "nature" of things and according to divine plan and the order of the universe that society be male dominated. Within this context, a *mystification of roles* takes place: The husband dominating his wife represents God "himself." The images and values of a given society have been projected into the realm of dogmas and "Articles of Faith," and these in turn justify the social structures which have given rise to them and which sustain their plausibility.[6]

Philosopher Simone de Beauvoir was well aware of the function of patriarchal religion as legitimizer of male power. As she wrote:

> Man enjoys the great advantage of having a god endorse the code he writes; and since man exercises a sovereign authority over women it is especially fortunate that this authority has been vested in him by the Supreme Being. For the Jew, Mohammedans, and Christians, among others, man is Master by divine right; the fear of God will therefore repress any impulse to revolt in the downtrodden female.[7]

This brief discussion of the psychological and political effects of God religion puts us in an excellent position to begin to understand the significance of the symbol of Goddess for women. In discussing the meaning of the Goddess, my method will first be phenomenological. I will isolate a meaning of the symbol of the Goddess as it has emerged in the lives of contemporary women. I will then discuss its psychological and political significance by contrasting the "moods" and "motivations" engendered by Goddess symbols with those engendered by Christian symbolism. I will also correlate Goddess symbolism with themes that have emerged in the women's movement in order to show how Goddess symbolism undergirds and legitimates the concerns of the women's movement, much as God symbolism in Christianity undergirded the interests of men in patriarchy. I will discuss four aspects of Goddess symbolism here: the Goddess as affirmation of female power, the female body, the female will, and women's bonds and heritage. There are, of course, many other meanings of the Goddess that I will not discuss here.

The sources for the symbol of the Goddess in contemporary spirituality are traditions of Goddess worship and modern women's experience. The ancient Mediterranean, pre-Christian European, Native American, Mesoamerican, Hindu, African, and other traditions are rich sources for Goddess symbolism. But these traditions are filtered through modern women's experiences. Traditions of Goddesses' subordination to Gods, for example, are ignored. Ancient traditions are tapped selectively and eclecticly, but they are not considered authoritative for modern consciousness. The Goddess symbol has emerged spontaneously in the dreams, fantasies, and thoughts of many women in the past several years. Kirsten Grimstad and Susan Rennie reported that they were surprised to discover widespread interest in spirituality, including the Goddess, among feminists around the country in the summer of 1974.[8] *WomanSpirit* magazine, which published its first issue in 1974 and had contributors from across the United States, expressed the grass-roots nature of the women's spirituality movement. In 1976, a journal devoted to the Goddess emerged, titled *Lady Unique*. In 1975, the first women's spirituality conference was held in Boston and attended by 1,800 women. In 1978, a University of Santa Cruz conference on the Goddess drew over 500 people. Sources for this essay are these manifestations of the Goddess in modern women's experiences as reported in *WomanSpirit*, *Lady Unique*, and elsewhere, and as expressed in conversations I have had with women who have been thinking about the Goddess and women's spirituality.

The simplest and most basic meaning of the symbol of Goddess is the acknowledgment of the legitimacy of female power as a beneficient and independent power. A woman who echoes Ntosake Shange's dramatic statement, "I found God in myself and I loved her fiercely," is saying, "Female power is strong and creative." She is saying that the divine principle, the saving and sustaining power, is in herself, that she will no longer look to men or male figures as saviors. The strength and independence of female power can be intuited by contemplating ancient and modern images of the Goddess. This meaning of the symbol of Goddess is simple and obvious, and yet it is difficult for many to comprehend. It stands in sharp contrast to the paradigms of female dependence on males that have been predominant in Western religion and culture. The internationally acclaimed novelist Monique Wittig captured the novelty and flavor of the affirmation of female power when she wrote in her mythic work *Les Guerilleres*:

> There was a time when you were not a slave, remember that. You walked alone, full of laughter, you bathed bare-bellied. You say you have lost all recollection of it, remember. . . You say there are not words to describe it, you say it does not exist. But remember. Make an effort to remember. Or, failing that, invent.[9]

While Wittig does not speak directly of the Goddess here, she captures the "mood" of joyous celebration of female freedom and independence that is created in women who define their identities through the symbol of Goddess. Artist Mary Beth Edelson expressed the political "motivations" inspired by the Goddess when she wrote:

> The ascending archetypal symbols of the feminine unfold today in the psyche of modern Everywoman. They encompass the multiple forms of the Great Goddess. Reaching across the centuries we take the hands of our Ancient Sisters. The Great Goddess alive and well is rising to announce to the patriarchs that their 5,000 years are up—Hallelujah! Here we come.[10]

The affirmation of female power contained in the Goddess symbol has both psychological and political consequences. Psychologically, it means the defeat of the view engendered by patriarchy that women's power is inferior and dangerous. This new "mood" of affirmation of female power also leads to new "motivations"; it supports and undergirds women's trust in their own power and the power of other women in family and society.

If the simplest meaning of the Goddess symbol is an affirmation of the legitimacy and beneficence of female power, then a question immediately arises, "Is the Goddess simply female power writ large, and if so, why bother with the symbol of Goddess at all? Or does the symbol refer to a Goddess 'out there' who is not reducible to a human potential?" The many women who have rediscovered the power of Goddess would give three answers to this question: (1) The Goddess is divine female, a personification who can be invoked in prayer and ritual; (2) the Goddess is symbol of the life, death, and rebirth energy in nature and culture, in personal and communal life, and (3) the Goddess is symbol of the affirmation of the legitimacy and beauty of female power (made possible by the new becoming of women in the women's liberation movement). If one were to ask these women which answer is the "correct" one, different responses would be given. Some would assert that the Goddess definitely is *not* "out there," that the symbol of a divinity "out there" is part of the legacy of patriarchal oppression, which brings with it the authoritarianism, hierarchicalism, and dogmatic rigidity associated with biblical monotheistic religions. They might assert that the Goddess symbol reflects the sacred power within women and nature, suggesting the connectedness between women's cycles of menstruation, birth, and menopause, and the life and death cycles of the universe. Others seem quite comfortable with the notion of Goddess as a divine female protector and creator and would find their experience of Goddess limited by the assertion that she is not *also* out there as well as within themselves and in all natural processes. When asked what the symbol of Goddess means, feminist priestess Starhawk replied:

> It all depends on how I feel. When I feel weak, she is someone who can help and protect me. When I feel strong, she is the symbol of my own power. At other times I feel her as the natural energy in my body and the world.[11]

How are we to evaluate such a statement? Theologians might call these the words of a sloppy thinker. But my deepest intuition tells me they contain a wisdom that Western theological thought has lost.

To theologians, these differing views of the "meaning" of the symbol of Goddess might seem to threaten a replay of the trinitarian controversies. Is there, perhaps, a way of doing theology that would not lead immediately into dogmatic controversy, would not require theologians to say definitively that one understanding is true and the others are false? Could people's relation to a common symbol be made primary and varying interpretations be acknowledged? The diversity of explications of the meaning of the Goddess symbol suggests that symbols have a richer significance than any explications of their meaning can express, a point literary critics have long insisted on. This phenomenological fact suggests that theologians may need to give more than lip service to a theory of symbol in which the symbol is viewed as the primary fact and the meanings are viewed as secondary. It also suggests that a *thea*logy of the Goddess would be very different from the *theo*logy we have known in the west. But to spell out this notion of the primacy of *symbol* in thealogy in contrast to the primacy of the *explanation* in theology would be the topic of another paper. Let me simply state that women, who have been deprived of a female religious symbol system for centuries, recognize the power and primacy of symbols. I believe women must develop a theory of symbol and thealogy congruent with their experience at the same time as they "remember and invent" new symbol systems.

A second important implication of the Goddess symbol for women is the affirmation of the female body and the life cycle expressed in it. Because of women's unique position as menstruants, birthgivers, and those who have traditionally cared for the young and the dying, women's connection to the body, nature, and this world has been obvious. Women were denigrated because they seemed more carnal, fleshy, and earthy than the culture-creating males.[12] The misogynist antibody tradition in Western thought is symbolized in the myth of Eve who is traditionally viewed as a sexual temptress, the eptiome of women's carnal nature. This tradition reaches its nadir in the *Malleus Maleficarum (The Hammer of Evil-Doing Women)*, which states "All witchcraft stems from carnal lust, which in women is insatiable."[13] The Virgin Mary, the positive female image in Christianity, does not contradict Christian denigration of the female body and its powers. The Virgin Mary is revered because she, in her perpetual virginity, transcends the carnal sexuality attributed to most women.

The denigration of the female body is expressed in cultural and religious taboos surrounding menstruation, childbirth, and menopause in women. While menstruation taboos may have originated in a perception of the awesome powers of the female body,[14] they degenerated into a simple perception that there is something "wrong" with female bodily functions. Menstruating women were forbidden to enter the sanctuary in ancient Hebrew and premodern Christian communities. Although only Orthodox Jews still enforce religious taboos against menstruant women, few women in our culture grow up affirming their menstruation as a connection to sacred power. Most women learn that menstruation is a curse and grow up believing that the bloody facts of menstruation are best hidden away. Feminists challenge this attitude to the female body. Judy Chicago's art piece "Menstruation Bathroom" broke these menstrual taboos. In a sterile white bathroom, she exhibited boxes of Tampax and Kotex on an open shelf, and the wastepaper basket was overflowing with bloody tampons and sanitary napkins.[15] Many women who viewed the piece felt relieved to have their "dirty secret" out in the open.

The denigration of the female body and its powers is further expressed in Western culture's attitudes toward childbirth.[16] Religious iconography does not celebrate the birthgiver, and there is no theology or ritual that enables a woman to celebrate the process of birth as a spiritual experience. Indeed, Jewish and Christian traditions also had blood taboos concerning the woman who had recently given birth. While these religious taboos are rarely enforced today (again, only by Orthodox Jews), they have secular equivalents. Giving birth is treated as a disease requiring hospitalization, and the woman is viewed as a passive object, anesthetized to ensure her acquiescence to the will of the doctor. The women's liberation movement has challenged these cultural attitudes, and many feminists have joined with advocates of natural childbirth and home birth in emphasizing the need for women to control and take pride in their bodies, including the birth process.

Western culture also gives little dignity to the postmenopausal or aging woman. It is no secret that our culture is based on a denial of aging and death, and that women suffer more severely from this denial than men. Women are placed on a pedestal and considered powerful when they are young and beautiful, but they are said to lose this power as they age. As feminists have pointed out, the "power" of the young woman is illusory, since beauty standards are defined by men, and since few women are considered (or consider themselves) beautiful for more than a few years of their lives. Some men are viewed as wise and authoritative in age, but old women are pitied and shunned. Religious iconography supports this cultural attitude towards aging women. The purity and virginity of Mary and the female saints is often expressed in the iconographic convention of perpetual youth. Moreover, religious mythology associates aging women with evil in the symbol of the wicked old witch. Feminists have challenged cultural myths of aging women and have urged women to reject patriarchal beauty standards and to celebrate the distinctive beauty of women of all ages.

The symbol of Goddess aids the process of naming and reclaiming the female body and its cycles and processes. In the ancient world and among modern women, the Goddess symbol represents the birth, death, and rebirth processes of the natural and human worlds. The female body is viewed as the direct incarnation of waxing and waning, life and death cycles in the universe. This is sometimes expressed through the symbolic connection between the twenty-eight-day cycles of menstruation and the twenty-eight-day cycles of the moon. Moreover, the Goddess is celebrated in the triple aspect of youth, maturity, and age, or maiden, mother, and crone. The potentiality of the young girl is celebrated in the nymph or maiden aspect of the Goddess. The Goddess as mother is sometimes depicted giving birth, and giving birth is viewed as a symbol for all the creative, life-giving powers of the universe.[17] The life-giving powers of the Goddess in her creative aspect are not limited to physical birth, for the Goddess is also seen as the creator of all the arts of civilization, including healing, writing, and the giving of just law. Women in the middle of life who are not physical mothers may give birth to poems, songs, and books, or nurture other women, men, and children. They too are incarnations of the Goddess in her creative, life-giving aspect. At the end of life, women incarnate the crone aspect of the Goddess. The wise old woman, the woman who knows from experience what life is about, the woman whose closeness to her own death gives her a distance and perspective on the problems of life, is celebrated as the third aspect of the Goddess. Thus, women learn to value youth, creativity, and wisdom in themselves and other women.

The possibilities of reclaiming the female body and its cycles have been expressed in a number of Goddess-centered rituals. Hallie Austen Iglehart and Barbry MyOwn created a summer solstice ritual to celebrate menstruation and birth. The women simulated a birth canal and birthed each other into their circle. They raised power by placing their hands on each other's bellies and chanting together. Finally they marked each other's faces with rich, dark menstrual blood saying, "This is the blood that promises renewal. This is the blood that promises sustenance. This is the blood that promises life."[18] From hidden dirty secret to symbol of the life power of the Goddess, women's blood has come full circle. Other women have created rituals that celebrate the crone aspect of the Goddess, especially at Halloween, an ancient holiday. On this day, the wisdom of the old woman is celebrated, and it is also recognized that the old must die so that the new can be born.

The "mood" created by the symbol of the Goddess in triple aspect is one of positive, joyful affirmation of the female body and its cycles and acceptance of aging and death as well as life. The "motivations" are to overcome menstrual taboos, to return the birth process to the hands of women, and to change cultural attitudes about age and death. Changing cultural attitudes toward the female body would help to overcome the spirit-flesh, mind-body dualisms of Western culture, since, as Ruether has pointed out, the denigration of the female body is at the heart of these dualisms. The Goddess as symbol of the revaluation of the body and nature thus also undergirds the human potential and ecology movements. The "mood" is one of affirmation, awe, and respect for the body and nature, and the "motivation" is respect for the teachings of the body and the value of all living beings.

A third important implication of the Goddess symbol for women is the positive valuation of will in Goddess-centered ritual, especially in Goddess-centered ritual magic and spellcasting in womanspirit and feminist witchcraft circles. The basic notion behind ritual magic and spell casting is energy as power. Here the Goddess is a center or focus of power and energy; she is the personification of the energy that flows between beings in the natural and human worlds. In Goddess circles, energy is raised by chanting or dancing. According to Starhawk, "Witches conceive of psychic energy as having form and substance that can be perceived and directed by those with a trained awareness. The power generated within the circle is built into a cone form, and at its peak is released—to the Goddess, to reenergize the members of the coven, or to do a specific work such as healing."[19] In ritual magic, the energy raised is directed by willpower. Women who celebrate in Goddess circles believe they can achieve their wills in the world.

The emphasis on the will is important for women, because women traditionally have been taught to devalue their wills, to believe that they cannot achieve their will through their own power, and even to suspect that the assertion of will is evil. Faith Wildung's poem "Waiting," from which I will quote only a short segment, sums up women's sense that their lives are defined not by their own will, but by waiting for others to take the initiative.

> Waiting for my breasts to develop
> Waiting to wear a bra
> Waiting to menstruate
>
> . . . .
>
> Waiting for life to begin, Waiting–
> Waiting to be somebody
>
> . . . .
>
> Waiting to get married
> Waiting for my wedding day
> Waiting for my wedding night
>
> . . . .
>
> Waiting for the end of the day
> Waiting for sleep. Waiting. . .[20]

Patriarchal religion has enforced the view that female initiative and will are evil through the juxtaposition of Eve and Mary. Eve caused the fall by asserting her will against the command of God, while Mary began the new age with her response to God's initiative, "Let it be done to me according to thy word" (Luke 1:38). Even for men, patriarchal religion values the passive will subordinate to divine initiative. The classical doctrines of sin and grace view sin as the prideful assertion of will and grace as the obedient subordination of the human will to the divine initiative or order. While this view of will might be questioned from a human perspective, Valerie Saiving has argued that it has particularly deleterious consequences for women in Western culture. According to Saiving, Western culture encourages males in the assertion of will, and thus it may make some sense to view the male form of sin as an excess of will. But since culture discourages females in the assertion of will, the traditional doctrines of sin and grace encourage women to remain in their form of sin, which is self-negation or insufficient assertion of will.[21] One possible reason the will is denigrated in a patriarchal religious framework is that both human and divine will are often pictured as arbitrary, self-initiated, and exercised without regard for other wills.

In a Goddess-centered context, in contrast, the will is valued. *A woman is encouraged to know her will, to believe that her will is valid, and to believe that her will can be achieved in the world*, three powers traditionally denied to her in patriarchy. In a Goddess-centered framework, a woman's will is not subordinated to the Lord God as king and ruler, nor to men as his representatives. Thus a woman is not reduced to waiting and acquiescing in the wills of others as she is in patriarchy. But neither does she adopt the egocentric form of will that pursues self-interest without regard for the interests of others.

The Goddess-centered context provides a different understanding of the will than that available in the traditional patriarchal religious framework. In the Goddess framework, will can be achieved only when it is exercised in harmony with the energies and wills of other beings. Wise women, for example, raise a cone of healing energy at the full moon or solstice when the lunar or solar energies are at their high points with respect to the earth. This discipline encourages them to recognize that not all times are propitious for the achieving of every will. Similarly, they know that spring is a time for new beginnings in work and love, summer a time for producing external manifestations of inner potentialities, and fall or winter times for stripping down to the inner core and extending roots. Such awareness of waxing and waning processes in the universe discourages arbitrary ego-centered assertion of will, while at the same time encouraging the assertion of individual will in cooperation with natural energies and the energies created by the wills of others. Wise women also have a tradition that whatever is sent out will be returned, and this reminds them to assert their wills in cooperative and healing rather than egocentric and destructive ways. This view of will allows women to begin to recognize, claim, and assert their wills without adopting the worst characteristics of the patriarchal understanding and use of will. In the Goddess-centered framework, the "mood" is one of positive affirmation of personal will in the context of the energies of other wills or beings. The "motivation" is for women to know and assert their wills in cooperation with other wills and energies. This of course does not mean that women always assert their wills in positive and life-affirming ways. Women's capacity for evil is, of course, as great as men's. My purpose is simply to contrast the differing attitudes toward the exercise of will *per se*, and the female will in particular, in Goddess-centered religion and in the Christian God-centered religion.

The fourth and final aspect of Goddess symbolism that I will discuss here is the significance of the Goddess for a revaluation of women's bonds and heritage. As Virginia Woolf has said, "Chloe liked Olivia," a statement about a woman's relation to another woman, is a sentence that rarely occurs in fiction. Men have written the stories, and they have written about women almost exclusively in their relations to men.[22] The celebrations of women's bonds to each other, as mothers and daughters, as colleagues and coworkers, as sisters, friends, and lovers, is beginning to occur in the new literature and culture created by women in the women's movement. While I believe that the revaluing of each of these bonds is important, I will focus on the mother-daughter bond, in part because I believe it may be the key to the others.

Adrienne Rich has pointed out that the mother-daughter bond, perhaps the most important of women's bonds, "resonant with charges. . . the flow of energy between two biologically alike bodies, one of which has lain in amniotic bliss inside the other, one of which has labored to give birth to the other,"[23] is rarely celebrated in patriarchal religion and culture. Christianity celebrates the father's relation to the son and the mother's relation to the son, but the story of mother and daughter is missing. So, too, in patriarchal literature and psychology the mothers and daughters rarely exist. Volumes have been written about the oedipal complex, but little has been written about the girl's relation to her mother. Moreover, as de Beauvoir has noted, the mother-daughter relation is distorted in patriarchy because the mother must give her daughter over to men in a male-defined culture in which women are viewed as inferior. The mother must socialize her daughter to be subordinate to men, and if her daughter challenges patriarchal norms, the mother is likely to defend the patriarchal structures against her own daughter.[24]

These patterns are changing in the new culture created by women in which the bonds of women to women are beginning to be celebrated. Holly Near has written several songs that celebrate women's bonds and women's heritage. In one of her finest songs she writes of an "old-time woman" who is "waiting to die." A young woman feels for the life that has passed the old woman by and begins to cry, but the old woman looks her in the eye and says, "If I had not suffered, you wouldn't be wearing those jeans/Being an old-time woman ain't as bad as it seems."[25] This song, which Near has said was inspired by her grandmother, expresses and celebrates a bond and a heritage passed down from one woman to another. In another of Near's songs, she sings of a "a hiking-boot mother who's seeing the world/For the first time with her own little girl." In this song, the mother tells the drifter who has been traveling with her to pack up and travel alone if he thinks "traveling three is a drag" because "I've got a little one who loves me as much as you need me/And darling, that's loving enough."[26] This song is significant because the mother places her relationship to her daughter above her relationship to a man, something women rarely do in patriarchy.[27]

Almost the only story of mother and daughters that has been transmitted in Western culture is the myth of Demeter and Persephone that was the basis of religious rites celebrated by women only, the Thesmophoria, and later formed the basis of the Eleusinian mysteries, which were open to all who spoke Greek. In this story, the daughter, Persephone, is raped away from her mother, Demeter, by the God of the underworld. Unwilling to accept this state of affairs, Demeter rages and withholds fertility from the earth until her daughter is returned to her. What is important for women in this story is that a mother fights for her daughter and for her relation to her daughter. This is completely different from the mother's relation to her daughter in patriarchy. The "mood" created by the story of Demeter and Persephone is one of celebration of the mother-daughter bond, and the "motivation" is for mothers and daughters to affirm the heritage passed on from mother to daughter and to reject the patriarchal pattern where the primary loyalties of mother and daughter must be to men.[28]

The symbol of Goddess has much to offer women who are struggling to be rid of the "powerful, pervasive, and long-lasting moods and motivations" of devaluation of female power, denigration of the female body, distrust of female will, and denial of the women's bonds and heritage that have been engendered by patriarchal religion. As women struggle to create a new culture in which women's power, bodies, will, and bonds are celebrated, it seems natural that the Goddess would reemerge as symbol of the newfound beauty, strength, and power of women.

NOTES

1. From the original cast album, Buddah Records, 1976. Also see *for colored girls who have considered suicide when the rainbow is enuf* (New York: MacMillan, 1976).
2. See Susan Rennie and Kristen Grimstad, "Spiritual Explorations Cross-Country," *Quest* 1, no. 4 (1975): 49–51; and *WomanSpirit* magazine.
3. See Starhawk, "Witchcraft and Women's Culture," in *Womanspirit Rising*, ed. Carol P. Christ and Judith Plaskow (New York: Harper & Row, 1979), 260.
4. Clifford Geertz, "Religion as a Cultural System," in *The Interpretation of Cultures* (New York: Basic Books, 1973), 90.
5. Ibid., 98-108.
6. Mary Daly, *Beyond God the Father* (Boston: Beacon Press, 1974), 13, italics added.
7. Simone de Beauvoir, *The Second Sex*, trans. H.M. Parshleys (New York: Alfred A. Knopf, 1953).
8. See Grimstad and Rennie, "Spiritual Explorations Cross-Country."
9. Monique Wittig, *Les Guerilleres*, trans. David LeVay (New York: Avon Books, 1971), 89. Also quoted in Morgan MacFarland, "Witchcraft: The Art of Remembering," *Quest* 1, no. 4 (1975): 41.
10. Mary Beth Edelson, "Speaking for Myself," *Lady Unique* 1 (1976): 56.
11. Personal communication.
12. This theory of the origins of the Western dualism is stated by Rosemary Ruether in *New Woman/New Earth* (New York: Seabury Press, 1975), and elsewhere.
13. Heinrich Kramer and Jacob Sprenger, *The Malleus Maleficarum*, trans. Montague Summers (New York: Dover, 1971), 47.
14. See Rita M. Gross, "Menstruation and Childbirth as Ritual and Religious Experience in the Religion of the Australian Aborigines," *Journal of the American*

Academy of Religion 45, no. 4 (1977): 1147–81.

15. Judy Chicago, *Through the Flower* (New York: Doubleday & Company, 1975), plate 4, 106–7.
16. See Adrienne Rich, *Of Woman Born* (New York: Bantam Books, 1977), chs. 6 and 7.
17. See James Mellaart, *Earliest Civilizations of the Near East* (New York: McGraw-Hill, 1965), 92.
18. Barbry MyOwn, "Ursa Maior: Menstrual Moon Celebration," in *Moon, Moon*, ed. Anne Kent Rush (Berkeley, Calif., and New York: Moon Books and Random House, 1976), 374–87.
19. Starhawk, "Witchcraft and Women's Culture," *Womanspirit Rising*, 266.
20. In Judy Chicago, 213–217.
21. Valerie Saiving, "The Human Situation: A Feminine View," *Journal of Religion* 40 (1960): 100–12.
22. Virginia Woolf, *A Room of One's Own* (New York: Harcourt Brace Jovanovich, 1928), 86.
23. Rich, *Of Woman Born*, 226.
24. De Beauvoir, *The Second Sex*, 448–49.
25. "Old Time Woman," lyrics by Jeffrey Langley and Holly Near, from *Holly Near: A Live Album*, Redwood Records, 1974.
26. "Started Out Fine," by Holly Near from *Holly Near: A Live Album*.
27. Rich, *Of Woman Born*, 223.
28. For another version of the story see Charlene Spretnak, *Lost Goddesses of Early Greece: A Collection of Pre-Hellenic Myths* (Boston: Beacon Press, 1984), 105–18.

Crowned Snake Goddess. From Neolithic Crete.

9. Symbols of Goddess and God in Feminist Theology

"God," Paul Tillich wrote cryptically, "is a symbol for God." For years, the meaning of that statement eluded me, but now Tillich's aphorism seems a perfect introduction to feminist work on the symbol of God, for it expresses the central thesis I will explore here: that *God* is a symbol that may have outlived its usefulness as an exclusive mediator between humans and the ultimate reality that grounds and sustains our lives. I believe we are living in a revolutionary time when new religious symbols are being formed by a process by syncretism and creativity that includes discovering new meanings in biblical and nonbiblical symbolisms, tapping the unconscious through personal and communal dream and fantasy work, trusting intuition and poetic inspiration, and even bringing the process the symbol creation to consciousness. It is my belief that the work that feminists are doing to transform the image of God has profound but subtle and not easily observable consequences for social life.

The subject of this paper can be threatening. To those without theological training the word *God* refers to the Father and Lord of biblical tradition. This God may be accepted or rejected, but to play with, change, or transform the image or word *God* is something most people never consider. Even theologians who have rejected naive biblical faith often hold symbols in a kind of reverence, asserting that they arise by mysterious, unconscious, or poetic processes that elude the rational mind. While they will question theological dogmas and muse on alienation from biblical symbolisms, such people often grant an honored status to other previously created symbolisms, such as those found in Greek mythology, Jewish kabbala, Christian mysticism, medieval alchemy, or the works of some modern poets. If someone suggests that people do not need to cite the authority of past tradition or poetic genius for symbols, many liberal scholars of religion become almost as quick as biblical literalists to cry heresy.

Theologians' views about the process of symbol creation are often derived from Freud and Jung via Tillich, and therefore these men's views need to be considered. Following Sigmund Freud, Carl Jung asserted that symbols often arise from a deep part of the mind that is below consciousness and never fully subject to conscious control. This depth dimension of the mind, the unconscious, is a repository of imagery and feelings, many but not all of them stemming from childhood experiences or traumatic experiences of later life that our conscious minds have repressed because they do not coincide with conscious self-images. These symbols emerge in dreams and fantasies and become expressed in the myths and symbols of a culture. While Freud had a unidimensional method of interpreting symbols, Jung believed that a symbol's ability to express more than could be put into words was essential to its meaning. Jung developed the theory that dreams and cultural symbols often express the human quest for meaning, the desire for connection to a wellspring of life power and creativity deeper than that offered by modern science. He believed that modern life was truncated by a slavish adherence to rationality and that people needed to be open to an irrational and mysterious dimension of life in order to find meaning. For Jung, connection to symbols is connection to a meaning that transcends rationality, a depth dimension in life.[1]

Jung and many of his patients were alienated from the symbols found in institutional religions, but they derived solace from connection to transpersonal mythic patterns that emerged in their dreams and fantasies. While Jung remained open to the notion that symbols connected individuals to divine power existing outside themselves, his primary focus was on the divinities or powers of symbol creation within people. Though Jung encouraged his patients to create new symbol systems through attention to their dreams and fantasies, the second-generation Jungians rigidified the notion of archetype and used it to stifle the creation of new symbols.[2]

While Jung emphasized the inner meaning of symbols, Protestant theologian Paul Tillich[3] stressed their transcendent reference. He asserted that humankind's ultimate concern must be expressed symbolically because symbolic language alone is able to express the ultimate. The influence of depth psychology can be seen in Tillich's definition. Like Jung, he believed that symbols transcend rational analysis, arise from the unconscious, and mediate meaning in human life. But for Tillich it is not enough to say that symbols arise in the soul; it must also be said that they point to and participate in transcendent reality. For Tillich, this transcendent reality, which he preferred to call humankind's "ultimate concern," is not simply a shared human sense of meaning but is grounded in Being itself, that which traditional theology has called God. For Tillich, Being is not an entity existing outside human life but is more appropriately understood as the ground of Being, which transcends finite existence, but in which finite beings participate and without which they would not be. Because humans are finite and ultimate concern is infinite, it is impossible to adequately represent ultimate concern. Thus for Tillich, primary religious language must be symbolic, because symbolic language points beyond itself to that which can never be fully or finally expressed. Tillich also believed that symbols cannot be produced intentionally, but that they grow and die by mysterious unconscious processes and therefore can never be subject to human control or conscious manipulation.

The insistence of Jung and Tillich on the importance of symbols in the human quest for meaning underscores the importance of feminist work on symbols. While the differences between Tillich's and Jung's views of the ultimate referent of symbols is not important for the purposes of this essay, the insistence of second-generation Jungians on the eternal archetype and Tillich's proposition that symbols cannot be consciously manipulated must be demystified if feminist symbol creation is to be understood. For feminists are engaged in the process of creating symbols that deviate from the so-called archetypes, and they are doing so consciously.

What is left out in the Tillichian and Jungian analyses of symbols is the interaction between symbol systems and culturally relative systems of value. Cultural anthropology fills in these gaps in symbolic theory. According to Clifford Geertz, religious symbols are both models "of" divine reality and models "for" human behavior. Moreover, religious symbol systems enforce attitudes and behaviors by labeling those who deviate from them outside the divine order.[4] Geertz's theory of the reciprocal relation between social and political attitudes and behaviors and religious symbol systems does not postulate a rigid one-to-one correlation between religion and politics, but it does alert us to the social and political ramifications of all symbols, even of the eternal archetypes of the Jungians and the "broken" symbol discussed by Tillich.

Putting these theories of symbols together, we can see that symbols are tremendously important in human life. If Jung is correct, rational life is but the tip of our total life, and many of our deepest feelings and attitudes stem from the unconscious, which is a repository of symbolic thinking. Both Tillich and Jung agree that symbols are the mediators of meaning in life and that life is truncated without symbols. Geertz tells us further that symbols affect behavior and social attitudes and policies.

Recognizing the importance of symbols calls attention to a feminist dilemma, because the primary symbol systems of both religious and secular culture in the modern West are male-centered. If symbols are important, then the lives of modern feminists are impoverished and thrown into conflict if they are not grounded in a compatible symbolic order. Feminists have alleged that the symbol of God as male, Father, Son, Lord, and King induces powerful, pervasive and long-lasting moods and motivations that are contrary to feminist values. Those who are influenced by the symbol of God as (exclusively) male are led to believe that men should rightly have all significant and legitimate power in society. Reciprocally, the fact that men hold most of the significant and legitimate power in society reinforces the notion that God is most appropriately symbolized as male.

After recognizing the influence of biblical religion on social policy and attitudes, feminists might well conclude that the demise of religion would be the best thing that could happen in Western society. But if symbols are important in human life, then this solution is inadequate. Humans have a need for symbols that can express the depth and ultimacy of life and ground our strivings in what Geertz has called "the conception of a general order of existence." Feminists who focus exclusively on social policy issues may experience the emptiness and meaninglessness that Jung said occurs in a life without symbols, or alternatively may experience profound conflicts between the symbol systems that provide depth in our lives and the social changes we strive to achieve.

Thus the cultural and symbolic dimension of feminism is critically important. The creation of new symbolisms in art, literature, music, religion, and ritual will make feminist goals easier to achieve. Instead of a discontinuity between symbols in the deep mind and desired social change, there will be a continuity and reciprocal reinforcement. If a feminist symbol system were created, then feminists might be able to overcome the feeling we sometimes have that we are struggling against the tide of nature and history, against, as it were, the "general order of existence." Instead of being devalued in songs, stories, rituals, and symbols, feminist moods and motivations would be reinforced by cultural symbol systems. Instead of remaining unarticulated, feminist conceptions of a general order of existence could be expressed. Feminist songwriters, artists, and writers, like Holly Near, Chris Williamson, Mary Beth Edelson, Judy Chicago, Adrienne Rich, Marge Piercy, and others are listening to their inner muses in conscious knowledge that they are engaged in the process of creating new symbols that will express feminist visions. Feminist work on language and symbol in religion is an important part of this process.

The feminist critique of the God symbolism in the biblically based religions of the West includes two principal arguments. The first is that in religions in which God is primarily imaged in language associated with the male gender, maleness is deified as the source of all legitimate power and authority. Proponents of this argument ask that genderized God language be eliminated in favor of sex-neutral or androgynous language or that genderized language associated with the female sex be included alongside male generic language. The second feminist argument is that the attributes associated with God, both in biblical symbolism and in philosophical tradition, are based on a model of perfection derived from alienated male experience that distorts the concept of divinity. According to this argument, changing the gender of the language associated with God would not be sufficient to overcome the sexism in the symbol of God. Other aspects of both biblical imagery and the philosophic concepts associated with God would also have to be changed. While these two arguments are fundamental to feminist work on the symbol of God, some feminist theologians focus more attention on one or the other of them.

Mary Daly is well known for her articulation of the first argument about God symbolism. In "After the Death of God the Father" and in *Beyond God the Father*,[5] she argued that the identification of divinity with maleness through the relentless use of masculine pronouns and genderized titles, such as Father, Son, Lord, and King, in Scripture, liturgy, and theology communicates a message to the deep mind that male power is divine. Daly is of course aware that philosophical and theological traditions also doggedly assert that God transcends sexuality, that God does not have a long white beard or a penis, and that God is not a member of the male sex. Her quarrel is not with philosophic conceptions of deity (at this point), but rather with what may be called the core symbolism of the tradition. Daly cited McLuhan, "the medium is the message"—the message communicated by the language of tradition is that maleness is divine.

A response to Daly's argument might draw on Tillich's notion that a symbol points beyond itself to the transcendent ground of being in which it participates. The male pronouns and titles point beyond human male power to a notion of infinite power that judges all finite power, including that of human males. Without denying that the symbol of God as Father may *on occasion* point beyond itself, Daly would respond that the symbol of God as Father in most cases functions as an idol and does not point beyond itself but instead allows humans to deify a finite power. "God" in Tillich's terms is no longer a symbol for the genuine ultimate God.

A second premise implicit in the first argument is that as male power is legitimated, female power is denigrated by the image of God as male. Elizabeth Janeway has brilliantly argued (in a different context) that female power is not altogether denied in patriarchy but is not recognized as legitimate power. Power that is not recognized as legitimate cannot be openly and directly expressed. Janeway has further noted that power that can only be expressed deviously, secretly, or through manipulation is always suspected of being dangerous or evil. The illegitimacy and danger of female power within the Western tradition is epitomized in the story of

Eve, which is the fountainhead of a woman-hating tradition within biblical religion. In Genesis, Eve's power is outside the law and commandment of God. She is perceived as evil in exegetical tradition. Within the biblical traditions, there are only two ways in which the power of women can be positively affirmed: when it is subordinated to the power of males—as loyal daughter, wife, or mother of sons—or when it is neuterized. In several of the Gnostic gospels and in the writings of some of the church fathers the notion that a woman must become *vir* ("man") before she can enter the kingdom of God is expressed. Since that which most obviously makes a woman female is sexual relationships and the bearing and nursing of children, it was a tenet of early Christian and medieval theology that a woman who denied her sexuality and remained virgin became like a man, not tainted with the evil and malignancy of her sex. The Virgin Mary and the female saints, symbols of female power in Western religion, are revered because they have transcended female sexuality. But Western religious tradition has never been able wholly and fully to affirm female power as female.

It might be argued that biblical religion has never been about the affirmation of the power of any creature, whether male or female. Some would point out that the biblical tradition affirms the transcendence and power of God above all and affirms human male power only insofar as it is subordinated to the divine will. But this argument fails to recognize the dual trajectories of Christian God symbolism. One is to point to the absolute transcendence of God, and the other is to point to the participation of finite beings in the divine ground. God symbolism couched in the male generic does not point equally to the participation of females and males in the divine ground. Male language allows males to participate fully in it, while females can do so only by abstracting ourselves from our concrete identities as females. Even the notion of God as transcendent other who limits the power of finite beings affects males and females differently, for if both males and females are limited by the power of God, we are limited in different ways. Though limited by God, male power is also affirmed by the generic language used in God symbolism—men can see themselves as "like God" in their relationships to women and children. Women receive no such compensation, and thus our power is doubly denied. In her book *The Mermaid and the Minotaur* Dorothy Dinnerstein provides an intriguing explanation of why both males and females find it comfortable to defer to the power of men in religion and society. According to Dinnerstein all mother-reared children develop a deep ambivalence toward the power of women because of their early intimate dependence on women for food, clothing, comfort, relief from dirty diapers—quite literally, for life. As they begin to assert their independence of the mother, mother-reared children wish to forget their total dependence on her, and thus they willingly transfer their allegiance to the father, whose power, because it is more distant and less connected to intimate bodily dependence, seems more manageable.

The second feminist argument against traditional God symbolism makes the point that even if all the male generic language were corrected, the symbolism of divine power would still be distorted because it is based on an alienated male experience of power. This argument is spelled out in a variety of ways. For example, I have argued that the image of God as a holy warrior, leading his people out of Egypt with a mighty arm and destroying the horses and chariots of the Egyptians, cannot be salvaged with a simple change of genderized language. A female or neuter holy warrior would still be an alienated image of deity based on the male glorification of conquest and domination, not an image that appropriately describes the nature of divine power. The problem with the symbol of God is deeper than the comparatively simple matter of changing genderized language.

Rosemary Ruether[6] has developed this argument into an important critique of what she calls the alienated dualistic and hierarchical mentality that has informed Western theology. According to Ruether, the breakdown of tribal and national cultures, increasing urbanization, and centuries of imperialistic domination produced a spirit of world negation that gave rise to a dualistic habit of thought. Transcendent and immanent, rational and irrational, spirit and flesh, soul and body, spirit and nature, male and female were conceived of as opposites and ordered hierarchically. Much of Ruether's work has shown how the negative image of women in Western tradition is rooted in the fact that women were identified with despised flesh, nature, and irrationality. But she has also noted that these dualisms gave rise to an alienated paradigm of divine power, a paradigm of domination requiring subjection. It could be argued that this image of God is integrally linked to the authoritarian and oppressive attitudes that feminists have labeled patriarchal. Moreover, power so conceived is not merely transcendent of but alienated from the powers of the body and nature that had been celebrated in earlier religions. This alienated image of God gave rise to distorted notions of sexuality that led to the notion that only the celibate are truly holy. It also made possible the domination of nature that has produced the ecological crisis. These dualisms became the pattern used to dominate women and other groups such as Jews, blacks, and third-world peoples, all of whom, like women, are perceived by the dominant males to be less spiritual and rational as well as more carnal and natural. According to Ruether, the key to the cultural transformation that feminists seek is the overcoming of classical dualisms and the alienated, hierarchical mentality they have produced.

Mary Daly has elaborated Ruether's critique of the dualistic, hierarchical mentality that informs Western theology and images of God. In *Beyond God the Father*, Daly argues that the distorted image of divine power has given rise to a mentality of conquest and domination, which she labels an "unholy trinity" of rape, genocide, and war which she says forms the base of Western culture.

The two arguments that we have examined are the basis of the feminist critique of God symbolism found in the work of feminist thinkers as diverse as Mary Daly, Rosemary Ruether, Sheila Collins, Letty Russell, Virginia Mollenkott, Phyllis Trible, Elisabeth Schüssler Fiorenza, Naomi Janowitz, Maggie Wenig, Judith Plaskow, Rita Gross, Starhawk, Christine Downing, Z Budapest, Naomi Goldenberg, and myself.

Feminist theologians agree on the outline of the critique of God symbolism, but we propose different solutions to the problem. Feminist theologians differ both in our assessment of and allegiance to Scripture and tradition, and in our visions of what God symbolism ideally should be. Because of these two variables, it is difficult to chart feminist theologians neatly on a scale of conservative to radical, for some feminist theologians might be considered conservative in their allegiance to tradition but radical in their vision of what tradition has been and can become (or vice versa). The views of tradition held by feminist theologians fall into three main types: in Type 1 tradition contains an essentially nonsexist vision or intentionality that becomes clear through proper interpretation; in Type 2 tradition contains elements of an essentially sexist and elements of an essentially nonsexist vision: the nonsexist vision must be affirmed as revelation, while the sexist vision must be repudiated on the basis (warrant) of the nonsexist vision *and* the contemporary experience of the full humanity of women; and in Type 3 tradition contains an essentially sexist vision and must therefore be repudiated, and new traditions must be created on the basis of present experience and/or nonbiblical religion. (It should be noted, however, that some feminist work on God symbolism does not discuss this last issue.)

On the issue of visions of what God symbolism ideally should be, feminist theologians hold four views. Type A: male symbols of God (and Jesus) may be interpreted in nonoppressive ways because what is oppressive is not the language associated with the male gender, but the notions of domination and oppression often associated with male symbolism. Type B: God language should be neuterized or made androgynous because language associated with one sex or the other inevitably is oppressive and also fails to symbolize the transcendence of God. Type C: female symbolism for God as discovered within tradition or found outside it and/or Goddess symbolism must be introduced alongside male God symbolism because the transcendence or bisexuality of God is best symbolized by dual imagery. Type D: male symbolism for God must be abandoned and/or deemphasized as the female God or Goddess returns to ascendency.

Individual feminist thinkers may propose more than one of these solutions, or different solutions in different contexts or at different stages of their thinking about the issue. I will discuss the various feminist positions on God symbolism in light of these basic positions.

Letty Russell, Virginia Mollenkott, Phyllis Trible, and Leonard Swidler are Christian thinkers who consider the tradition to be essentially nonsexist if properly interpreted. While not denying that there are sexist elements within tradition, they attribute these elements to the patriarchal cultures in which the Bible arose and claim that the core vision or intentionality of the biblical faith is salvific and liberating for all people. Sexist elements within tradition do not need to be repudiated but properly interpreted. Rosemary Ruether, Elisabeth Schüssler Fiorenza, *the early* Mary Daly, Rita Gross, and others hold a more complex view of tradition. They believe that tradition includes an essentially liberating vision but acknowledge that elements of sexism have crept into this vision. Freeing tradition of sexism is not simply a matter of being faithful to biblical or traditional intentionality, but also of repudiating parts of Bible or tradition on the basis of present experience and theological insight. Elisabeth Schüssler Fiorenza[7] states the hermeneutical principle of this group most radically when she says that only those parts of Scripture that are free of sexism can be considered authentic revelation. Clearly this is not a hermeneutical principle that can be derived from Scripture itself. Rather, it is based on Schüssler Fiorenza's experience and interpretation of what is revelatory within Scripture—on the theological principles that are informed by, but not wholly derived from, Scripture itself. *The middle and later* Daly, Naomi Goldenberg, Starhawk, Z Budapest, Merlin Stone, Christine Downing, and I fit into the third group, which, while not denying elements of nonsexism within Scripture and tradition, see them as essentially or fundamentally sexist. This group claims that the core symbolism and the preponderence of teachings within tradition add up to an intentionality or vision that is essentially and profoundly sexist. This group argues that the attempt to transform tradition on the basis of selected liberating passages is doomed to failure.

Within the first group (Type 1 thinkers) who believe that Scripture or tradition is essentially nonsexist, different views of the solution to the problem of God symbolism are held. Many thinkers in this group are influenced by Phyllis Trible's discussion of feminine symbolism of God within biblical tradition.[8] While admitting that the Bible comes from a patriarchal culture, Trible argues that the existence of elements within tradition that challenge patriarchal norms testifies to a biblical intentionality or alternative vision that transcends sexism. This intentionality or alternative vision is found, for example, in certain passages from the Hebrew Bible in which God is imaged in terms derived from women's experience or traditional roles, including giving birth, nurturing children, and providing clothing or food. For example, in Isaiah 66:9 Yahweh speaks of himself as a mother giving birth: "Shall I bring to the birth and not cause to bring forth? says Yahweh. Shall I, who cause to bring forth, shut the womb? says your God." That such imagery could arise at all within a patriarchal culture such as that of ancient Israel is astonishing and is evidence, Trible argues, of a fundamental biblical insight that God transcends sexuality. Trible thus finds a biblical warrant to justify a theology and liturgy in which God may be symbolized in both male and female terms. The fact that such imagery was commonly associated with Goddesses who were worshiped throughout the ancient Near East and even in the official worship of ancient Israel, to my mind, weakens Trible's argument. A simpler explanation is that the biblical writers attributed qualities associated with Goddesses to Yahweh, in attempts to break the power of Goddess symbolism in the hearts and minds of the Hebrew people.

Letty Russell and Virginia Mollenkott[9] hold theological positions that are strongly biblically based and similar to Trible's. According to Russell, the biblical message is essentially one of liberation, but this liberating potential has been partly obscured for women by patriarchal language. While not denying the need for female God language and the biblical warrant for it, Russell's constructive proposals tend to emphasize the need for an inclusive neutral or androgynous language in which pronouns are eliminated altogether by repetition of words like God; neutral terms like Creator, Redeemer, Liberator, and Ruler are substituted for the traditional Father, Lord, and King. Virginia Mollenkott, a Protestant evangelical, likewise claims biblical warrant for feminine imagery for divinity but also focuses on the sex-neutral solution to the problem of God symbolism. The work of Tom and Sharon Neufer Emsweiler[10] in creating nonsexist liturgies illustrates the position defended by Russell and Mollenkott. In their liturgies, for example, female imagery is occasionally used, but more often, male imagery is neuterized. For example, in the confession of faith, the Emsweilers speak of "the living God, the Parent of humankind," instead of "God, the Father Almighty," and of "God incarnate on earth," not "his only begotten Son."

The reluctance of these theologians whose work is strongly based in the Bible to insist on the necessity of female God language may perhaps be attributed to their loyalty to the Bible. They are aware that the number of places in which the Bible uses female imagery for God is small, whereas there is certainly no dearth of male imagery for divinity in the Bible. The requirement that female God language be used more than occasionally in liturgy constitutes a more fundamental alteration of the biblical pattern than these authors seem ready to embrace. The regular use of female language for God would require a radical change in the image people hold of the reality to which God symbolism points. The change to a sex-neutral language eliminates the direct offense to women created by male God symbolism without necessarily forcing people to change their understanding of divinity. One can use sex-neutral language and still imagine that God is male or abstractly neutral, but when female language and symbolism is introduced, people's minds are jarred and they are forced to think about the positive inclusion of the female in the nature of God and also to rethink their prejudices about women's roles in society.

Jesus presents an important challenge to feminist theology since tradition holds that he is both a historical figure and the decisive incarnation of divinity. Because of his alleged historicity, Jesus' maleness cannot be neutralized or supplemented with female imagery, and this seems inevitably to point to the notion that God is also to be identified with the male sex. Several sectarian leaders of the nineteenth century, including Mother Ann Lee, founder of the Shakers, and Mary Baker Eddy, founder of the Christian Science, solved this problem by asserting that in the second coming the messiah would be female. While a few feminist theologians have proposed that the second person of the Trinity could be referred to as the Daughter as well as the Son of God, neither this nor the nineteenth-century solution has had much appeal to contemporary feminist theologians. Instead, following the lead of Leonard Swidler,[11] they call attention to Jesus' alleged feminism and a purported absence of sexism in the early Christian movement. Swidler's argument is that even though Jesus is a male figure, the New Testament tradition never identifies him with the hierarchical, authoritarian symbolism associated with patriarchy, and it never pictures him as expressing negative attitudes toward women. Following the line of thinking about God symbolism discussed here as Type A, Swidler alleges that the maleness of Jesus as a historical figure is not problematic, since Jesus' life points beyond sexist ideology to a vision of the world in which sexism is transcended. Views similar to Swidler's are adopted and elaborated by Russell, Mollenkott, the Emsweilers, and by Type 2 thinkers, such as Ruether, Schüssler Fiorenza, and others.

A number of interesting solutions to the problem of God symbolism are proposed by Type 2 thinkers, who view the tradition as both sexist and nonsexist. Rosemary Ruether,[12] whose important theories on dualism and hierarchicalism have already been discussed, has sketched out a reinterpretation of the alienated symbolisms of transcendence that have been associated with the male symbols of God and Christ. Ruether argues that the sexist symbolism of domination, which compare Christ to a male patriarch and the church to his obedient bride and which can be found in the New Testament itself, must be repudiated by Christian feminists. But she believes there is also a "feminist Jesus" who points toward a nonsexist, nonalienated God. According to Ruether, Jesus' model of community (which she finds in the New Testament) was one in which the "orders of domination and subjugation are replaced by a community of brothers and sisters related to each other in mutual service." She even speculates, in a radical reinterpretation of the Greek doctrine of *kenosis* ("self-emptying"), that, in Jesus, God overcomes the modeling of God's power on "male leadership and class domination" and "overthrows the masculine alienation of the divine by being poured out with the flesh." Ruether suggests that it is not the maleness of God and Christ that give rise to sexist attitudes, but rather the patriarchal models of maleness as dominance and femaleness as subjugation. If understood in nonsexist ways that stress the giving up of power on the part of the male, then the maleness of Jesus and even of God need not be alienating for women.

Ruether also states that she thinks of God as the "Great Matrix [which] is neither male nor female" and prefers to think of "Her as She in personal prayer," though she "would not want to dogmatize that preference."[13] Nonetheless, Ruether has shown much less interest in female symbolism for God than many other feminist theologians.

Much feminist work on God symbolism clusters in Type 2C and

is an attempt to introduce female God symbolism into Christianity and Judaism. The thinkers in this group draw on the work of Trible and others that provides biblical and traditional warrant for female God symbolism. They often call attention to the work of Jewish or Christian mystics who have used feminine imagery for God. An essential tenet of Type 2C is that while the Bible and tradition provide warrants for female symbolism, both have distorted the image of God through primary use of male symbolism. These thinkers believe further that it is not enough to neuterize the image of God, but that female imagery must be positively included if women are to become full members of the worshiping community and the society it projects. A stated or unstated premise of this position is that (at least at this point in religious history and in the development of the English language) sex-neutral language used about God is still likely to conjure up the image of a male God that has been firmly fixed in the unconscious by repeated use of male symbolism for God within the Jewish and Christian traditions. If the being of women is to be affirmed by God language, then female symbolism must be positively included. A recent psychological study[14] confirms the allegation of some feminist theologians that sex-neutral language does not include women. When asked what image was connoted for them by supposedly sex-neutral terms like *student,* most female subjects drew a blank, while most male subjects imagined a male like themselves.

Rita Gross argues for the introduction of female God language into Jewish ritual.[15] Her views and those of Wenig, Janowitz, and Plaskow, discussed below, can also be applied to the critique of Christian symbolism. She argues that though the deity may transcend sexuality, language does not. Since Jews are committed to the notion of a personal God who may be addresed in prayer and ritual, they are committed to personal or anthropomorphic language. The exclusion of female God language from traditional Jewish practice means the exclusion of women from full participation in the religious community. Though advocating that change begin with pronouns, Gross stated that further changes in core symbolism would follow. Her prediction has been proved correct with the publication by Maggie Wenig and Naomi Janowitz[16] of some of the prayers used in a Jewish women's *minyan*, or worshiping community, at Brown University. Not only is God referred to as *She*, but startling and profoundly important imagery of the female body and female experience is used to point toward God. In one of the prayers, the women say:

> Blessed is She who spoke and the world became.
> Blessed is She.
> Blessed is She who in the beginning gave birth.
> Blessed is She who says and performs
> Blessed is She who declares and fulfills.
> Blessed is She whose womb covers the earth.

In this rewriting of a traditional prayer women reaffirm the traditional notions of creation and covenant, but they affirm them of a God symbolized as female, thus allowing women to picture the qualities of power and faithfulness as part of their own being. And they also introduce into Judaism the notion of a female God who gives birth through her womb, thus allowing women to see that the creativity of their own bodies points to the divine creativity. Such affirmations of female power, creativity, and faithfulness are especially important to women who have been taught to subordinate themselves to a male God (and to fathers, husbands, and sons who reflect his power), who have been taught that they are unclean during menstruation and following childbirth, and who have been told stories of the faithlessness and treachery of women.

In "The Right Question Is Theological," Judith Plaskow takes the Jewish feminist discussion of female God language a step further by arguing that the word *Goddess* must be spoken again within Judaism. Acknowledging that for some this raises "the specter of paganism," Plaskow poses the following challenge:

> While it might seem that we are now distant enough from paganism to understand the suppression of the Goddess without feeling the need to refight this struggle, the deep resistance called forth by naming her indicates that the needs she answered are still with us. It is precisely because she is not distant that the Goddess must be recognized as part of God. For the God who does not include her is an idol made in man's image, not the relativizer of all gods and goddesses who nonetheless includes them as part of God's self. Acknowledging the many aspects of the Goddess among the names of God becomes a measure of our ability to incorporate

the feminine and women into a monotheistic religious framework.[17]

Catholic theologian Elisabeth Schüssler Fiorenza[18] points out the resources in Marian symbolism for a female language and imagery of divinity. With Mary Daly, Rosemary Ruether, and others, she argues that though every Catholic schoolchild is taught that Mary is not God, on an emotional, imaginative, and experiential level Catholics experience the love of God in the symbol of Mary, and thus they experience Mary as a symbol of God. Catholic feminist theologians are rightly aware of the destructive elements in Marian tradition, particularly its function as one pole of the virgin/whore, virgin/witch polarity that has been used to oppress women. Also they recognize that Catholic doctrine has limited the power of Mary by insisting that Mary is Mother of God, but not God the Mother—a figure whose power is derived from her relationship to the Father and the Son. Catholic theologians have yet to articulate a full theology of Mary as symbol of God from a feminist perspective and to show how they will reconcile new interpretations of Marian symbolism with Catholic tradition and dogma.

Sheila Collins,[19] following the arguments of Ruether and Daly concerning male language and authoritarian symbolism for God, elaborates the feminist argument that God symbolism is distorted by the exclusive use of symbolism derived from the male experience. She urges women to learn about the history of the Goddess worship that preceded Christianity and Judaism and to use it as a resource for resymbolizing God. She also argues that women must not reject the so-called feminine qualities of emotionality, intuitiveness, relatedness, and closeness to nature, which have been denigrated as the negative side of the classical dualisms, but rather women must reclaim those qualities and integrate them into a wholistic value system and symbolism of divinity that transcends the classic polarities. She argues that prepatriarchal, premonotheistic cultures where Goddesses were worshiped have much to teach about the integration of so-called masculine and so-called feminine qualities. The great Goddesses were not only birth givers but also the givers of just law and the arts of civilization.

Collin's work is in many ways transitional between Type 2C and Types 3C and 3D. She does not clearly state whether the revisioning of God that will come about through renewed contact with ancient Goddesses will reform biblical religions, or whether it will move beyond the boundaries of Judaism and Christianity into a new religious future. This refusal to draw clear boundaries may be a virtue in a transitional phase of religious history that may result in the renewal of traditional faiths, the creation of new religions, or both.

Type 3 thinkers neither claim allegiance to the biblical faiths nor attempt to transform them. They consider the essential core or intentionality of biblical religions to be essentially linked with male dominance in society. They believe that to strip away or transform the male images of God or salvation in these traditions would change them so profoundly that they would not be the same religions.

In *Beyond God the Father*, Mary Daly argued that sexist language and symbolism was essential to the core of Judaism and Christianity and proposed that women abandon those religions. At that time she argued that androgynous or sex-neutral language replace the male God language of tradition. Emphasizing the transcendent divinity spoken of by philosophers and pointed to in the mystical traditions of *via negativa*, she did not then see the clear need for female symbolism for God. Instead she proposed that God be named Verb in order to point to the dynamism of Be-ing which is always moving toward transcendence. In *Gyn/Ecology*,[20] Daly embraces gynomorphic symbolism for divinity, including the ancient term Goddess.

Other thinkers and symbologists, such as Christine Downing, Nelle Morton, Rita Gross, Merlin Stone, Starhawk, Z Budapest, and I, also advocate the reemergence of the symbol of the Goddess in Western religious consciousness. Those who call for the reemergence of Goddess in modern life have different visions of the symbolic context in which Goddess imagery will emerge. Some believe that the Goddess is the most adequate symbol for divine reality, or include her son as a distinctly secondary figure. Others believe that the Goddess and God together point toward a single divine ground that transcends sexuality. Others believe that images of God and the Goddess reflect an ultimately plural reality. But in order to avoid misunderstanding, let me state that envisioning the Goddess does not necessarily imply substituting the Goddess for God and thereby creating yet another single-sex system.

The suggestion that the Goddess be reintroduced into Western religion sounds strange to many. Even the word *Goddess* seems to some to have only a vague and shadowy meaning, connoting perhaps a fertility fetish, a Greek myth, or the beliefs of so-called primitive peoples. What do feminists mean when we say *Goddess*? We may have in mind a bas-relief painted perhaps eight thousand years ago on the walls of a shrine in Çatal Hüyük, which pictured her with legs spread wide, giving birth. Or the image of the lady who was invoked by peoples throughout the ancient world:

> Hear O ye regions, the praise of Queen Nana; magnify the Creatress; exalt the dignified; exalt the Glorious One; draw nigh to the Mighty Lady.
>
> In the beginning was Isis: Oldest of the Old, She was the Goddess from whom all becoming arose. She was the Great Lady (Egypt, fourteenth century B.C.E.).[21]

We may have in mind also the Goddesses of all lands including those of Africa and Asia as well as the more familiar Goddesses of Greece and the ancient Near East.

In *When God Was a Woman* Merlin Stone discusses the power ancient symbols of the Goddess can have for modern women. She believes that the discovery that "at the very dawn of religion, God was a woman" can aid modern women's quest to liberate ourselves from beliefs and attitudes of female subordination fostered by patriarchal religion. Learning that God was a woman can help women to view ourselves as being in the image and likeness of the Goddess, as creators of our own destinies and responsible for our own lives.

In "Persephone in Hades" and in *The Goddess*,[22] former president of the American Academy of Religion, Christine Downing discusses her lifelong connection to the Greek Goddesses, for example, through the myth of Demeter and Persephone, the story of mother and maid which was central to the religion of Greece for several thousand years. Downing tells how the story of Persephone, the daughter born with the spring flowers and taken away to the underworld by a male God, gave depth to her own experiences of girlhood, sexual initiation, and depression, while the story of Demeter's grief at the loss of her beloved daughter helped her to accept her feelings of anger and loss when her own children grew up. Knowing that her life fit a mythic pattern helped Downing to accept its rhythms of joy and grief, anger and depth. It is important for women, she argues, to connect mythic stories of female divinities whose experiences elucidate women's lives more completely than stories of Gods and heroes can.

The recent interest in Goddesses is part of a widespread grassroots movement of women's spirituality that has emerged spontaneously in the United States and elsewhere. The image of the Goddess that is reemerging in the psyches of modern women is symbolic of women's sense that the power we are claiming for ourselves through the women's movement is rooted in the ground of being itself.[23]

Though nourished by ancient symbols of Goddesses from around the world, women's imagination is by no means subject to the authority of the past. Instead, modern women joyfully discover what is useful to us in the past and reject what is not. We understand that many symbols of the Goddess have come down to us from patriarchal cultures, and, using feminism as a principle of selection, we reject those aspects of ancient mythologies that picture Goddesses as legitimizers of the power of men. In a spirit captured by Monique Wittig,[24] we seek to remember a past where women were not slaves. What we cannot remember we invent joyfully, recognizing that modern women can create symbols that express our quest for authenticity and power.

Several feminist scholars analyze the significance of the emerging Goddess symbol. Drawing on her expertise in Hinduism, Rita Gross[25] argues that the symbol of the Goddess has five things to teach modern Westerners. First, the Goddess's obvious strength, capability, and transcendence validate the power of women as women that has been denied in Western religion and culture. Second, Goddess symbolism involves the coincidence of opposites —of death and life, destruction and creativity—that reminds humans of the finitude of life and points to its transcendent ground. Third, Goddess religion values motherhood as symbolic of divine creativity, but without limiting female power to biological destiny. Fourth, Goddess symbolism also associates women with a wide range of culturally valued phenomena, including wealth, prosperity, culture, artful living, and spiritual teaching.

Fifth, the Goddess requires the explicit reintroduction of sexuality as a religious metaphor in a symbol system where God is imaged as both male and female.

In "Why Women Need the Goddess," I discuss four meanings of modern symbolism of the Goddess in the women's spirituality movement. First, the Goddess is symbol of the legitimacy and beneficence of female power in contrast to the image of female power as anomalous or evil in biblical religion. Second, the Goddess validates women's bodily experiences, including menstruation, birth, lactation, and menopause, and validates the human connection to finitude, which has been denigrated in Western religions. Third, the Goddess symbol in the context of feminist Goddess worship values the female will, which has been viewed as the origin of evil in biblical mythology. Fourth, the Goddess points to the valuing of woman-to-woman bonds, including the mother-daughter relation, which is celebrated in the story of Demeter and Persephone but which has scarcely been mentioned in the religion and culture of the past several thousand years. The symbol of Goddess, I argue, legitimates and undergirds the moods and motivations inspired by feminism just as the symbol of God has legitimated partriarchal attitudes for several thousand years.

In *The Journey is Home* [26] Nelle Morton argues that the experience of women that has been unarticulated for centuries is the source of a new imaging of humanity and divinity. She argues that the names God the Mother and Goddess have a metaphoric power that God the Father lacks today. God the Father is taken for granted and assumed after centuries of use in a male-dominated culture, whereas God the Mother or Goddess points to the new and requires change and movement on the part of the speaker and hearer. While not claiming that God the Mother or Goddess will be the final resting point in the transformation of religious language occurring today, she argues that using the names Goddess and God the Mother is probably the only way to shatter the hold of idolatrous male God on the psyche.

While not denying the importance of all the feminist work on the symbol of God, it seems to me that the challenge posed by God the Mother and Goddess is the one most important to the success of feminist theology. The absence of the Goddess in biblical religion is no mere oversight, nor can it be blamed on the cultural milieu in which the biblical canon was shaped. The active suppression of symbols of the Goddess and God the Mother is at the heart of the process of the formation of the Hebrew and Christian Bibles, as I have argued. Both the victorious Yahweh only groups within ancient Hebrew culture and the victorious Christian groups did battle with Goddess religions and suppressed them. Moreover, as Elaine Pagels[27] has shown, one of the characteristics of the groups labeled heretical by emerging orthodox Christians was their use of female symbolism for divinity.

The symbol of the Goddess was not merely omitted from the Jewish and Christian canons but forcibly evicted from them. This suggests to me that there is an unanswered question at the heart of the biblical traditions. This question is why the symbol of the Goddess was suppressed and what was the meaning of that suppression. The suppression of the symbol of female power cannot have been without consequence for women and men within those traditions. While there is no convincing evidence to support the theory that the transition from God the Mother and the Goddess to God the Father and King reflects a simple transition from matriarchy to patriarchy, the widely held theory that the transition was from the orgiastic excesses of nature religion to the higher morality of a religion of covenant and history seems tainted with apologetic pleading.

What is significant here is the meaning of the reemergence of the symbols of God the Mother and the Goddess today. Whatever God the Mother and the Goddess may have meant in ancient cultures, today God the Mother and the Goddess symbolize the emerging power of women, the celebration of the powers of the female body, and an acceptance of humankind's rooting in nature and finitude. It seems to me that these three issues—female power, the female body, and finitude—have consistently been denied in Western religion and that the symbol of the Goddess forces their recognition more clearly than any other symbol. God the Mother and God/She have considerable power to bring these issues to consciousness, as the liturgies of Janowitz and Wenig suggest; but I would argue that the word *Goddess* must also be spoken. As long as Goddess remains unspeakable, female power is not fully expressed. God/She jars the imagination, but God/She is still a hybrid symbol, made up of the word *God* (which in common usage will connote maleness) and a female pronoun. Goddess is a more clear validation of the legitimacy and autonomy of female power. Some might object that it is unwise to press this argument, since God/She and God the Mother might become acceptable symbols within Christianity and Judaism, but Goddess never will. If this is so, and I do not believe it *must* be so (since historical traditions can change), then it may be that the conscious rejection of the symbol of female power in the formative periods of these religions means that they will never be able to affirm female power or the participation of women in the divine ground fully and wholeheartedly.

The symbols of God the Mother, God/She, and the Goddess have the power to begin to transform deeply held attitudes and beliefs. It would be foolish to argue that the reemergence of God the Mother, God/She, and the Goddess alone will ensure equal rights for women. Clearly, there are many contemporary and historical societies in which Goddesses are or were worshiped and women were or have not been granted full social equality. Nonetheless, most feminists who are interested in the symbols of God/She and the Goddess have an intuitive sense that the reemergence of God/She and the Goddess will not be without enormous social and political consequences. These women talk about how their connection to the symbols of God/She and the Goddess have enabled them to integrate feminist beliefs and ideals on a deeper level. They say that the Goddess and God/She have made them more comfortable in accepting their own power and the power of other women, and that their unconscious needs for male approval have lessened as the Goddess and God/She symbols begin to transform the hold of the male-father-savior on their minds. They say that they no longer feel that the feminist political struggle is against the tide of history and the course of nature, that they feel more confident about eventual feminist success, since they have discovered a symbol that points to the rooting of feminism in the nature of being.

Perhaps what we can safely say about the symbols of God/She and the Goddess is not the grandiose claim that they will ensure equal rights for women, but the more minimal—but certainly not insignificant—claim that they will help to bring the attitudes and feelings of the deep mind into harmony with feminist social and political goals, *and* reciprocally, that they will express and bring to articulation the feminist intuition that the struggle for equal rights is supported by the nature of reality.

NOTES

1. Carl G. Jung, *Psychological Reflections*, ed. Jolande Jacobi (New York: Harper & Row, 1961).
2. Naomi Goldenberg, *Changing of the Gods* (Boston: Beacon Press, 1979).
3. Paul Tillich, *The Dynamics of Faith* (New York: Harper & Row, 1957).
4. Clifford Geertz, "Religion as a Cultural System," in *The Interpretation of Cultures* (New York: Basic Books, 1973), 87–125.
5. Mary Daly, "After the Death of God the Father," *Commonweal* (March 12, 1971); reprinted in *Womanspirit Rising*, ed. Carol P. Christ and Judith Plaskow (New York: Harper & Row, 1979), 53-62; and *Beyond God the Father* (Boston: Beacon Press, 1973).
6. Rosemary Ruether, *Liberation Theology* (New York: Paulist Press, 1972); and *New Woman/New Earth* (New York: Seabury Press, 1975).
7. Elisabeth Schüssler Fiorenza, "Feminist Spirituality, Christian Identity, and Catholic Vision," *National Institute for Campus Ministries Journal* (Fall 1978); reprinted in *Womanspirit Rising*, 136–148.
8. Phyllis Trible, "Depatriarchalizing in Biblical Interpretation," *Journal of the American Academy of Religion*, 41, no. 1 (1973): 31, 33; partially reprinted in *Womanspirit Rising*, 74-83, and *God and the Rhetoric of Sexuality* (Philadelphia: Fortress Press, 1978).
9. Letty M. Russell, *Human Liberation in a Feminist Perspective* (Philadelphia: Westminster Press, 1974); and *The Liberating Word* (Philadelphia: Westminster Press, 1976); Virginia Mollenkott, *Women, Men, and the Bible* (Nashville: Abingdon, 1977).
10. Tom and Sharon Neufer Emsweiler, *Women and Worship* (New York: Harper & Row, 1974), 61.
11. Leonard Swidler, "Jesus Was a Feminist," *Catholic World* (January 1971); and *Biblical Affirmations of Woman* (Philadelphia: Westminster, 1979). But see the critique of Swidler in Judith Plaskow, "Christian Feminism and Anti-Judaism," *Cross Currents* 28 (1978): 306–309.
12. Rosemary Ruether, "Christology and Feminism," *WomanSpirit* (Summer 1977): 42.
13. Rosemary Ruether, "A Religion for Women," *Christianity & Crisis* (December 10, 1979): 310.
14. "Ms. Gazette," *Ms.* (August 1978): 24; the study by Wendy Martyna was published in *The Journal of Communications.*
15. Rita Gross, "Female God Language in a Jewish Context," *Davka* 17, reprinted in *Womanspirit Rising*, 165–173.
16. Naomi Janowitz and Maggie Wenig, "Sabbath Prayers for Women," in *Womanspirit Rising*, 176.
17. Judith Plaskow, "The Right Question Is Theological," in *On Being a Jewish Feminist*, ed. Susannah Heschel, (New York: Schocken Books, 1983), 230.
18. Elisabeth Schüssler Fiorenza, "Feminist Spirituality, Christian Identity, and

Catholic Vision," in *Womanspirit Rising*, 136–48.

19. Sheila Collins, *A Different Heaven and Earth* (Philadelphia: Judson Press, 1974).
20. Mary Daly, *Gyn/Ecology* (Boston: Beacon Press, 1978).
21. Merlin Stone, *When God Was a Woman* (New York: Dial Press, 1976), X.
22. Christine Downing, "Persephone in Hades," *Anima* 4, no. 1 (Fall 1977) and *The Goddess* (New York: Crossroad, 1981).
23. See *WomanSpirit* magazine, published from 1974-1984. Back issues available from 2000 KMT, Sunny Valley, OR 97497; Zsuzsanna Budapest, *Holy Book of Women's Mysteries*, Vols. 1 and 2 (Los Angeles: Susan B. Anthony Coven no. 1, 1979, 1980); Starhawk, *Spiral Dance* (San Francisco: Harper & Row, 1979); Naomi Goldenberg, *Changing of the Gods* (Boston: Beacon Press, 1979); *Heresies* (Summer 1978); Charlene Spretnak, ed., *The Politics of Women's Spirituality* (New York: Doubleday, 1981).
24. See *Les Guerilleres*, trans. David LeVay (New York: Avon Books, 1971), 89.
25. Rita Gross, "Hindu Female Dieties as a Resource for the Contemporary Rediscovery of the Goddess," *Journal of the American Academy of Religion* 46, no. 3 (1978): 269-291.
26. Nelle Morton, "Beloved Image" in *The Journey Is Home*, (Boston: Beacon Press, 1985), 122-46.
27. Elaine Pagels, *The Gnostic Gospels* (New York: Random House, 1980).

Goddess and Priestesses with Sacred Trees. From Minoan Crete.

10. Reclaiming Goddess History

My experience of the power of Goddess symbolism and ritual has led me to question the view that Goddesses always and everywhere support male power.[1] I have not been satisfied to set history aside, to say that the past does not matter. Therefore I have chosen to search the historical and prehistorical record for clues to times and places when religions were, to quote Anne Barstow, "created at least in part by women"[2] and reflected female power.

This requires a paradigm shift in our understanding of Goddess history and prehistory,[3] a subject that is being pursued by other scholars as well. Goddess history goes back to the Upper Paleolithic. The so-called Paleolithic "Venuses" such as the "Venus of Willendorf" date from approximately 32,000–10,000 B.C.E. In the Neolithic era (c. 9000–3500 B.C.E.) in Old Europe and the Near East, Goddess symbolism was prominent. These times are called prehistoric because they left no written records. Writing was invented in Sumer in the fourth millennium B.C.E., tens of thousands of years after Goddess images first emerged in the Upper Paleolithic, several thousand years after the Neolithic revolution. According to anthropologist Ruby Rohrlich,[4] whose conclusions are shared to a large extent by historian Gerda Lerner,[5] a patriarchal, militaristic, hierarchical, class-based, slave-holding society arose in Sumer during the third millennium B.C.E. Though women continued to retain some power in religion and society in Sumer and the societies which succeeded it, their power was gradually diminished as power passed more completely into the hands of the warrior kings.

The mythological writings from Sumer reflect a patriarchal society. The earliest Sumerian literary documents date from about 2400 B.C.E. The well-known *Enuma Elish*, often said to reflect Sumerian mythology, is a Babylonian document dated at about 668–626 B.C.E.[6] In Greece, the writings of Homer (eighth century B.C.E.), Hesoid (early seventh century B.C.E.), the *Homeric Hymns* (eighth to fifth centuries, B.C.E.) and the tragedies (fifth and fourth centuries, B.C.E.) are even later, all dating from the first millennium B.C.E., long after the matrifocal, prosperous, artistic, earth- and sea-bound Goddess cultures of Old Europe had come to an end about 3500 B.C.E.[7] Though these texts can be read for clues about earlier times when the Goddesses reigned supreme and women may not have been subordinate in religion and society, they reflect many centuries of androcentric shaping of tradition in which the powers of the Goddesses, the priestesses, the women had been diminished.

The work of Elisabeth Schüssler Fiorenza in reconstructing the history of early Christian women provides an interpretative model and methodological theory that is relevant to feminist research on the Goddesses. Schüssler Fiorenza writes that "androcentric texts and linguistic reality constructions must not be mistaken as trustworthy evidence of human history, culture, and religion." This is as true of the "androcentric traditioning" in the transmission of Goddess history as it is of the transmission of the history of the Jesus movement. Schüssler Fiorenza continues, "Rather than take androcentric texts as informative 'data' and accurate 'reports' we must read their 'silences' as evidence and indication of that reality about which they do not speak." According to Schüssler Fiorenza, the "feminist critical method could be likened to the work of a detective in that it does not rely solely on historical 'facts' nor invents [sic] its evidence but is engaged in an imaginative reconstruction of reality." Feminist critical reconstruction as method does not oppose itself to other forms of history that are based solely on the "facts," but rather points out that all history is told within the framework of a "unifying vision" that involves all scholars in an imaginative selection and reconstruction of the past. In the case of the New Testament, Schüssler Fiorenza argues that any scrap of evidence about leadership within the Jesus movement must be given weight, because it was not in the interests of the increasingly androcentric church to preserve such information.[8]

Feminist scholars who wish to reconstruct Goddess history are faced with a more difficult task than those wishing to reconstruct early Christian history, because much of Goddess history comes from the time before written records. Nonetheless, Schüssler

Fiorenza's methodology can be useful to us. Feminist scholars must be aware that androcentric biases are found in interpretations of Goddess artifacts as well as in primary texts and interpretations of them.

Marija Gimbutas, for example, has argued that contemporary male views of sexuality have affected interpretations of the so-called "Paleolithic Venuses." She writes, "To us, naturally, the vulva, breasts, and buttocks are sex symbols—we cannot escape the ideals of the century we live in—to them [prehistoric peoples] they apparently were symbols of birth, life-giving, fertility, and regeneration. The rounded parts of the female body were the sacred and magic parts of the Creative Goddess, the Giver-of-All."[9]

In the androcentric scholarly traditions of anthropology and prehistory, it is often conceded that women were the likely inventors of agriculture, a hypothesis based both on the prominence of female figures in myths about the origins of agriculture, and on the theory that as the primary gatherers in the gathering and hunting societies that preceded agriculture, women would have been the ones to discover the relationship between the dropping of a seed and the springing up of a plant. Mircea Eliade writes that in the Neolithic "women and feminine sacrality are raised to the first rank. Since women played a decisive role in the domestication of plants, they became the owners of the cultivated fields, which raised their social position."[10] Since it is not in the interest of the androcentric scholarly tradition to hypothesize that women were responsible for one of the great advances of civilization, we ought, according to Schüssler Fiorenza's methodology, to take this concession very seriously. It should not surprise us that anthropologists and prehistorians have not generally used the theory that women invented agriculture to hypothesize that this marvelous invention must have led, at least for a time, to enhanced social roles for women. Nor is it surprising that theory about the social and economic roles of women in the Neolithic era has not been combined (except in the work of a few scholars) with the evidence we have about the importance of Goddesses in Neolithic religion to challenge the patriarchal assumption that men have always and everywhere been dominant in religion and culture and that Goddesses have never correlated with female power. For to entertain hypotheses about female equality or preeminence in prehistory is too threatening to the androcentric paradigm to be taken seriously by those who function within it.

Similar points can be made about the historical or written records concerning the Goddesses. If even the misogynist Hesiod records that Gaia was the first to arise from Chaos, or if Aeschylus records that Gaia was the first to be worshiped at Delphi, followed by her daughters Themis and Phoebe, and last by Phoebus Apollo, this may be taken to imply a vast amount of information about the prehistory of the Goddesses which was not preserved.[11]

The loss of the works of Sappho vividly illustrates the problem facing feminist historians of religion. Sappho, who lived on the island of Lesbos in the sixth century B.C.E. (between the time of Homer and that of Aeschylus) was known as the greatest lyric poet of Greece and was compared to Homer, the greatest epic poet. Socrates called her "the beautiful," a term referring to her work, in the *Phaedrus*, and Plato was said to have called her the tenth Muse. The works of Sappho, estimated at 9000 lines, were collected into nine volumes in the Alexandrian era. Her poetry was destroyed during the burnings of the libraries at Alexandria and Constantinople, and on occasion by orders of popes and bishops. We have access to fragments of her work today (estimated at perhaps five percent of the total), through quotations by Greek and Roman authors, and from discarded copies of her poems that were shredded and used as scrap to wrap mummies. If the works of Sappho and other women poets from antiquity, such as Erinna and Corinna, had survived, students of the classical curriculum would study Sappho's poetry as seriously as they now study the surviving works of Homer and Aeschylus. The question whether there had ever been a female genius would never be asked. Social historians would be forced to acknowledge that the Aegean islands provided a climate in which female genius could thrive. If Sappho's society was not a matriarchy (and evidence does not support this hypothesis), it must have been at least as supportive of female creativity as our own.[12]

If the works of Sappho were available for study, we would have a body of literature that would provide insight into the roles that the Greek Goddesses played in female imagination. The fragments of Sappho's work suggest that Greek Goddesses were viewed quite differently by Greek women than they were by

Greek men. As Paul Friedrich notes, Sappho's Aphrodite differs sharply form Homer's. "Sappho is unique in early Greece for the directness and prominence of her tie to a single divinity: in the sense of presence, immediacy, and reality she creates for her Aphrodite. . . Sappho incarnates the [G]oddess' most fundamental trait: her subjectivity working through the heart, the synthesis of wild emotion and high sophistication." Eve Stehle Steigers shows that Sappho, in contrast to male lyric poets, is not simply overpowered by Aphrodite, but rather treats her as a confidant and ally. Page duBois argues that Sappho responds to Homer's largely negative depiction of Helen with a positive evaluation of Helen's active pursuit of her desire.[13] What we have lost then, in losing Sappho, is data that could be used to reconstruct the meanings and functions of Goddesses in women's lives. Without this information, we are faced with a far more difficult task of historical reconstruction.

The gaps and silences in the androcentric tradition deny women a potentially empowering knowledge of history. When Goddesses are dismissed without careful consideration of all the evidence from prehistory and history, scholars perpetuate an inexcusable ignorance about the prehistoric Goddesses and the power of women in prehistory, an ignorance that serves to bolster patriarchy. In this essay I will sketch a feminist approach to the history and prehistory of the Goddesses in Old Europe, the ancient Near East, and Mediteranean through a consideration of a small part of the data that awaits more thorough feminist consideration. As will become clear, feminist historical reconstruction of this period, as opposed to Jungian and other ahistorical methodologies, takes seriously the historical changes in society that led to the development of patriarchy and with it, the transformation of myth and symbolism.

One of the earliest and most enduring images of the Goddess is the Goddess Creatress, the Lady of the Animals. She is known to readers of the classics as Aphrodite with her dove, Athene with her owl, Artemis with her deer. But the image of Lady of the Animals goes back much further than the classical age of Greece (fifth and fourth centuries B.C.E.), much further back than Homer (before 700 B.C.E.). She goes back to prehistory, certainly to the Neolithic era (began c. 9000 B.C.E. in the Near East), if not to the

Paleolithic (32,000–10,000 B.C.E.). The Lady of the Animals is found in almost all cultures.

Because prehistory has left no written records, interpretations of the meaning of the earliest images of the Lady of the Animals is not a matter of certainty. We cannot know if she was known to her earliest worshipers as "Mother of All the Living" (a term used to refer to Eve in Gen. 3:20), as "Creatress," as "Goddess," as "Clan Mother," as "Priestess," or simply as "Ma" or "Nana." Whatever she was called, the Lady of the Animals is an image of the awesome creative power of woman and nature.

The *Homeric Hymns*, dated c. 800–400 B.C.E., many of which reflect much earlier religious conceptions, provide us with two powerful written images of the Lady of the Animals, which can help us interpret earlier drawn and sculpted images. The *Homeric Hymns* present her thus: "well-founded earth, mother of all, eldest of all beings. She feeds all creatures that are in the world, all that go upon the goodly land, and all that are in the paths of the seas, and all that fly. . ." Also, "she is well-pleased with the sound of rattles and timbrels, with the voice of flutes and the outcry of wolves and bright-eyed lions, with echoing hills and wooded coombes."[14] In these songs the Lady of the Animals is cosmic power; she is mother of all; the animals of earth, sea, and air are hers; the wildest and most fearsome animals, the wolves and the lions, and human beings as well, praise her with sounds. The Lady of the Animals is also earth: she is the firm foundation undergirding all life. The hills and valleys echo to her. In these images she is not yet Lady of the Plants, which suggest that the conceptions reflected in these hymns may have their origin in preagricultural times. Jane Harrison in *Prolegomena* has suggested that the Lady of the Wild Things becomes Lady of the Plants, or Corn Mother, only after human beings become agriculturalists.[15]

Marija Gimbutas, G. Rachel Levy, and E.O. James are among those who concur with Harrison in tracing the Goddess symbolism of the Neolithic and later periods to the Upper Paleolithic or Old Stone Age (c. 32,000–10,000 B.C.E.). Therefore we must ask whether the image of the Lady of the Animals also goes back to the Paleolithic age.

Many small figures of so-called pregnant "Venuses" have been dated to the Upper Paleolithic. These abundantly fleshed unclothed women have prominent breasts, bellies, and pubic triangles, and often they were painted with red ochre, which seems to have symbolized the blood of birth, the blood of life. These images have been variously interpreted as symbolizing the Goddess, the Clan Mother, and the awesome female powers of birth and transformation. Their designation as mere fertility fetishes does not do justice to them. Paleolithic people lived in a universe in which magic and religion were not yet separate, and in which divinity and humanity and nature were not understood as inhabiting separate planes of existence. If these images are to be called Goddesses, then Goddess must not be understood as separate from humanity and nature; if they are to be called fertility images, then fertility must be understood as the cosmic principle of life, death, and renewal.

These images must be interpreted in relation to the cave art of the Paleolithic era, when the labyrinthine paths and inner recesses of caves were decorated with abstract line patterns and with drawings and paintings of animals such as bison and deer. Small human figures, both male and female, were sometimes painted in the vicinity of the much larger animals. The drawings and paintings of these animals and the rituals practiced in the inner reaches of the caves have often been understood as hunting magic, done to ensure the capture of prey. But G. Rachel Levy in *Religious Conceptions of the Stone Age* argues that the purposes of these rituals cannot have been simple "magic compulsion" but must have involved a desire for a "participation in the splendor of the beasts."[16] If, as surely later was the case, Paleolithic peoples also understood the caves and their inner recesses to be the womb of Earth, then is it not possible to recognize the aniconic image of the Lady of the Animals in the womb-cave onto which the animals were painted? And can we not also see the Lady of the Animals in the well-known Paleolithic carving of an unclothed, apparently pregnant woman holding a bison horn found in Laussel? And must we not then interpret prehistoric rituals in the labyrinthine recesses of caves as a desire to participate in the transformative power of the Creatress, the Lady of the Animals?

We cannot know with certainty the religious and social roles of women in the Paleolithic times. But there is no reason to assume that women were subordinate. Feminist anthropologists are beginning to rethink the role of women in the development of human society. We now recognize that theories based upon the favorite of anthropological theorists, "man the hunter," must be complemented by theories about the contributions of "woman the gatherer."[17] Comparisons with other gathering and hunting groups, which cannot be undertaken uncritically, nonetheless suggest that sex roles were probably strongly differentiated in early human groups, and that both sexes were valued for their contributions to the survival of all. In small-scale societies, which must have been the norm in the Paleolithic, everyone's voice could be heard, and the kinds of status differentiation and hierarchy that develop in large-scale societies were not possible. Women and men were probably roughly equal in Paleolithic society, men being valued for hunting and women for giving birth and gathering.

Anthropomorphic images for the Lady of the Animals appear in abundance in the Neolithic or early agricultural period, which began about 9000 B.C.E. in the Near East. In *The Goddesses and Gods of Old Europe*, Marija Gimbutas presented the results of her exhaustive study of the civilization of Old Europe (c. 6500–3500), a Neolithic and Chalcolithic (or Copper Age) civilization that included the lands surrounding the Aegean and Adriatic seas and their islands, extending as far north as Czechoslovakia, southern Poland, and the western Ukraine. There is reason to believe that Neolithic-Chalcolithic cultures developed along similar lines in other parts of the world, including for example, Africa, China, the Indus Valley, and the Americas. In Old Europe, Gimbutas found a pre-Bronze Age culture that was "matrifocal and probably matrilinear, agricultural and sedentary, egalitarian and peaceful." This culture was presided over by a Goddess as Source and Giver of All. Originally the Goddess did not appear with animals but herself had animal characteristics. One of her earliest forms was as the Snake and Bird Goddess, associated with water, and represented as a snake, a water bird, a duck, goose, crane, diver bird, owl, or as a woman with a bird head or birdlike posture. She was the Goddess Creatress, the Giver of Life. The Old European Goddess was also connected with the agricultural cycles of life, death, and regeneration. Here she appeared as or was associated with bees, butterflies, deer, bears, hares, toads, turtles, hedgehogs, and dogs. The domesticated dog, bull, male goat, and pig became her companions. To the Old Europeans the Lady of the Animals was not a power transcending earth, but rather the power that creates, sustains, and is manifest in the infinite variety of life forms on earth. Old Europe did not celebrate humanity's uniqueness and separation from nature but rather humanity's participation in and connection to nature's cycles of birth, death, and renewal. The Creatress manifest as animal or with animal parts did not diminish but rather enhanced human understanding of her creative power: many animals, such as the rapidly growing piglet, the caterpillar/chrysalis/butterfly, the bird who flies in the air and walks on the earth, the snake who crawls above and below the earth, express the creative powers of the universe more fully than human form alone.[18]

In Old Europe the Goddess Creatress as Lady of Animals was the primary image of the divine. According to Gimbutas, the "male element, man and animal, represented spontaneous and life-stimulating—but not life-generating—powers."[19] Gimbutas believes that women were preeminent in the society and religion of Old Europe. If women were the first agriculturalists, perhaps initially guarding the secrets from men, then there is a social and economic basis for the primacy of the Goddesses in the earliest agricultural societies.

The Neolithic town of Çatal Hüyük (6500–5700 B.C.E.) in Anatolia (central Turkey), excavated by James Mellaart, reflects a culture similar to that found by Gimbutas in Old Europe. Like Gimbutas, Mellaart found a culture where women and Goddesses were prominent, a culture that he believed to have been matrilineal and matrilocal and peaceful, and in which the Goddess was the most powerful religious image. In Çatal Hüyük the Lady of the Animals was prominent. Wall paintings in the shrines frequently depict the Goddess with arms and legs outstretched, giving birth, sometimes to cow or bull and ewe or rams' heads. Other shrines depict rows of cow or bull heads with rows of breasts; in one shrine rows of breasts incorporate the lower jaws of boars, or skulls of foxes, weasels, or vultures. In a small clay statue, she is imaged seated on a throne or chair, apparently giving birth, her hand resting on the heads of her two leopard companions. Mellaart also found a sculpture of a woman in leopard skin robes, standing in front of a leopard. One shrine simply depicts two leopards standing face to face. Wall paintings of bulls were also frequent. Mellaart believes the religion at Çatal Hüyük centered around life, death, and rebirth. The bones of women, children, and some men were buried under platforms in the living quarters and shrines, apparently after having been picked clean by vultures. Mellaart believes vultures were also associated with the Goddess, thus showing that she was both Giver and Taker of life.[20]

In the Mediterranean islands that were more difficult to invade, the Goddess-centered cultures survived and developed into Bronze Age civilizations, such as that of Minoan Crete. In Crete, the Lady of the Animals remained supreme until the Minoan civilization fell to the Mycenaeans about 1450 B.C.E. In the Old and New Palace periods of Minoan Crete (c. 2000–1450 B.C.E.), a highly developed pre-Greek civilization based on agriculture, artisanship, and trade emerged. From existing archaeological evidence (Linear A, the written language of the Minoans has not been translated), it appears that women and priestesses played prominent roles in religious rituals. There is no evidence that they were subordinate in society. Indeed, it is now deemed plausible by several scholars, including Jacquetta Hawkes, Stylanios Alexiou, Helga Reusch, and Ruby Rohrlich, that the celebrated "Throne of King Minos" found by excavator Sir Arthur Evans may have been occupied by a priestess queen.[21]

In Minoan Crete the Goddess was worshiped in natural sites, in caves or on mountaintops, or in small shrines in the palaces and homes. She was known especially as the Mountain Mother and as Lady of the Animals. In a small statue found in the treasury of the Palace of Knossos (c. 1700–1450 B.C.E.), she stares as if in trance, her outstretched arms holding two striped snakes, her breasts exposed, a small animal perching on her head. In an image on a seal ring, she emerges from the mountain top bare-breasted, attended by two lions and a young male. In Crete the Lady of the Animals is commonly found in the company of snakes, doves, and trees, particularly the olive tree cultivated by Minoan farmers. In a seal ring found in the Dictean cave the Goddess appears with bird or snake head between two winged griffons, the same animals that flank the throne of "Minos." Other pervasive symbols in Crete include the stylized horns of consecration, evoking not only the cow or bull but the crescent moon and the upraised arms of Minoan Goddesses and priestesses, and the double axe, interpreted by Gimbutas as a stylized butterfly. Heiresses and heirs to Neolithic religion, the Minoans continued to understand the divine as the power manifesting in the cycle of nature. Cretan pottery and frescoes abound in rhythmical forms: images of waves, spirals, frolicking dolphins, undulating snakes, graceful bull leapers are everywhere. The Minoans captured life in motion. Exuberant movement must have represented to them the dance of life, the dance of the Lady.

As Mellaart states in *Earliest Civilizations of the Near East*, the land-based matrifocal, sedentary, peaceful, agricultural societies of the Near East were invaded by culturally inferior northern peoples starting in the fifth and fourth millennia B.C.E. According to Gimbutas, similar developments occurred in Old Europe where proto–Indo-Europeans who were patriarchal, nomadic, and warlike, infiltrated the matrifocal agricultural societies between 4500 and 2500 B.C.E.[22] As a result, in both the Near East and Old Europe, the Goddess Creatress was deposed, slain, or made wife, daughter, or mother to the male divinities of the warriors. The Goddess Creatress, the Lady of the Animals, did not disappear—religious symbols linger long after the end of the cultural situation that has given rise to them—but her power was diminished. No longer understood to be the great power of the universe, she was subordinated to Gods, such as Zeus or Marduk, who claimed preeminent power.

Eventually all the Neolithic and (isolated) Bronze Age cultures where the Lady was supreme fell to patriarchal and warlike invaders. By the time of decipherable written records, we begin to see evidence that societies are ruled by warrior kings; Goddesses are no longer supreme, and women are subordinated by law to their husbands. Societies become class- and slave-based and hierarchical. On mainland Greece, Apollo took over the holy site of Delphi, sacred first to Earth and her prophetess, after slaying the python, the sacred snake that guarded the sanctuary. This may be viewed as one record of the dethronement of the Goddess Creatress. In the Olympian mythology of Homer and the tragedies, Zeus, the Indo-European sky God, is named father and ruler of all the Gods and Goddesses. Hera, an indigenous Goddess whose sanctuary at Olympia was older than that of Zeus, becomes the never fully subdued wife of Zeus. Athena is born from the head of Zeus, but her temple on the mountain, the rock outcropping of the Parthenon hill, and her companions, the owl and the snake, remind us of her connection to the Mountain Mother and the Lady of the Animals. Aphrodite retains her connections to the dove and the goose. Artemis is the Goddess of the untamed lands, mountain forest, and wild animals, especially bears, and deer. Though she is named Virgin, she aids both human and animal mothers in giving birth. Of all the Olympian Goddesses, Artemis retains the strongest connection to the Lady of the Animals. What happened to the Goddesses in Greece happened everywhere. They were slain or tamed or made defenders of patriarchy and war or relegated to a place outside the city. They were not allowed to challenge the patriarchal order that everywhere became the norm.[23]

The transformation of the Goddess Creatress or Lady of the Animals into the more familiar Virgin Goddess illustrates how the power of the prehistoric Goddesses was reinterpreted to serve patriarchal interests. The Virgin Goddess of urban patriarchal societies did not in fact emerge full-grown from the head of Zeus as is claimed in the *Homeric Hymn* "To Athena." The Virgin Goddesses have their origins in the prehistoric Goddesses of the Paleolithic and Neolithic eras. According to Marija Gimbutas, Goddess images gradually became differentiated into two aspects, The Giver and Taker of All, and Rebirth and Regeneration. Eventually these two aspects became the Mother and the Maiden. The Mother was the sustaining power, represented especially by the enduring earth, the bedrock that undergirds all life. The Maiden aspect, the forces of renewal and regeneration, was represented especially by the new life, plant and animal, that emerges in spring. The Mother, the eternal, the Maiden, the ephemeral power of nature, were understood to be two aspects of the same whole. As Jane Ellen Harrison says "They are in fact, merely the older and younger form of the same person."[24] They did not require the male to complete or justify their power. In the patriarchal societies that emerged after 3500 B.C.E. in the Near East and Greece, none of the Goddesses retained their full power. In

Sumer, Marduk established his power by slaying the primordial Goddess Tiamat. In Greece, Zeus married and attempted to subdue the indigenous Goddess Hera. "With the coming of patriarchal conditions," Harrison wrote in 1903 in *Prolegomena*, "women [G]oddesses are sequestered to a servile domesticity, they become abject and amorous.[25] More than seventy years later classicist Sarah Pomeroy in *Goddesses, Whores, Wives, and Slaves* put it even more bluntly: "The distribution of desirable characteristics among a number of females rather than their concentration in one being is appropriate to a patriarchal society. . . A fully realized female tends to engender anxiety in the insecure male."[26] Such anxiety is also manifest in the androcentric theory of Erich Neumann, who in *The Great Mother* wrote, "The negative anima [is] the seductive young witch and the positive anima [is] the Sophia-virgin."[27]

In a patriarchal and patrilineal society, it is necessary to control women's sexuality so that a man can be certain that his children are "his." In earlier matrilineal societies all children were legitimate offspring of the mother. Thus it was decreed that women must be virgin at marriage and refrain from sexual intercourse with any man but their husbands. In this context the polarity between virgin and wife developed. In Greek this polarity is expressed in the opposition between *gynē*, which means both woman and wife refers to married women, and *parthenos*, which means maiden or girl and virgin, and refers to unmarried girls.

The Virgin Goddess reflects a separation of the Maiden from the Mother. The Mother becomes defined as Wife, while the Maiden becomes defined as unmarried, hence Virgin. The designation of the female divinities as married or virgin reflects the desire to control women and female sexuality. As Pomeroy comments, "Among the [G]ods there are no virgins, and sexual promiscuity—including rape—was never cause for censure even among the married ones."[28]

Though the appellation Virgin Goddess stems from patriarchal societies, the Goddesses designated Virgin were never fully subordinated to the interests of the patriarchal city state. The Virgin Goddess is not always entirely innocent of sexuality but may be virgin in the sense of being unmarried or even in the sense of not being defined by marriage. The complex nature of the Virgin

Goddess is further explicated by noting that in patriarchal societies the unmarried girl or woman poses a threat to the social order because her sexuality is not under the control of a man. Thus *parthenos* also carries the connotation of being wild or untamed.[29] The title Virgin Goddess signifies both limitation and independence within a patriarchal context. The Virgin Goddess is separated from her primordial power as Mother. But as virgin rather than wife, she remains independent of patriarchal marriage and the subordination it requires. In addition, as virgin she retains access to the wildness that would be considered inappropriate in the wife. This wildness can manifest in at least three forms: as connection to wild places and wild animals not tamed or under control of the city; as passion for the shedding of blood, which draws hunters and warriors away from the city and the family; and as untamed sexuality.

According to the *Homeric Hymn* "To Aphrodite" there are only three Aphrodite cannot sway: the Virgin Goddesses, Athena, Artemis, and Hestia.[30] Hestia, the aniconic Goddess of the hearth fire, represents the home as the ancient sphere of women. Even in patriarchal societies this is one sphere in which men are not in full control. Her virginity represents the ancient matrilineal ties among women. Moreover, since she was never really anthropomorphized, it was unnecessary to provide her with a husband. Artemis and Athena are more fully Virgin Goddesses.

Artemis, the Goddess of the moon and the wild places, is known as *Potnia Theron* or Lady of the Wild Animals in the *Iliad*, but as slayer of wild beasts in the *Homeric Hymns*. She is *parthenos*, both unmarried and virgin. Yet she is also invoked as *Eleitheia* and *Locheia*, Goddess of childbirth. These seemingly contradictory aspects can be understood if it is recognized that Artemis derives from the prehistoric Goddess. Artemis as Giver and Taker of Life was the Mother Deer as is indicated by the legend that pregnant does swim to her island in order to give birth. She was also the Mother Bear: her temple on the Acropolis was dedicated to Artemis *Brauronia*, and there she was served by young girls who dressed as bears, though the tradition of Artemis the Bear is thought to have originated in Arcadia. As Taker of Life, Artemis was also the one to whom animals of all kinds, including deer and bears, were sacrificed. Her wildness was acceptable in a patriarchal culture only if it was understood that she was not like other women. Thus her Maiden aspect was transformed to Virgin, and she was imaged as a masculinized huntress, clad in short tunic, slaying wild animals with arrows from her quiver. Yet, paradoxically, she remained the Goddess of women. Except for her brother Apollo, she shunned men. She danced with her companion nymphs in the forests by moonlight. Her association with the moon also expressed her connection to women, for the menstrual and birth cycles of women have long been connected with the waxing and waning of the moon. Her aspect as Mother reemerged in the image of Artemis the Midwife, who did not herself give birth, but who always came to the aid of animal and human mothers.[31]

Athena, the *parthenos* worshiped in her temple the Parthenon, expressed a different image of the Virgin Goddess, for she was identified with the city and with men. Said to have been born from the head of her father Zeus, Athena in the *Eumenides* of Aeschylus declared that she sided with the father against the mother in all things except marriage—which she shunned. She was born fully armed as a warrior and usually was imaged wearing a helmet and holding a spear and shield. Her title *Polias* indicated the city was her home; her titles *Promachos* and *Nike* named her victorious against its enemies. She avoided the company of women but nurtured heroes such as Odysseus, Theseus, Hercules, Perseus, and Erichthonius. Her virginity meant she could consort with men as an equal and engage in the masculine pursuit of war. Yet even Athena's roots in the prehistoric Goddesses were not fully obscured. Her companion animal the owl, the snake hiding behind her shield, and the olive tree that she caused to spring up on the Parthenon hill, indicate her chthonic origins. Athena secretly fostered the infant Erichthonius whom Gaia produced from the semen spilled in Hephaestus's attempt to rape her. Even Athena's warlike character probably derives from an earlier image as protectress of the city. Moreover, she was patroness not only of the masculine art of warfare but also of the arts originally associated with women, including pottery, weaving, and healing. One ritual performed in her honor involved the weaving and presentation of a new *peplos* or robe for her ancient wooden statue; girls and women played important roles in these rites. Today the bridal wreaths once offered to the Virgin Athena are presented to the Virgin Mary at the church of *Panaghia Kapnikarea* in Athens.[32]

Though the power of the prepatriarchal Goddesses as Mother and Maiden can still be felt in Artemis and Athena, these Goddesses are diminished and distorted by being cut off from their sexual power. They are more independent and powerful than women who submit to patriarchal marriage, but there is a coldness about them.[33] Athena barely remembers that the city too is dependent upon the powers of nature and sexuality. And when the Taker of Life is cut off from the Giver of Life, she can degenerate into a bloodthirsty huntress or warrior who glories in the shedding of blood for its own sake.

Though both are sexual, and according to Olympian mythology they are married and bear children, Aphrodite and Hera also deserve mention as Maiden Goddesses. Jane Ellen Harrison reminds us that both were honored with Athena as part of a Maiden Trinity that comes down in distorted form as a beauty contest in the so-called Judgment of Paris.[34]

Hera, though known as wife of Zeus and as mother of Hebe, Eleitheia, Ares, and Hephaestus, was also known as a Virgin Goddess. Before Zeus entered Greece, Hera was indigenous to Argos, and to the island of Samos, which was once called *Parthenia*; even at Olympus her temple is older than that of Zeus. In Arcadia she was worshiped as Child, Full-Grown, and Widow, the three stages of a woman's life echoing the three seasons of spring, summer, and winter. Her union with Zeus as presented in the *Iliad* was a sacred marriage that brought fertility to the earth. But another legend tells us that every year she renewed her virginity at a sacred spring called Canathus in Nauplia. As Jane Harrison explains, "Virginity was to these ancients in their wisdom a grace not lost but perennially renewed."[35] This custom reflects the prepatriarchal understanding that at all stages of her life a woman belongs primarily to herself; both her virginity and her sexuality are hers, not something she gives to another to control.

Fully and joyously sexual, Aphrodite remains Virgin in that her sexuality is unbridled, untamed, and her own. Though married to Hephaestus according to Olympian mythology, she is neither submissive nor faithful to him. Though she is a mother, her child *Eros*, Love or Desire, is but a reflection of her sexuality. Her birth from the sea, an *anodos* (rising up or emergence) of the Maiden, can be interpreted as the ritual bath of her ever-renewed virginity. Often misunderstood as a trivial Goddess of love and beauty, Aphrodite is clearly rooted in the ancient Goddess of Renewal and Regeneration. Historian of religion Mircea Eliade writes that Aphrodite represents "one of the most profound sources of religious experience: the revelation of sexuality as transcendence and mystery."[36] An island Goddess who entered Greece through Phoenecian ports in Cytheria and Cyprus, Aphrodite's temples were often found in the marshy ground where sea transforms into land, or on the cliffs where the sea rises as mist to the land. Her sacred places, like her sexuality, symbolize transformation. Aphrodite is also connected to the Near Eastern Goddesses of Renewal and Regeneration, Ishtar and Astarte. Like them, she was identified with the morning and evening stars, marking the transformation between night and day. Like Ishtar and Astarte she was served by priestesses who engaged in sacred sexual rituals, which degenerated into sacred prostitution as the status of women declined under patriarchy. Her connection to the ancient Goddess as Giver of Life is evident from her companions the amorous doves and her birth from the sea. The *Homeric Hymn* "To Aphrodite" portrays her as followed by wolves, lions, bears, and leopards, in whom she awakens the spark of desire.[37]

Hera and Aphrodite, like the Goddesses of the Near East, Innana, Ishtar, Astarte, Artemis of Ephesus, and Cybele, but unlike the Greek Artemis and Athena, are Virgin in the sense of being independent of patriarchal marriage, but not in the sense of denying their sexuality. These Goddesses fit Jungian M. Esther Harding's often-quoted definition of the Virgin Goddess from *Women's Mysteries*: "She is essentially one-in-herself. She is not merely the feminine counterpart of a male god."[38] The virginity of Aphrodite, Hera, and the other sexual Goddesses is an expression of the prepatriarchal idea that sexuality is transformative power, not a matter of possessing or being possessed. Sexuality is an aspect of the eternal renewal contained within the cycles of birth, fullness, death, and regeneration within nature and all life. Just as the seed and the moon wax to fullness and wane again, so the Goddess returns to her Maiden state, and the cycle begins again.

Though not a Goddess according to orthodox theological interpretation, the Virgin Mary inherits many aspects of the Virgin Goddesses and functions as Goddess to many of her worshipers. Throughout the Near East, Europe, and Latin America, churches to the Virgin Mary were built at places holy to the Goddesses. Though she is not prominent in the New Testament, the myths and imagery surrounding her grew as the Goddesses were finally suppressed in Christian culture. To the Greeks she is *Panaghia*, which means simply "the All Holy." In the Gospel of Matthew, a prophecy from Isaiah, which reads, "Behold a virgin shall conceive and bear a son" (1:23), is applied to the birth of Jesus. Though the Hebrew word *'almah* in the original prophecy might be translated "young woman" without the necessary imputation of "virgin," both the Greek translation of the Hebrew Bible, the Septuagint, and the Gospel of Matthew use *parthenos*. Lest there be any ambiguity as to its interpretation, the author of Matthew clarifies, Joseph "knew her not [a biblical euphemism for intercourse] until she had borne a son" (1:25). The contradictions lurking in the background of the Virgin Goddesses of patriarchy were elevated to the level of theological paradox when it was later affirmed that Mary was virgin before, after, and during the birth of Jesus. Though in Mary, the Mother and Maiden aspects of the Goddess, which were severed in patriarchy, were reunited in a single image, the power of the Goddess was not restored. Like Artemis and Athena, Mary was cut off from her sexuality, which was the original source of her power. Moreover, Christian theology affirms the Father, the Son, and the Holy Spirit—but not the Mother or the Maiden—as God. Reluctantly the church agreed at the Council of Ephesus in 431 (held at one of the most important ancient sites of the worship of Artemis), that Mary could be called *Theotokos,* The God Bearer, as long as it was understood that she was not God. Though many Christians have continued to worship Mary as God, few have questioned the patriarchal fear of female (and ultimately all) sexuality implicit in her title as Virgin.[39] Until and unless the virginity of Mary is recognized in the ancient sense as the power of Regeneration and Renewal expressed in sexuality, Mary, like Artemis and Athena, will remain a truncated image of the Goddess.

NOTES

1. Rosemary Radford Ruether, *Sexism and God-Talk* (Boston: Beacon Press, 1983), esp. 50.
2. Anne L. Barstow, "The Prehistoric Goddess," in *The Book of the Goddess*, ed. Carl Olson (New York: Crossroad Press, 1983), 8.
3. See Carol P. Christ, "Toward a Paradigm Shift in the Academy and Religious Studies," in *The Impact of Feminist Research in the Academy*, ed. Christie Farnham (Bloomington: Indiana University Press, 1987); James Mellaart, *Çatal Hüyük* (New York: McGraw-Hill, 1967), and *Earliest Civilizations of the Near East* (New York: McGraw-Hill, 1965); Marija Gimbutas, "Women and Politics in Goddess-Centered Old Europe," in *The Politics of Women's Spirituality*, ed. Charlene Spretnak (New York: Doubleday, 1982), 22–31, and *The Goddesses and Gods of Old Europe 6500–3500 B.C.* (Berkeley and Los Angeles: The University of California Press, 1982); Charlene Spretnak, *Lost Goddesses of Early Greece: A Collection of Pre-Hellenic Mythology* (Boston: Beacon Press, 1984); and Christine Downing, *The Goddess: Mythological Representations of the Feminine* (New York: Crossroad, 1983).
4. Ruby Rohrlich, "State Formation in Sumer and the Subjugation of Women," *Feminist Studies* 6, no. 1 (1980): 76–102.
5. Gerda Lerner, *The Creation of Patriarchy* (New York: Oxford University Press, 1986).
6. See Samuel Noah Kramer, *The Sumerians* (Chicago: University of Chicago Press, 1963), esp. ch. 5. Kramer notes that the earliest mythological text is dated c. 2400 B.C.E., but that the plot is unintelligible.
7. See Gimbutas, "Women and Politics in Goddess-Centered Old Europe."
8. Elisabeth Schüssler Fiorenza, *In Memory of Her* (New York: Crossroad Press, 1983), 29, 41, 69.
9. Marija Gimbutas, "Vulvas, Breasts, and Buttocks of the Goddess Creatress," *The Creative Woman Quarterly* 6, no. 4 (1983): 8–11, esp. 11.
10. Mircea Eliade, *A History of Religious Ideas*, Vol. 1, trans. Willard Trask (Chicago: University of Chicago Press, 1978), 40; see also "To Demeter," in *The Homeric Hymns*, trans. Thelma Sargent (New York: W.W. Norton, 1973); Ruby Rohrlich-Leavitt, "Women in Transition: Crete and Sumer," in *Becoming Visible: Women in European History*, ed. Renate Bridenthal and Claudia Koonz (Boston: Houghton Mifflin, 1977), 36–59.
11. See "Theogony," *The Poems of Hesiod*, trans. R.M. Frazier (Norman, Oklahoma: University of Oklahoma Press, 1983), 30; Aeschylus, *The Eumenides* in *The Complete Greek Tragedies*, Vol. 1, ed. David Grene and Richmond Lattimore (Chicago: University of Chicago Press, 1959), 135.
12. See *Greek Lyric I*, trans. David A. Campbell (Cambridge: Harvard University Press, 1982), 46–47, 3, 48–49, xiii; Paul Friedrich, *The Meaning of Aphrodite* (Chicago: University of Chicago Press, 1978), 126.
13. Friedrich, *The Meaning of Aphrodite*, 123; Eve Stehle Steigers, "Sappho's Private World," in *Reflections of Women in Antiquity*, ed. Helen P. Foley (New York: Gordon and Breach Science Publishers, 1981), 45–61; Page duBois, "Sappho and Helen," in *Women in the Ancient World*, ed. John Peradotto and J. P. Sullivan (Albany, NY: State University of New York Press, 1984), 95–105.
14. "To Earth, The Mother of All," and "To the Mother of the Gods," in *Hesoid: The Homeric Hymns and Homerica*, trans. Hugh G. Evans-White (Cambridge: Harvard University Press, 1914), 457, 439.
15. Jane Ellen Harrison, *Prolegomena to the Study of Greek Religion* (London: Merlin Press, 1962), 271.

16. Levy, *Religious Conceptions*, in *The Stone Age* (New York: Harper & Row, 1963), 20.
17. Frances Dahlberg, *Woman the Gatherer* (New Haven: Yale University Press, 1981).
18. Gimbutas, *Goddesses and Gods of Old Europe*, esp. 9.
19. Ibid.
20. See James Mellaart, *Çatal Hüyük*; also see Barstow, "The Prehistoric Goddess."
21. Jacquetta Hawkes, *Dawn of the Gods* (New York: Random House, 1968), 153–55; Stylianos Alexiou, *Minoan Civilization*, 3d ed., trans. Cressida Ridley (Heraclion: Spyros Alexiou Sons, n.d.), "Women in Transition: Crete and Sumer," in *Becoming Visible*, 49; also see Marymay Downing, "Prehistoric Goddesses: The Cretan Challenge," *Journal of Feminist Studies in Religion* 1, no. 1 (1985): 5–22.
22. James Mellaart, *Earliest Civilizations of the Near East*, 134; also see Gimbutas, "Women and Politics."
23. See Aeschylus, *The Eumenides*; Harrison, *Prolegomena*, esp. ch. 6; and Spretnak, *Lost Goddesses*.
24. Harrison, *Prolegomena*, 274.
25. Ibid., 272.
26. Sarah Pomeroy, *Goddesses, Whores, Wives and Slaves: Women in Classical Antiquity* (New York: Schocken Books, 1975), 8.
27. Erich Neumann, *The Great Mother*, trans. Ralph Manheim (Princeton: Princeton University Press, 1955), 75.
28. Pomeroy, *Goddesses*, 8.
29. See Helen King, "Bound to Bleed: Artemis and Greek Women," in *Images of Women in Antiquity*, ed. Averil Cameron and Amelie Kuhrt (Detroit: Wayne State University Press, 1983), 111.
30. Sargent, trans. "To Aphrodite," p. 46.
31. See *The Homeric Hymns*; Harrison, *Prolegomena*, 299–300; Harrison, *Mythology*, (New York: Harcourt Brace, 1963), 82–92; Spretnak, *Lost Goddesses*, 75–83; Eliade, 278-80; Christine Downing, 157-85; Gimbutas, *Goddesses and Gods*, 196–200.
32. See *The Homeric Hymns*; Harrison, *Prolegomena*, 300–7; *Mythology*, 70–74; Spretnak, *Lost Goddesses*, 97–101; Eliade, 280–2; Christine Downing, 98–130; Gimbutas, *Goddesses and Gods*, 147–9, 234-5; also see "Byzantine Athens," in C. Gouvoussis, *Athens* (Athens: Editions K. Gouvoussis, n.d.), n.p.
33. Harrison, *Prolegomena*, 299.
34. Ibid., 286–300.
35. Ibid., 312, 315–18; *Mythology*, 68–70; Spretnak, *Lost Goddesses*, 87–94; Eliade, 277–8; Christine Downing, 68–98; Gimbutas, *Goddesses and Gods*, 149–50.
36. Eliade, 283.
37. See *The Homeric Hymns;* Harrison, *Prolegomena*, 307-15; *Mythology*, 74-82; Spretnak, *Lost Goddesses*, 69-72; Eliade, 282-83; Christine Downing, 186-216; Gimbutas, *Goddesses and Gods*, 95, 149.
38. See M. Esther Harding, *Women's Mysteries: Ancient and Modern* (New York: G. P. Putnam's Sons, 1971), 125.
39. Marina Warner, *Alone of All Her Sex* (New York: Alfred A. Knopf, 1976); also see Margaret Miles, "The Virgin's One Bare Breast," in *The Female Body in Western Culture* ed. Susan Suleiman (Cambridge: Harvard University Press, 1986), 193-208.

Profile of Goddess with Flowing Hair. Cave of Skotino, Crete.

11. Laughter of Aphrodite

At the beginning of his novel *The Gates of the Forest*, Elie Wiesel tells a story about a rabbi who went to a special place in the forest whenever a disaster was about to befall his people. There he lit a fire, said a prayer, and the disaster was averted. In another generation, another rabbi went to the forest and said the prayer. Though he had forgotten how to light the fire, still the miracle was accomplished. Time passed, and another rabbi remembered only the place in the forest. Still, it was enough. Yet later, another rabbi remembered only the story. It was sufficient.[1] Elie Wiesel's story describes the struggle of a community to retain communication with the divine power even though the memory of the original revelation had dimmed through time. It expresses the Hasidic belief that even though the prayer, the ritual, and the sacred space have been lost, the heartfelt desire to communicate with God is enough. Though Elie Wiesel's story reflects the experience of a people who have retained the memory of their relationship with the divine power in community, it sheds light on the desires of those who seek to enter into relationship with ancient Goddesses.

Many whose contemporary experiences impel us "in search of Her,"[2] as Christine Downing writes, know neither the prayers, rituals, places, nor stories as preserved in an ongoing community. Yet we can find some of the places and can piece together fragments of stories, rituals, and prayers, taking our clues from archaeological and historical records and from fragments of Goddess images, symbols, and rituals that have survived in Christianity and Judaism. We can trust our own intuitions and listen for the echoes of the still resounding voices of ancestors, and of the Goddesses.

My initiation into the symbols and rituals of the Goddesses began a number of years ago when my own experiences of the silencing of the voice of my experience and perception within patriarchal religious and academic structures led me to desire a validating female God language. Though I had experimented with female names for God, it was not until I found myself engaged in the dialogue inspired by Wiesel's story of God and Man changing places that I found her in a concrete way. In retrospect, I would name the night when I heard a still small voice saying, "God is a woman like yourself," as the beginning of my initiation into the mysteries of the Goddesses. My struggles to understand the meaning of Wiesel's stories for myself and for God could be viewed as a kind of spiritual discipline. Wiesel was my "teacher," even though he probably would not have recognized or validated the words that came to me in the night. In the next several years I learned that the Goddess had made her presence felt in the lives of many other women as well. I began to read and teach the history of the Goddesses and began creating and participating in rituals celebrating the Goddesses in connection with the cycles of the moon and the yearly seasons.

When I was invited by Ellen Boneparth to teach in the Aegean Women's Studies Institute in Mithimna, Lesbos, I resisted the Greek Goddesses because I felt there was too much focus on them already. I thought I should learn about the Grandmothers of the American land, about the Goddesses of my Swedish, German, Irish, Scottish, and English ancestors, and about the Goddesses whose presence lingers in the stories of the God of Israel. Moreover, I was not satisfied with what I knew of the Greek Goddesses from the patriarchal myths and stories told about them. Yet I went to Greece and have returned each year. Without my choosing them the Greek Goddesses have chosen me. The stories that follow depict my encounters with these Goddesses.

IN THE BEGINNING, THE CAVE

> Rocks are very slow and have sat around since the beginning, developing powers. Rocks . . . can show you what you are going to become. They show you lost and forgotten things.[3]

Before I went to Greece a friend said to me, "Whenever you visit a temple, look for the cave. The places were known as sacred because of the caves, long before the temples were built." In ancient times the Greeks knew Gaia, the Earth, to be the oldest of the Goddesses and Gods, source and sustainer of all. Though our culture's images of the feminine might predispose us to think Mother Earth to be a flowering hillside or gently flowing stream, the Greeks knew her as the bedrock beneath the thinly layered soil, the seed and the flower, the coursing stream. She exposed her power on craggy peaks, majestic towering breasts, and she revealed her mysteries in dark caves with labyrinthine passageways leading to her center, the place of emergence and return. Giver and Taker of life, Gaia endures while all else comes into being and passes away.

According to Aeschylus, Gaia was the first to be worshiped at Delphi.[4] The Pythia, the prophetess, was always a woman, even after Apollo's priests took over the oracle.[5] It is likely that the Pythia originally prophesied in the Cornycian cave, not far from Apollo's temple.[6]

At Delphi, I bathe my hair in the spring of Canathus and chew a laurel leaf as the prophetess was said to have done. I have heard that there is a small cave somewhere on the site. My scrambling and broken Greek do not reveal it. So I set off to the Cornycian cave, accessible by taxi from the next village, Arachova. Alighting from the bus, I speak a few words to the taxi drivers and find myself ushered into a car driven by an old man who speaks not a word of English. As we drive, the mountains open on a deep green brown valley studded with farms, edged by rocky pine-covered slopes. We ascend a steep and winding dirt road to the small dark mouth of the cave. The old man gets out of the car, lights a cigarette, and gestures that he will wait.

As my eyes adjust, I see that I am in an enormous room filled with folded stalagmite shapes emerging and receding in the cave's wet darkness. "The Shape Shifter," I think remembering *The Clan of the Cave Bear*,[7] as I watch lime-whitened forms become now human, now animal, now male, now female. "*Meter*, Mother," I call into the blackness and hear my words echo from deep recesses. I sit on the floor of the cave looking out to the light, and I feel myself become a woman grinding seeds while children play before her. "If you had eyes like the stones, you could explore the universe . . . Yes, you could go back to ancient times."[8]

"We'll look for the cave tomorrow at Sunion," says my rationalist friend Diane, inspired by my stories of Delphi and her first

Temple of Aphrodite. Mesa, Lesbos.

breath of Greek air. "But there are no caves at Sunion," I respond, "I've been there." "We'll find them," she insists. And so we do, swimming around the rocky cliffs that shelter the bay of Sunion, but not before we are each separately tested by dark currents of the open sea beyond the spot marked by Poseidon's shimmering temple. The cave we find is a small womb at the edge of the threatening sea, one side dry, the other filled with just enough water to make her glisten yellow, green, lavender in a translucent light pouring down through a tunnel in the cliff. A tiny red starfish clings to the rock where we sit, our feet in clear water, turning over stones, meditating, sharing our stories.

In Crete Roger and I flee the shrill shouts of tour guides filling the rooms of the palace of Knossos and set off to find the cave at Skotino, sacred to the Minoans. The small church perched atop the cave is dedicated to *Aghia Paraskevi*, patron saint of eyesight, successor to the powers of the seeress entwined with snakes whose trancelike gaze once penetrated the cave's dark mysteries. We arrive on *Paraskevi's* birthday as the Greeks are leaving the church, the icons inside garlanded with sweet-scented basil. We follow them down the steep hillside to the cave's mouth where they start the barbecue and begin to play a Greek instrument, the bouzouki. Young boys run deep into the cave with flashlights. We descend into an enormous cool cathedral that could hold thousands. What rites once were practiced here, I wonder, as I touch clammy limestone walls looking up into silky soft shapes formed by dripping water. We find a naturally formed limestone basin and bless ourselves with clear water just before a tiny black-clad crone hobbles over to fill her vial with healing water and vanishes. We look into the depths of the cave and when we turn again to the light, I see her, stalagmite Goddess with long, flowing hair in profile guarding the cave's entrace. I know I am not the first nor the last to see her here.

YOU KNOW THE PLACE

In my class in Lesbos we read my book *Diving Deep and Surfacing* in conjunction with Christine Downing's *The Goddess*. We write in our journals about our experiences of nothingness, awakening, insight, and naming, and about our relation to Downing's visions of the Greek Goddesses. We share what we have written in groups of two and three in the sunlight in view of the Aegean sea below. An atmosphere of openness, intimacy, and trust develops.

After writing about our experiences of nothingness, Alexis and I share our stories of being left by men we had loved too much. We speak of how we had felt whole, alive, sexual, creative, and then empty, devastated. A few days later we discuss Downing's chapter on Aphrodite. Downing writes of Aphrodite as cosmic life force, associated especially with the transformative power of sexuality. Aphrodite's temples often stood at places of transformation: where mists rise from the sea, where sea and dry land meet. Imaged rising from the sea on a shell, Aphrodite is known as the golden one because she prefers the sunlight. Downing mentions Aphrodite's laughter.

After we write in our journals about Aphrodite, Alexis and I speak of going to Aphrodite's temple in Lesbos to reclaim our sexuality. The tension builds within each of us until we know that we must go.

While wandering through town agitatedly, waiting for the time we had agreed to meet, I suddenly understand why temples to other deities are often in the vicinity of a major temple: those who visit make offerings to other Gods and Goddesses so that they can approach the major divinity free from distraction. We must make offerings to other Goddesses before we can approach Aphrodite. Objects begin to beckon to me from shop windows—a bottle opener picturing Priapus with enormous erection, another with an owl, golden worry beads, a postcard of a Greek woman weaving, and finally the white gauze dress woven with golden threads and a golden shawl I had admired the night before. I would go to Aphrodite's temple in white, symbolizing my desire to be initiated into her mysteries. I would wear the golden shawl to honor her goldenness and my own. When I meet Alexis at my friend Axiothea's tourist shop, she is wearing the white dress she had found in Athens. We bedeck ourselves in golden bronze necklaces and buy a handmade pottery pitcher and bowl, white with rose and indigo flowers. Alexis decides that she too must wear a golden shawl. Our last stop is the grocery shop where we find red wine and golden retsina, golden biscuit cookies, milk and honey, yogurt. On impulse we each pick out a pair of double shells. Alexis's yellow, mine pink, which will become one of the central symbols of our ritual. We ask for directions to the temple, but all we can learn is that we must turn down a small unmarked road several kilometers from the next town. Someone writes the words *Naos Aphrodite* on a scrap of paper in Greek letters.

When we get to the bus stop, we discover we have missed the afternoon bus. At the edge of town we catch a ride with two young Greek men in a Toyota. We don't want them at the temple, so we tell them we are only going to the next town. From there we walk a little way and try to hitch again, with no luck. On the way back to town we see Alexis's watch on the ground where she had dropped it. At the taxi stand we show our slip of paper and say *Naos Aphrodite* and are met with blank stares. Soon there are ten old men passing the paper around, shouting and gesturing in Greek in the middle of the street. Eventually one of them comes over to us and tells us he knows the way to the temple. Later we learn that the Greeks call the temple *Naos Messon*, which means "inside." He drives some distance from town, across three bridges, and then, just after the sea has appeared, down a rough dirt road. He lets us out of his Mercedes taxi and offers to show us the temple or wait. We tell him we will find our own way back.

The temple is at the end of a farm road in marshy ground within sight of a enormous womblike bay. Despite its proximity to a farm with goats and turkeys, the temple itself, surrounded by barbed wire and unmarked, appears deserted. We have arrived during the afternoon nap time. We are alone. The temple is small, and though none of its columns still stand, its light gray stone floor is clearly exposed, and fragments of columns are strewn about the site. Two trees grow at the center of the temple. The crumbling walls of a tiny Byzantine church built over the rear part of the temple are visible. A freshly whitewashed altar in the ruins of the church and a couple of dusty icons and oil lamps indicate it is still used.

Our excitement builds as we scramble over a barbed-wire fence and find ourselves standing amidst thorns and thistles in what must have been the temple's forecourt. We begin to take things out of our bags. We haven't planned much. We fill the flowered pitcher with red wine and the bowl with water and set the rest of the wine and the food aside. We put our offerings into the bowl.

I begin. On an exposed flat rock, I place the postcard of a Greek woman weaving and the golden worry beads. This is my altar to Hestia, Goddess of hearth and home. I speak to Hestia, telling her how honored I am to live in her realm, continuing the traditions of homemaking I have learned from my mother and grandmothers, a bond I share with women across the ages. Though I also work outside the home, I affirm my connection to Hestia. I spend a good deal of my time working on my home and in my garden. But I also speak to Hestia of how much she demands. I tell her that when I wake on a weekend morning thinking of what needs to be done, rather than of my husband, she asks too much. I pour out libations to her, begging her to leave me time to worship Aphrodite. She seems very thirsty, and Alexis has to stop me before I pour out a whole pitcher of wine.

My second altar is to Athena. On it I place the owl, Athena's sacred animal. For me, as for Christine Downing, Athena symbolizes my intellectual self, my ability to move in the world of men, like the patriarchal Athena, as well as my ability to draw upon the wisdom of night, the realm of the prepatriarchal Athena. I tell Athena I am honored to live in her realm, proud of my academic credentials and training, proud also to remember the wisdom of my mother. But I remind her that she too can be a demanding Goddess. As I pour out red wine offerings to her, I plead with her to leave me time and space for Aphrodite. Athena too drinks deeply and Alexis takes the pitcher from my hand.

Alexis's altar is to Demeter and Persephone. On a small rise, she arranges the black scarf of Demeter's mourning next to green worry beads for Persephone. She pours out her story to the Mother, telling Demeter of the loss of her beloved daughter, of a husband who threatened to take her children where she would never see them again if she sued for custody. She shares with Demeter her joy at learning that her daughter soon would be returning to live with her after many years of separation. Finally she tells Demeter her fear that her Persephone might try to destroy her relationship with her lover. She offers libations at the altar.

We are ready to enter the temple. Excited and apprehensive, we await Aphrodite. We do not know what that will mean. We gather the retsina and food and our shells, pouring the last of the red wine and water into the pitcher. Pausing at the threshold of the temple, I pour out the water and wine. All of a sudden I hear what I can only describe as the laughter of Aphrodite, as clear as a bell. I hear Aphrodite saying through her golden laughter, "Whoever told you that you could know sexual ecstasy without pain?" And then she begins to laugh again, saying, "What can you do but laugh?" I begin to laugh with her. I laugh with joy and pain. Alexis laughs too.

We step into the temple. She is everywhere. We find womblike spirals and vaginal roses carved in stone. We start to make an altar on one of the broken columns, but I feel myself drawn to the space between the two trees, at the center of the temple. I go to the spot, remove my shoes and my dress. I sit between the trees, opening my body to the midday sun, my golden shawl reflecting rays of golden light. I anoint my body with milk and honey, saying to myself, surely this is the land flowing with milk and honey. I pour milk and honey into the rose-colored shells, which open and close like my own. The sun warms and transforms my body. Though Alexis is standing nearby, I am alone with the Goddess in her sacred space. I feel myself opening. I become Aphrodite.

After Alexis has performed her own ritual in the space between the trees, we sit together eating from our shells, drinking retsina, and sharing stories. We speak of our first lovers, our current lovers, and many in between. When we finish, we each fill one of our shells with milk and honey and leave it for the Goddess. We pour out a libation of retsina and toss Priapus into the air. A bit of milk and yogurt is left, and we offer it on the whitewashed altar with a prayer that Greek women also might reclaim their connections to Aphrodite.

Packing our things, we make our way past goats and turkeys and small farms along the dirt road leading back to the main road. We walk a long way down the road before a German tourist bus picks us up and brings us back to our town.

We are glowing, and when we tell our story, three women ask us to take them to the temple. When we return, Alexis and I know that we have become priestesses of Aphrodite. One of the women is a virgin. We begin to understand what it means for women to initiate other women into the mysteries of sexuality. Our rites are sensual, not sexual: each woman discovers that her sexuality is her own. We all give the virgin lots of advice—much of it contradictory. Some time later, I take another woman to the temple. This time I lose my watch. It is a small price to pay.

APHRODITE AND THE NYMPH

Claire the nymph wants to know everything about my love affair with Dimitris. Each morning she comes to my room and I tell her. He is very beautiful. His skin is black. His hair is black and coarse. The earth moves. We move. *Prasina matia,* "green eyes," he says, "I love you." No one ever called me green eyes before.

Claire is at the end of her twelfth year. She has not yet started to bleed, but she will soon. Womanhood is just beginning to shape her body. She does not know whether she wants to be a child or a woman. She is not certain she wants a womanhood ritual. Helen, her mother, and I decide to take her to Aphrodite's temple at Mesa, Lesbos. We do not ask her, we tell her. Now is the time and this is the place. She does not resist. She will wear the white seersucker dress with handmade lace Helen bought her for an early thirteenth birthday gift.

On the way to the temple in the taxi we tell Claire about the Goddesses. I tell her about the Paleolithic Goddesses with huge breasts and bellies, the givers of life. I speak of the time when women invented agriculture, and weaving, and pottery, all great mysteries, and of how the Goddess came to symbolize the creative power women knew, of how there was a time when we were not afraid but walked upright, confident in our powers. Briefly I speak of how and why this power was lost, of how religion became the domain of fathers and sons. I tell her that Aphrodite is Goddess of transforming cosmic power, especially as it is known in sexuality, that she is by no means Goddess only of love and beauty. We tell Claire how lucky she is to be becoming woman now when women are beginning to understand again that our bleeding is not curse but mystery, sacred gift. We tell her our blood is not dirty, that in some cultures men even mimic women's bleeding in their rituals in order to participate in our power.

We re-member ourselves and Claire as we speak of the mysteries of sexuality and love. "The reason I am Aphrodite's priestess," I say to Claire, "is because for me sexuality is a mystery. I am her priestess not because I understand, but because I do not." "Yes," Claire's mother responds, her first year of law school behind her, "women like ourselves—and you Claire—can learn how to be successful in the world, but sexuality and love remain uncertain." "And Claire," I say, "every moment of joy is a gift, every hour, every second. Even if we know it only briefly, it is enough."

The taxi brings us to the temple. The spring that flows over the road is gurgling. We take off our shoes, get our feet wet. Outside the temple, I look and see that the feather, the stones, and the thistle another friend and I left on the altar of Hera and Hestia a week or two earlier are now on the ground near the altar. Time changes everything. We change. The beautiful pink-centered conch shell I had filled with honey and left inside the temple as a thank offering for the transforming romance of the past summer has been taken, my gift to the universe, returned to the source. I am released. The flowers, the grain, and the thistle left on the altar of Demeter and Persephone are still there beneath the grasses, but they have shriveled, the power and the pain they represent diminished. Helen and I prepare altars to the other Goddesses, taking care of our obligations to them so that we can be free to meet Aphrodite. Claire watches, too young or too unaware to join us.

Now we are ready to approach the temple of Aphrodite. We pour out a final libation at the threshold. Inside, I show Claire a beautiful carved image of a flower within a vaginalike oval shape. I tell her that she must understand that her vagina, her sexuality, is her own, that she may share it when she chooses, but she must never give her power to anyone. We pour honey for our sexual juices, and red wine for our blood onto the flower. It glistens in the sun. "Nothing about our sexuality is dirty," we say. "Remember this image. Hold it in your mind all your life."

Then we show her a spiral, symbol of the power within, and lead her to a spot between the trees at the center of the ancient temple. I spread out a black shawl for Claire to sit on, so that her white dress will stay clean. "Know that you come from the Crone, from the Earth," I say. "Know that you can call on the power of old women, the Earth, whenever you need it." We read to Claire from the poems of Sappho, lyric poet from this island, a poem for two voices:

Virginity O
my virginity!

Where will you
go when I lose
you?

I'm off to
a place I shall
never come back from

Dear [girl]
I shall never
come back to you

Never![9]

And then I read Sappho's invocation to Aphrodite:

You know the place: then

Leave Crete and come to us
waiting where the grove is
pleasantest, by precincts

sacred to you; incense
smokes on the altar, cold
streams murmur through the

apple branches, a young
rose thicket shades the ground
and quivering leaves pour

down deep sleep; in meadows
where horses have grown sleek
among spring flowers, dill

scents the air. Queen! Cyprian!
fill our gold cups with love
stirred into clear nectar.[10]

Claire's embarrassment turns to smiles as we give her gifts. "This golden shawl comes from the Crone," I say, "our friend Lily gave it to me when she left the island. But I don't need it. I still have my own golden shawl, which I got for my first visit to the temple. Now I know that she left it for you. And that she is here in spirit. This shawl symbolizes the goldenness of Aphrodite, her love of the sunlight, her honey, her sweetness, her joyous sexuality. Whenever you wear this shawl, remember that this goldenness is yours, that you are Aphrodite." Claire smiles widely as I place her golden shawl on her shoulders. "And this golden bracelet, made here on Lesbos, etched with spirals, symbolizes your connection to Aphrodite and to me. I was given my golden bracelet covered with spirals, which I am wearing, when I was initiated at this temple. Know that you can turn to me whenever you need guidance. And for you, Helen, I have a gift, a golden bracelet, etched with triangles, symbolizing the power of women's sexuality. Know that we too are connected through this symbol and this ritual."

Helen has also brought gifts. "For you, Claire," she says, "I have brought this beautiful double shell, which opens and closes, just as our vaginas open and close. This large double shell is for me, the smaller, more delicate one for you, whose sexuality is just beginning." We feed Claire honey from her shell, saying, "You will know the sweetness of love and sexuality." Then we feed her salt, saying, "You will know tears." "We will fill our shells with honey and wine," Helen says, "and leave one half here for the Goddess, and take the other home. And for each of us," Helen continues, " I have brought a small golden knife (actually a letter opener) with spirals and snakes on the handles. I give these as symbols that your sexuality belongs to no one but yourself. Do not give your power away. Always remember that no one may own or control your body. When you hold this knife in your hand, know that whatever you have shared, you have shared because it is yours. Claire," she says, "I don't know if you will ever have an altar, but I want you always to keep your shell and your knife in a special place." Claire continues to smile, saying nothing.

I pour out a full bottle—"Yes it must be a full bottle," I tell Helen—of red wine to Aphrodite thanking her for sending me Dimitris. "Tell me again how you met Dimitris," Claire asks. And so, as we eat yogurt and honey and golden cookies and drink retsina in the sunlight, Helen and I speak of the loves we have known, the joy and the pain. At some point Claire reveals that she has been kissed. "Of course it was a boy at school," she says. We tease her about Stavros, the Greek boy who has a crush on her. "Learn about your sexuality at your own pace," we tell her.

"There is no need to rush." "And don't forget," I add, "you may love women too." "Yes," Helen says, "all love is a gift." I read to Claire from my journal:

Whoever you love openly
with your body
becomes part of you
lives woven together.
the Goddess does not lie:
we do not forget our lovers
there are, as my good friend who has had many, says,
no one night stands.

Then I read to Claire one of the poems I had written the previous summer in Lesbos.

TRYING TO MAKE LOVE ON THE BEACH AT ANAXOS

Eating in the taverna
elbow to elbow
our faces drawn close
retsina calamari
calamari retsina
not touching

was it words. . .mine?
or touch. . .yours?
the rush of passion

going off to a secluded spot
trembling
the rush of passion
falling to the sand
touching kissing
the sun
hot on my arms my face your back
the sun
the heat
the passion
Aphrodite
the sun

the man emerging from the sea
goggles breathing tube black trunks
stocky Greek
assuming he would walk past

continuing
then seeing him watching
us
unclothed embarrassed half oblivious
the passion intense
the heat

you hurt your knee on the sand
we go swimming
embrace in the water
you draw me down
words about drowning
in a sea of passion
flash in my mind
"You'll drown me," I say
"No I won't," you say

swimming back to the rocks
we had struggled to swim over
my foot on the rock
your hands on my breasts
holding tight
the urchins underfoot
my passion
your passion
Aphrodite
the sea

my body
your body
the sea
the sea

Claire is embarrassed again. We sit for a long time talking and laughing.

Then we each take time for our own private rituals with the Goddess. While Helen sits alone between the trees, I show Claire the place where once we found a turtle near the spring. Then she too wanders off alone. Later we find her making patterns with yogurt and golden cookies, her offerings, her altar to the Goddess.

We leave our shells in the sacred place, gather our things, and walk together down the dirt farm road in the hot afternoon sun. A bit later we hitch a ride in the back of a farmer's truck. Three

Temple of Demeter and Persephone. Eleusis.

rides and some time later we are back. Claire and I rush to the sea. "Remember," I joke, "when you come out, you will be a woman."

As we emerge Dimitris comes up to tell me he loves me and that Stavros loves Claire. She's only twelve, I remind him. A bit later Dimitris and Stavros and Claire and I play a long and wild game of keep away in the waves, as Helen watches. Later that night, Dimitris and Stavros find the three of us sitting under the stars at a taverna. Claire, after being teased into drinking some wine because now she is a woman, entertains Stavros by pretending to be drunk. The golden laughter of Aphrodite is heard in the black night. Some days later when Dimitris runs from the depth of our passion and the complications of our romance, I remember my knife, my shell, and the mystery. Aphrodite smiles.

ELEUSINIAN MYSTERIES

In the Aegean Women's Studies Institute our learning begins with trips to the Parthenon and the National Museum, but our spiritual beginning comes at Eleusis, a site sacred to Demeter, the Grain Mother, and Persephone, her Daughter, Queen of the Underworld.

The rituals of Demeter and Persephone at Eleusis were practiced for some 2000 years, from the fifteenth century B.C.E. to the end of the fourth century C.E. Demeter and Persephone are Goddesses of the agricultural cycle, Goddesses of the death and rebirth of the seed crops, Goddesses whose rites were later spiritualized to symbolize the death and rebirth of the soul.[11] The rites of Demeter and Persephone are said to derive from agricultural rituals for women only known as the Thesmophoria. In classical times the rituals of Demeter and Persephone at Eleusis were among the most important in all Greece.[12]

We go to Eleusis because we too want to celebrate the mysteries of mother and daughter. For those of us who are reared on myths and stories of fathers and sons, it is healing to know that once the deepest mysteries of the universe were symbolized in a story about the relationship of mother and daughter. The story of Demeter and Persephone resonates with echoes of the powerful but little-celebrated relationship we each have had with our mothers and our daughters.

Our rituals at Eleusis in the summers of 1981 to 1986, are among the first to have been celebrated there in conscious recognition of the Goddesses since the forced closing of the ancient temples about 400 C.E. These rituals have been among the most powerful experiences of my life. It seems as if there is an enormous energy dammed up on the site waiting to be released. Whether that power is the natural energy of the place (all the Greek temple sites are at naturally powerful spots, as Vincent Scully has shown[13]), or the cumulative energy of worshippers, or the power of the Goddess, I do not know.

We travel to Eleusis by bus along a highway built in part over the sacred road that celebrants once walked. The ruins of the ancient temple (which is little visited by tourists) lie at the apex of the heart-shaped Bay of Eleusis. To the side of the sacred way is a shallow cave, undoubtedly once known as the womb of the earth, but later said to be the opening through which Persephone descended to the underworld. The site appears desolate. The temple can barely be distinguished from the other ruins. Only those who know can imagine that this was once one of the most important ritual centers in all of Greece. A single phrase runs through my mind, "So much has been lost, so much has been destroyed." I find myself thinking how different our world might have been if we had known a religion that celebrated womanhood and our bonds with our mothers, our daughters. We come to Eleusis to remember that once there was a time when we were not despised, when we did not learn to despise ourselves. The desecration of the site makes us feel in our bodies the desecration of ourselves. A solemnity overtakes us as we try to imagine how much has been lost, how much we have lost.

Joining hands in a women's circle we meditate on our coming together as women, something that is not so easy to do in our culture. "We have come together as women to learn about our history and to create a community. And so it is appropriate that we come to this place, where the bonds of women with women, mother with daughter, daughter with mother, were celebrated. We come with a sense of new beginning, and we call on ancient Goddesses to give us strength."

We make an altar on the base of what was once one of the columns within the temple. We bring grain, seeds, fruits, and flowers. A beautiful pattern emerges as each woman places her offering on the altar. Someone brings honey and then everything is wet and glistening. We join hands again, this time around the altar we have created. We breathe deeply and draw the beauty, the nourishing power the earth has given and we have brought to the site, into ourselves. Then we reenact the story. Our telling, inspired by Charlene Spretnak,[14] rejects the rape of Persephone as a patriarchal addition. We speak of season and cycle, mother and daughter. As one of us tells the story, two move to the center of the circle and enact the drama.

"In the beginning Demeter give birth to a daughter and named her Persephone. For a time, mother and daughter were as one. The mother stroked her daughter's hair and told her many things. As they danced together plants and flowers sprang up. The cycle of the seasons is the dance of mother and daughter. For aeons the cycles continued in the same way. Then one day Persephone realized she was a woman and knew that she must find her own way. Day by day she wandered farther and farther from her mother, until one day she could not find her way back. She was frightened, but she knew she must continue. In her wanderings Persephone learned many things. She knew joy. She knew pain. One day she came to a chasm and heard the cries of the dead. Taking a torch she climbed slowly down. The moans of the dead ceased when they saw the light she had brought them. When Persephone did not return, Demeter was desolate. She mourned and she raged. She draped herself in a dark cape and she cried until she could cry no more. 'No life will come forth from me until my daughter returns,' she said. All the growing things on the face of the earth began to wither and die. 'No life will come forth from me,' she said."

Here at the place of the separation of mother and daughter, we begin to tell our own stories. Our stories of separation between mother and daughter. We speak of daughters taken away from their mothers by angry husbands. We speak of times when our mothers did not understand our lives. We speak of times when we did not understand our mothers. We speak of alcoholic mothers. We speak of daughters who made their mothers fear. We speak of loss. We speak of separation. We speak of anger. We cry. We cry together. We embrace one another. We embrace each other as mother and as daughter. The healing begins. Demeter and Persephone run to embrace each other. We speak of reunions. We speak of daughters who learned to appreciate their mothers. We speak of mothers who can name their daughter's strengths and celebrate. We speak of moments when we saw how alike we are. And of how we learned to appreciate our differences. We embrace each other again. We anoint each other with water. We offer fruit to each other. We join hands again and thank the powers of the place. We close the circle. Each woman takes one flower from the altar and leaves it in a special place on the site. We say that in so doing, "we consecrate the site for women's mysteries once again."

PERSEPHONE VISITS ALUM ROCK PARK

It is important that we celebrate the land in which we live, forging connections to her. Several years ago I came to know well a particular group of trails in Alum Rock Park in San Jose by walking them several times a week. I saw the grasses dry out, watched the ground rejoice with the rains as the creeks filled with rushing water, and celebrated first green shoots emerging. It seemed natural to have a spring ritual in this place where I had followed the daily changes of the seasons. Because it was spring, I also wanted to celebrate Persephone's return and honor the ancient bonds of mother and daughter.

We meet in the parking lot. When we have all arrived we put on our flower crowns and walk to the alum (sulphur) springs. In a bowl filled with healing water, we dip our fingers and repeat the self-blessing ritual. "Bless my eyes to see your ways. Bless my ears to hear your sweet sounds. Bless my nose to smell your essence. Bless my lips to speak of you. Bless my breasts formed in strength and beauty. Bless my sex without which we would not be. Bless my feet to walk in your paths. Bless me, Mama, for I am your child."[15]

Then we walk up the steep hillside in silence, meditating on the journey of Persephone up from the underworld and on the recent journey of the green plants up from under the soil. After about half an hour, we arrive at a resting point.

Each woman is guided, one at a time, to the center of an enormous California bay laurel. There she is asked to fold herself into a fetal position, to feel herself in the womb of the mother, to know herself nutured and protected in the womb of the earth. Each woman stays here as long as she wants. When she is ready to be born, we help her out of the tree, shouting, "It's a girl! It's a girl! Oh good, it's another girl!" Our faces are radiant as we emerge.

After we have all been born, we proceed up to the meadow at the top of the hill. Each woman picks one green sprig or flower, which for her symbolizes the rebirth of spring. Each finds a stone in the meadow and places it under the oak tree next to the stones we had left the year before. (When I had looked a few days earlier to see if the stones were still there, a green-and-yellow-striped snake had slithered out between the rocks.) We put our flowers and green shoots on the stones, and offer the food and juice we have brought.

We make a circle, part a few lingering clouds, raise the power, and reenact the myth. We speak of the union of mother and daughter. Of their dance of creation. Of Persephone's need to find her own way. Of Demeter's loss and how she sat on a stone and wept. And of their joyous reunion.

Then each of us takes her stone and holds it in her hands. We name the loss, the bitterness, the grief that has turned to stone within us. We speak of mothers, fathers, grandmothers who have died, lovers who left us, separations too painful to bear. We cry and share our sorrow.

We return our stones to the altar, pour water over them, saying that just as water wears away stone, so the stones within us can be worn away. Each of us gives the flower or green shoot she has brought to one of the others, making a wish. "I give you my strength." "I give you my laughter." "I give you my ability to clean up messes." And so on, until we have each received a piece of new growth and a wish. And then we feast.

Later we close the circle and make our way down the hill.

RETURN TO ELEUSIS

My initiation deepens each time I visit the sacred places. During one of the rituals at Eleusis, I express my desire to give birth to a daughter, and am profoundly challenged. Unexpectedly, Caroll, a Jungian analyst who has been deeply influenced by my work but whom I have just met, steps into the center of the circle, looks me in the eyes, and says, "I don't know whether or not you will ever have a physical daughter, but you have many spiritual daughters, and I don't think you're taking responsibility for them." I feel as if I have been addressed by Demeter. Over the next days, weeks, and months, I think about what she has said.

During the previous years I had been deeply depressed about my work. The community of feminist scholars in religion had fragmented after the initial bonding created by our critique of patriarchal religion. As we each chose our own paths, we became aware of our differences. We had not yet come to the place where we could see the commonalities beyond the differences. Most of my friends had decided to continue to work within established traditions to transform them. Some of my closest friends and most admired colleagues had expressed serious reservations about Goddess religion and spirituality rooted in nature. Male theologians sympathetic to feminism drew the line at the Goddess. I felt profoundly isolated. While I had expected criticism from male colleagues, I had not expected it from other feminists. I felt I could not continue to write in face of their criticism. I stopped writing.

As I think about what happened at Eleusis, I realize that I had allowed myself to succumb to the illusion that I was powerless.[16] I had discounted the many women who had drawn strength from my work. I had denied the power of my own experiences, the power I had drawn from the earth, from the Goddesses. Later that summer I wrote in my journal: "I chose to view myself as a victim. I need to recognize that I have made choices, that the experiences I have had and the thinking I have done are powerful. I must understand that if I challenge the traditions, I will meet opposition. I must recognize that my thinking is not only my thinking, that if it is true, it comes from a source much larger than myself. I have drawn from the well of women's wisdom, from the earth, from the power I call Goddess. I am only one voice among many. When we disagree it is not entirely personal. If what I write contains truth, it will be heard. All I can do is to be faithful to the piece of vision and truth that I know because I have experienced it deeply within myself. The rest is not up to me." Since that time I have claimed my power and begun to write more freely, more boldly, and in a way that is more clearly connected to the sources of my vision. I worry much less about what others think. I have gained, what Aloudres, the Haitian priestess who initiated my friend Karen Brown, promised her, "plenty confidence in myself."[17]

NOTES

1. Elie Wiesel, *The Gates of the Forest*, trans. Frances Frenaye (New York: Schocken Books, 1982), i–vi.
2. Christine Downing, *The Goddess: Mythological Representations of the Feminine* (New York: Crossroad, 1981), 3.
3. Lynn V. Andrews, *Flight of the Seventh Moon* (New York: Harper & Row, 1984), 52.
4. Aeschylus, *The Eumenides*, in *The Complete Greek Tragedies*, Vol. 1, ed. David Grene and Richmond Lattimore (Chicago: University of Chicago Press, 1959), 135.
5. See Thomas Dempsey, *The Delphic Oracle* (New York: Benjamin Bloom, 1972), 52–57; also, H.W. Parke and D.E.W. Wormell, *The Delphic Oracle*, Vol. 1 (Oxford: Basil Blackwell, 1956).
6. Joseph Fontenrose, *Python* (Berkeley and Los Angeles: University of California Press, 1959), 406–7.
7. Jean M. Auel, *Clan of the Cave Bear* (New York: Bantam Books, 1980).
8. Andrews, *Flight of the Seventh Moon*, 51–52.
9. Mary Barnard, trans., *Sappho: A New Translation* (Berkeley: University of California Press, 1958), no. 32.
10. *Sappho*, no. 37.
11. See George Mylonos, *Eleusis and the Eleusinian Mysteries* (Princeton: Princeton University Press, 1961), 41; Mircea Eliade, *A History of Religious Ideas*, Vol. 1, trans. Willard Trask (Chicago: University of Chicago Press, 1978), 290–301.
12. Mara Keller, "The Mysteries of Demeter and Persephone," unpublished; Sarah Pomeroy, *Goddesses, Whores, Wives, and Slaves* (New York: Schocken Books, 1975), 77–78.
13. Vincent Scully, *The Earth, the Temple, and the Gods*, rev. ed. (New Haven: Yale University Press, 1962).
14. Charlene Spretnak, *Lost Goddesses of Early Greece* (Boston: Beacon Press, 1978), 105–7.
15. See Zsuzsanna E. Budapest, "Self-Blessing Ritual," in *Womanspirit Rising*, ed. Carol P. Christ and Judith Plaskow (New York: Harper & Row, 1979), 269–2.
16. This was particularly ironic given that I had written about Margaret Atwood's phrase, "This above all, to refuse to be a victim. . .give up the old belief that I am powerless," and had even taken it as a personal motto; see *Diving Deep and Surfacing*, 49.
17. Karen Brown, " 'Plenty Confidence in Myself': The Initiation of a White Woman Scholar into Haitian Vodou," *Journal of Feminist Studies in Religion* 3, no. 1 (1987), 67–76.

III. THE MEANING OF THE JOURNEY

The Meaning of the Journey

Modern culture has little connection with the earth—or, rather, normally fails to perceive a connection with it. But for the Greeks the earth embodied divinity.

—VINCENT SCULLY

As I complete this book in Lesbos under the invisible cloud of radioactive fallout from Chernobyl, I no longer eat yogurt or feta made from contaminated sheep's milk. I listen as a black-clad Greek housewife shouts to an old farmer selling vegetables from his horse, *Ekei radienergia*? "Are they radioactive?" and wonder if my beloved gray-blue Aegean sea now contains the isotopes that will bring me death from cancer. How much radioactive uranium and plutonium has already leaked into the ground? How soon will it seep into the water, travel to the Black Sea, and then to the Aegean? The Voice of America and *The International Herald Tribune*, my two source of news, interpret the disaster through cold war rhetoric of Russian secrecy and treachery, refusing to acknowledge it as a clear warning that nuclear energy and nuclear bombs can only bring destruction to all we love and hold dear.

"Finitude, Death, and Reverence for Life" fulfills the intention I had when I wrote the essay that became "Why Women Need the Goddess." The original title of that essay was, "Why Women and Other Living Things Need the Goddess," an allusion to the motto of the International Women's League for Peace and Freedom, "War is harmful to children and other living things." For me Goddess has always been more than a symbol of female power. Goddess symbolizes my profound conviction that this earth, our source and ground, is holy. I have always known this. I will never know anything with stronger conviction.

To watch the sun set over the sea as the swallows fly in and out of their nests, to be surprised by four beautiful kittens and then to watch helplessly as the one who has fallen into a crevice cries itself to death, to work, to talk with friends, to eat and drink, to love and lose and love again. This is life. *Zoe einai allagi.* "Life is change." While we live, we will never know any other life.

For me it follows that there is no cause or ideal more precious than life itself. And that there can be no possible justification for nuclear bombs or nuclear power plants with the capacity to destroy all the life on this planet.

As we read the news of Chernobyl, my Greek friend Nena cries for her children, throws up her hands, and says, *Ti na kanome?* "What can we do? They're going to kill us all." I feel a similar futility. I do not want nuclear power plants and nuclear bombs. I have voted against them, I have worked against them. And yet they are still threatening our lives. When I try to understand how we got to the point where our species is threatening life, I can only think that scientists, business leaders, and politicians are not inspired by the same love for this finite and changing earth that my friend and I share. Perhaps they, like Plato, feel that our goal is somehow to transcend the uncertainty, the ordinariness of life and change. I feel deeply that the flight from finitude and death is at the root of the problems we face. It seems so simple: if we truly love this life which ends in death, then however could we destroy it? It must be that we do not love earth and life enough. Maybe something went wrong, massively wrong, when Platonism and Christianity became the dominant symbol systems of our culture. Maybe the return of the Goddess can help us to re-member ourselves, to re-member this earth, which is our home. Maybe she can help us to turn away from our quest for immortality, our quest to escape change, our quest to control the conditions of our lives. Perhaps she can help us to love a life that ends in death.

"Finitude, Death, and Reverence for Life" is about the deepest meaning, the *ethos* and the ethic, that emerges from my journey to the Goddess. But I do not speak her name in this essay, because the issues of which I speak here are too critical to our survival to be reserved for those who know her.

NOTE

Epigraph: Vincent Scully, *The Earth, the Temple, and the Gods,* rev. ed. (New Haven: Yale University Press, 1979), xi.

Cave at Eressos. Lesbos.

12. Finitude, Death and Reverence for Life

At any moment this earth and all who live upon it could be destroyed in nuclear war. I believe that one of the reasons we face nuclear destruction is the failure to acknowledge our own finitude and death and the potential finitude and death of the earth. Our religious and philosophical traditions since Plato have attempted to deny finitude and death and have prevented us from fully comprehending our connections to this earth. Feminist thinkers who challenge these traditions and provide alternatives have much to contribute to our survival.

Jonathan Schell defines the crisis we face in *The Fate of the Earth*: "We live, then, in a universe whose fundamental substance contains a supply of energy with which we can extinguish ourselves. . . . As for the destruction of all the life on the planet, it would be not merely a human, but a planetary end—the death of the earth." Not content with describing the problem, Schell also evokes our deep connection to earth and the life forms on it: "We not only live on the earth but also are of the earth, and the thought of its death, or even its mutilation, touches a deep chord in our nature."[1] I live daily with the knowledge Schell so eloquently expresses, that at any moment this earth that I love could cease to be. While I write, the sound barrier breaks overhead like the crashing of thunder on a sunny day. I rush to the window and look out: the sky is clear. I do not see the nuclear warheads streaking over San Francisco. The knowledge that we could destroy this earth weighs heavily on me. I can imagine the end of our way of life. (Indeed, insofar as the American way of life is patriarchy, racism, and war, I hope for its end.) I can imagine my own death and do not really fear it. I can even imagine that the time of the human species could end just as the time of the dinosaurs ended. (Even this thought is not entirely negative for me, when I think of how much greater a chance for survival the rest of the earth would have without us.) But it fills me with enormous pain and anger to think I am part of a species that may be responsible for the death of all life on earth.

I find it difficult to comprehend the fact that I share this earth with those who can calmly calculate the risks of nuclear war and find them acceptable. I wonder if these scientists and politicians feel part of this earth, or whether in their hearts they despise their bodies, their lives, their families and friends, their mortality.

I share with theologian Gordon Kaufman the conviction that "there is no question that the possibility of nuclear holocaust is the premier issue which our generation must address." I agree further with Kaufman that as interpreters of our religious heritage: "we must be prepared to enter into the most radical kind of deconstruction and reconstruction of the traditions we have inherited, including especially their most central and precious symbols."[2]

One of the ways our religious and philosophical systems have contributed to the threat of extinction is by cutting us off from nature and from fully experiencing and acknowledging limitation. I believe that our political leaders can think about fighting a nuclear war only because they don't really think they (and almost all other human beings and life forms) will die. They imagine a nuclear war to be "survivable" despite the evidence to the contrary. Most of us are probably familiar with the story told in Robert Scheer's book *With Enough Shovels*. Scheer reports that a government official told him the way to survive a nuclear war is to dig a hole, climb into it, and pull a door down over it. The absurdity of this scenario, reportedly taken from a Russian survival manual, should not blind us to the fact that all schemes to survive a nuclear war are just as absurd.[3]

Paradoxically, the denial of finitude and death may express an even more profound failure of our culture, the failure to affirm this life on this earth, in these bodies. The underside of the denial of death may be despair about the meaning of a life that ends in death. And thus the very politicians who assert that "we" will "survive" nuclear war may not really care whether we do or not.

It might be argued that the denial of death expresses an affirmation of life. But life bounded by mortality is the only life we know, the only life we can know. We must learn to love this life that ends in death. This is not absolutely to rule out the possibility of individual or communal survival after death, but to say that we ought not live our lives in light of such a possibility. Our task is here.

Feminist thinkers and thealogians have a great deal to say about our survival. In *Woman and Nature* Susan Griffin evokes that "deep chord" of connection we feel to the earth when she writes: "This earth is my sister; I love her daily grace, her silent daring, and how loved I am *how we admire this strength in each other, all that we have lost, all that we have suffered, all that we know: we are stunned by this beauty*, and I do not forget: what she is to me, what I am to her."[4]

Like Griffin I know "this earth is my sister" more deeply than I feel or know anything. My spirituality stems from my sense of connection to this earth, to its cycles of changing seasons, to ocean, rivers, mountains, trees, grasses, birds, deer, roses, daffodils, and to my grandparents, to my mother, my father, my family, my friends, my dog, and to all the others whose lives have been intertwined with mine on this earth.

I believe that the inability to reverence the earth has deep roots in our culture, going back at least to Plato, roots intimately bound up with the denial of finitude. The finite is defined as "having boundaries; limited; capable of being bounded, enclosed, or encompassed; being neither infinite nor infinitesimal; existing, persisting, for a limited time only; impermanent, transient."[5] This definition encompasses the major reason finitude has been denied in most of the philosophies and theologies influenced by Plato. For Plato that which is limited by time or space is imperfect. In *The Symposium* Plato wrote that our true home is not this finite, imperfect world. He described the journey of the soul from love of beautiful bodies, to love of beautiful souls, to love of beautiful laws and institutions, to love of science and knowledge, until finally, the soul ascends to the vision of the good described as:

> that wondrous vision which is the very soul of the beauty he has toiled so long for. It is an everlasting loveliness which neither comes nor goes, which neither flowers nor fades, for such beauty is the same on every hand, the same then as now, here as there, this way as that way, the same to every worshiper as it is to every other.

> Nor will his vision of the beautiful take the form of a face, or of hands, or of anything that is flesh. It will be neither words, nor knowledge, nor a something that exists in something else, such as a living creature, or the earth, or the heavens, or anything that is—but subsisting of itself and by itself in an eternal oneness, while every lovely thing partakes of it in such sort that, however much the parts may wax and wane, it will be neither more nor less, but still the same inviolable whole.[6]

For Plato "the Good" is not affected by time (it does not come into being or die) and it is not essentially affected by relationships (it is an inviolable whole). The vision of the Good as totally transcending finitude is fundamental to Platonic philosophy. Susan Griffin aptly characterizes the Platonic vision when she writes:

> It is decided that matter is transitory and illusory like the shadow on a wall cast by firelight; that we dwell in a cave, in the cave of our flesh, which is also matter, also illusory; it is decided that what is real is outside the cave, in a light brighter than we can imagine, that matter traps us in darkness. That the idea of matter existed before matter and is more perfect, ideal.[7]

Griffin alludes to Plato's *Republic* where it is alleged that just as the shadows on the wall of a cave are poor reflections of physical objects, so our physical bodies are poor reflections of eternal ideas or forms.

Since Plato, Western thinkers have shared a dualistic philosophy in which mind and body are perceived as separable, and in which the body and nature (because impermanent, finite) have been perceived as less than the mind and the realm of ideas (imagined to be eternal, infinite). The contrast between finite and infinite is at the heart of Platonic dualism. Change and dependence are considered impediments to the soul's journey. In Platonic thought it is asserted that "man" is not essentially finite, that "his" mind or soul partakes in the infinite. (Philosophers and theologians have never been certain that women have minds or souls with the same rational capacity as the minds of men.)

Much Christian theology is built on the denial of finitude and death. The Platonic vision of the Good as immaterial, unchanging, and essentially unrelated to any other entity became the philosophical basis for Christian theology's doctrine of God. In classical Christian theology, God is declared as totally or absolutely transcending creation, the earth, and all creatures in it. God's absolute transcendence becomes the basis for doctrines such as God's aseity or inability to be affected in his essential nature by what happens to creation, God's omnipotence or total power, God's omniscience or knowledge of everything. The doctrine of God's absolute transcendence, like Plato's notion of the Good, correlates with a theology in which this earth, this body, and this life are despised, and in which the spiritual goal is to transcend the flesh and its desires and to seek a life after death in which the limitations of finitude are overcome.

It is sometimes asserted that the incarnation, the doctrine of God's full presence in the body of Christ, is an affirmation of the body. That God entered into this life is said to be an affirmation of life, and that God died on the cross an acceptance of death. But at best the incarnation is a partial affirmation of finitude. The doctrine of the incarnation was developed by theologians influenced by Platonism, who believed that the finite and the infinite are essentially opposed. For them it was paradox or mystery that the divine could be fully present in human flesh. There is no paradox if the finite is understood to be the natural home of the spirit or the divine. Because they polarized the finite and the infinite, the church fathers could not fully affirm finitude.

Nor did they affirm death but rather asserted, "He is risen." Without addressing the complex theological disputes about the nature of the resurrection, let me state the obvious: the statement "he is risen" is a denial that death marks the end of individual life. The hopes of Christians throughout the centuries have been based upon the expectation of an individual life after physical death in which the limitations of finitude are overcome.

The Christian doctrine of original sin asserts that since the fall, since Adam and Eve, we no longer have the choice not to sin, or, as it is often put, "we cannot *not* sin." Whatever we do, this doctrine states, is tainted with evil. This doctrine imposes an infinite standard on our finite lives. We are made to feel guilty for being human and told to long for a salvation that will release us from bondage to the finite. According to traditional theology, "the wages of sin is death." Because Adam and Eve sinned, death has entered into the world as punishment, it is said. Instead of being understood as an ordinary and accepted part of life, death is set up as an enemy of life, as something to be feared and avoided. To understand death as punishment, I believe, is to misunderstand the nature of life. Death is implicit in life. The cycles of nature include birth, fruition, and decay. We all die so that others may live. This is neither punishment nor sacrifice. It is simply the way things are.

Asceticism, the practice of self-denial, is a reflection of the Christian denial of finitude. Extreme ascetics deny themselves food, sleep, sex, comfort, baths. The number of vermin falling from an ascetic's body was once said to be a way of determining his holiness.[8] Self-flagellation is often practiced. The theory behind asceticism is dualism. It is said that the body is at war with the soul, and that by denying the body, one frees the soul.

While extremes of asceticism are frowned upon in most circles today, celibacy is stilled required of Catholic priests and nuns. The ascetic attitude toward the body has been reaffirmed in Pope John Paul II's teachings on sexuality, marriage, and celibacy. While these teachings take a more positive attitude toward sex within marriage than some earlier pronouncements, they nonetheless affirm the traditional view that celibacy is a higher calling.[9] Though Protestantism abolished the celibate ideal, ascetic attitudes remain. Many Protestants are taught that pleasure is a sin and are urged to practice mental asceticism by constantly dwelling upon their imperfections.

Apocalypticism takes the denial of finitude and death a step further. The apocalyptic vision alleges that the whole finite world will come to an end but affirms that God will create a new order. The Gospel of Mark states the apocalyptic view, "There will be such a distress as until now has not been equalled since the beginning when God created the world, nor will there ever be again. . . . Heaven and earth will pass away, but my words will not pass away" (13:19, 31). The Book of Revelation likewise envisions the destruction of this earth. "Then I saw a new heaven and a new earth, and the first earth had disappeared, and now there was no longer any sea" (21:1). To envision destruction of this earth and its recreation by God is to imagine that the limitations of finitude and death can be transcended in a new creation. The new fundamentalist movement, which has had a great deal of influence on American politicans and policy makers, accepts the apocalyptic vision, explicitly tying the possibility or even inevitability of nuclear war to God's apocalyptic will.

Modern science added a new dimension to the denial of finitude. Prior to the creation of modern technology, ideas about transcending the body and nature were located in ascetic practices and visions of a world other than this one: heaven or a "new" creation. Modern science gave rise to the notion that the rational mind could overcome the limitations of the body and nature within this world.[10] Elizabeth Kübler-Ross reflected on the assumptions of her medical training when she wrote:

> We believed that we could transplant kidneys, then livers, then hearts, then brains. People would no longer die. We [could] deep freeze them in a deep freeze chamber and 50 years from now, we [could] defrost them when we [had discovered] a cancer cure and they [would] live happily ever after.

Kübler-Ross adds, "I am not making up stories."[11] Kübler-Ross believed and many doctors continue to believe that their powers to control the body are not finite, and that the body is not finite. (This is not to say that there should not be attempts to cure disease, only that there should be no illusion of triumph over death.)

The nuclear mentality is built on the denial of finitude. It is believed that humans can control forces far more powerful than themselves. Plutonium 239, one of the substances created in nuclear power plants and used in the making of nuclear bombs, is deadly even in small amounts. Its radioactivity could contaminate the earth for 500,000 years.[12] Even if all nuclear bombs were dismantled and all nuclear power plants were closed tomorrow, we would still have to find a way to safely store radioactive material for half a million years. Scientists assume that when the time comes other scientists will find a way to clean up the mess they have created. They deny that the time is now: today containers in which nuclear waste is being stored are leaking into the ground and into the ocean. Scientists fail to contemplate the possibility that there is not way to control a deadly substance for 500,00 years. They do not accept finitude—their own or that of the earth. The fragility of the ecosystem, the limitations of our minds and our power to control are denied. The very real possibility that the human race and most complex species of plants and animals would be destroyed in a nuclear war is not faced.

Politicians share this denial. The architects of nuclear policies imagine that nuclear war can be justified in order to preserve an abstraction called "our way of life." Robert Scheer asked the following question of Eugene Rostow, one of the architects of American nuclear policy: "Would it be fair to say that you feel that the dangers inherent in the arms race, the dangers of accidental war, the dangers brought about by more and more weapons piling up, are a less serious threat to peace than the danger of not controlling the Soviets and of having the Western alliance break up?" To this question Rostow answered, "That is absolutely correct." He acknowledged that the damage that would be brought about by a nuclear war would be "worse" than that caused by the two world wars, yet he stated that Soviet expansionism posed a greater threat.[13] Apparently he had deceived himself into believing that a nuclear war is different only in magnitude, not in kind, from World War II.

Louis O. Giuffrida, appointed by Ronald Reagan to run the Federal Management Agency said this to ABC News about the consequences of nuclear war: "It would be a terrible mess, but it wouldn't be unmanageable." He apparently expected to be around afterwards to clean up the "mess." Ronald Reagan told Scheer that nuclear war is survivable. "It would be a survival of some of your people and some of your facilities [so] that you could start again."[14] He evidently did not comprehend the significance of the fact that a single one megaton bomb is eighty times the size of the Hiroshima bomb and would gut or flatten an area the size of the city of New York, and that it is highly unlikely that only one bomb would be dropped. He apparently did not wish to know that any areas of the United States not immediately vaporized, exploded, or burned by nuclear bombs would be poisoned by radiation, that all the major hospitals would be destroyed. He apparently did not know that this earth is finite. Ronald Reagan has since declared that he believes that a nuclear war is not survivable, yet his policies continue to bring us ever closer to the brink of disaster.[15]

Caspar Weinberger's statement to Scheer was more frightening. In his conversation with Scheer about nuclear war, he admitted that he expects the world to come to an end. "I have read the Book of Revelation, and yes, I believe the world is going to end—by an act of God, I hope . . . I think time is running out, but I have faith." [16] Weinberger seems not to take seriously the threat to survival posed by nuclear war, since he believes God is planning to bring this world to an end in any case. According to Pacifica radio programmer Joe Cuomo, American President Ronald Reagan eleven times publicly declared or implied his belief in Armageddon, the destruction of the world by the will of God.[17]

These men have not allowed consciousness of the finitude of life on this earth to affect their thinking about nuclear policy. They do not understand or do not care that nuclear war is likely to mean the end of civilization, the end of humanity, the destruction of all but a few species of plants and animals. Jonathan Schell's vision of the survivors of a nuclear war as a "republic of insects and grasses"[18] seems to me to be a more realistic assessment of the consequences of nuclear war. According to Schell, the short- and long-term effects of nuclear war would probably mean the destruction of all the complex species of plants and animals. Yet those who are making the decisions about the life and death of our planet seem to believe that they are not finite and that human life and all life is not capable of being "bounded, enclosed, or encompassed." Most frightening are those who contemplate total destruction but imagine that such might be the will of God.

It is easy to dismiss these men as mad. Indeed, they seem to have lost touch with reality. But they are not aberrations within Western civilization. They are its products, and their visions of reality are considered sane within a culture founded on the denial of finitude and death, a culture that clings to ideas about life, to ideologies, rather than to life itself. I am not suggesting that Platonic dualism as represented in theology and philosophy is the sole cause of these views. But the cultural habit of denying finitude and death, which is deeply embedded in Western thought, makes it easier to deny that nuclear war could destroy almost all the life on this planet.

I believe the crisis of our times calls upon us to point out the roots of our peril in the denial of finitude and also to begin to depict a religious vision compatible with the preservation of this finite earth. We must envision a spirituality that acknowledges finitude and death and that encourages us to affirm rather than deny our connections with the earth. From the perspective of our religious heritage it might seem that such a spirituality is a contradiction in terms. What is spirituality, it might be said, if not an answer to questions we have about finitude and death? What is religion if not a call to deny our limitations, to strive for a "more perfect way"? The spirituality we need for our survival, I would argue, is precisely a spirituality encouraging us to recognize limitation and mortality, a spirituality calling us to celebrate all that is finite. There are many resources for such a religious vision. The indigenous traditions of Africa, Asia, America, and Europe all have much to teach us. Feminist thinking and spirituality also have much to say about the overcoming of the Platonic legacy.

Feminist thinkers remind us that our ideas about finitude, the body, and nature are very much bound up with our ideas about women. As Rosemary Ruether, Mary Daly, and others have shown, in Western philosophy and theology women are associated with the negative side of the Platonic dualisms, with the body, nature, and finitude, while males (and the male God) are associated with the mind, the spirit, and the infinite. The root of the equation of women with the body, nature, and finitude can be found in the fact that those doing the equating were men. Male theologians, philosophers, and scientists have viewed women's cycles of menstruation, pregnancy, childbirth, lactation, and menopause as manifestations of our carnal nature, while conveniently denying their own bodily processes (such as birth, aging, and death, not to mention the uncontrollability of the penis), which just as definitively mark them as carnal. Recognizing the damage that has been done to women by dualistic philosophies equating us with the despised body, some feminist thinkers have begun to question this way of thinking. We have asserted that women's rational and spiritual capacities are equal to men's. And some feminist thinkers have also begun to question the dualistic patterns of thinking that separate mind and body, spirit and nature, finite and infinite.

One of the thinkers who has questioned dualism in her writing is Adrienne Rich. In her book *Of Woman Born: Motherhood as Experience and Institution*, Rich is forced by her position as a thinker who is also a mother to question the dualistic patterns that equate women with the body. She chooses to affirm both her mind and its creative capacities *and* her body and its creative capacities as equally relevant to her task of understanding motherhood. She therefore acknowledges herself as an embodied female thinker. She cannot accept the denial of the body in the work of some feminist thinkers. She writes that she understands why "many intellectual and creative women" have "minimized their physicality" in their affirmation of women's rationality. But she urges feminist thinkers to move beyond dualism: "feminist vision has recoiled from female biology for [obvious] reasons; it will, I believe, come to view our physicality as a resource . . . We must touch the unity and resonance of our physicality, our bond with the natural order, the corporeal ground of our intelligence."[19] When Rich writes that we must learn to "think through the body" (and I assume she means all of us, not just women), she is fully aware that she is proposing a fundamental break from the dualisms of Western thought. She is saying that we must recognize that all thought is finite. Thus she is denying the Platonic view that the mind can separate itself from the body in order to perceive and participate in the unconditioned.

Susan Griffin is another feminist writer whose work challenges the underlying metaphysic of Western thought. In *Woman and Nature* Griffin documents "how man regards and makes use of woman and nature,"[20] showing how man has categorized both woman and nature as inferior to himself, as matter to be shaped and controlled by his mind and will. The central movement of Griffin's book occurs when woman strips off this false naming. When she recognizes that she is more than matter to be shaped by man's will, woman finds herself in a cave where she has a vision. Susan Griffin's vision in "The Cave" provides us with a model for a spirituality based on the acceptance of finitude and death, a clear alternative to Plato's vision. In her vision the ego is transcended, but the earth and the body are not. Socrates's vision as recorded by Plato is of the union of the soul with that which is unchanging, independent, and immaterial. Susan Griffin's vision is of the connection of the body and spirit to that which is changing, dependent, and material. Socrates wanted to transcend the body and nature; Susan Griffin experiences deeply her connection to body and nature. To Socrates the shadows on the wall of a cave are a metaphor for the illusory nature of material reality. In Griffin's vision the cave *is* nature speaking to woman:

the shape of this cave is a history telling us with each echo of the sound of each wave rushing against its sides: "I was not here before; my shape changes daily. I was sand. I was mountain. I was stone. I was water, I was shellfish and sea anemone and sea snail, I was fish, eel, urchin. I was plankton. I was seaweed and sea grass. Here I am black and polished and round, here I am yellow, here I am covered with moss, here I gleam with a purple reflection when the light lies across me, here I curve outward, here I sink back.

"When the water approaches me, the shape of the wave is changed. And when the tibe ebbs, you will see, I, too, have changed.[21]

The voice in this passage is the voice of the cave speaking to us, telling us that it changes daily, that it is constantly transforming. The cave is made of the bodies of sea animals and sea plants long ago returned to mineral form, transformed to sand, transformed to rock. The cave would not be cave without water flowing in, wearing the rock away. The cave tells us that all is ever changing, transforming. Change is its essence; it is not permanent, it is connected to everything. When I read Griffin's words, I recognize that the cave's voice is also my voice. *I* was not here before; *my* shape changes daily. *I* was sand. *I* was mountain. *I* was stone. *I* was water, *I* was shellfish . . . Here *I* am black and polished and round, here *I* am yellow . . . I come from earth, my body is made of water, minerals, plant, and animal life; one day my body will become food for other animals, my molecules will become something other than what they are today. Like the cave, I am not permanent, I am changing and continually changed, I am connected to everything.

Later Griffin expresses these thoughts more explicitly. "We know ourselves to be made from this earth. We know this earth is made from our bodies." She challenges the Platonic longing for permanence when she writes, "Everything moves, everything changes.[22] She bridges the gulf between "man" and "nature" when she insists:

We are nature. We are nature seeing nature. We are nature with a concept of nature. Nature weeping. Nature speaking of nature to nature.[23]

When she says "we are nature," Griffin challenges the classical legacy of a categorical distinction between the human mind and what is called nature, namely finite, embodied, impermanent reality. Griffin rejects religious and philosophical traditions that place "man" halfway between "angels" and "animals." When she says "we are nature," Griffin is not saying, as the romantics might say, that the human ego encompasses the whole. Her suggestion is much more humble. She is asking us to consider that we are as much a part of nature as are plants, stones, and other animals. Griffin acknowledges that we "see" nature (a capacity we share with most other animals), that we have a concept of nature (a capacity that may be uniquely human), and that we speak of nature. But she does not conclude that we are set apart from nature by virtue of having a concept of it. Rather, she insists that "we are nature." This statement sounds paradoxical to us because the idea that nature is one thing and we are another is deeply embedded in our thinking. Griffin is asking us to reconsider one of the fundamental and unquestioned assumptions of our thought. It would be a mistake to conclude that Griffin "reduces man to nature." In asserting that we are nature, Griffin asks us to accept our finitude and our temporality. Like the cave, we are changing and continually changed. We too are made from other creatures; one day our bodies will become food for other creatures, our molecules will become something other than what we are today. But Griffin does not deny our ability to perceive, to think, to conceptualize. Rather than reducing us to "brute" nature, Griffin asks us to expand our concept of nature to include all that we are. It is important to stress this point, for it is easy to misread feminist thinkers like Griffin as denying human capacities for self-reflection and our limited freedom to shape our relation to the earth. I believe rather that Griffin is calling us to redefine self-consciousness and limited freedom within rather than in opposition to our fundamental grounding in nature. Griffin has not yet provided us with a fully developed alternative metaphysical theory, but she has named a vision suggesting the directions toward its development.

In *Diving Deep and Surfacing* I discussed visions like Griffin's as examples of nature mysticism, and I named nature mysticism as one of the sources of women's spiritual vision. In so doing, I confronted the fact that nature mysticism (if it is discussed at all by theorists of mysticism) is denigrated as an inferior form of mysticism.[24] This is because nature mysticism has been defined as union with the finite world, while so-called "higher mysticism" has been defined as union with the infinite, that which utterly transcends the finite, sometimes called the Void, or God. I argued that nature mysticism is an important source of spiritual insight. Now I ask us to consider whether there is any reality "higher" than the finite, the earth, that which changes. I believe that we cannot know such a reality if it exists, and that it is destructive of the reality we do know to focus on an imagined reality superior to the finite, embodied reality we do know.

During the past summers, while visiting the cave at Eressos in Lesbos, I have had visions similar to Griffin's. I refer to the cave as "she" in the words that follow, because for me (as for Griffin) the cave resonated with my knowledge that caves once were known as the womb and birth canal of earth, her opening.

She appears to me while I am floating in the embrace of the azure sea, rising up from the water in the shape of an enormous vagina. I swim her mouth and climb over anemone and urchin covered rocks to her opening. I see that iron ore has stained her mottled granite and sandstone folds the color of blood. I am startled yet comforted by a strong smell of salt and fish within. Watching the water flow in and out of her, I feel drawn to her center. I climb up and lean back into the crevice. As my body relaxes, I feel a surge of energy, the life force flowing through me. My rhythms merge with hers, the shapes of the rock become the shapes of my body pulsating with energy, flowing into the sea. When I stand up I feel dizzy.

Near the cave is a tiny white church dedicated to the *Panaghia*, the Greek name for Mary, which means *All Holy*. I know the church is here because once people knew the cave to be All Holy. I am struck by the contrast between the enormous cave formed by the sea, changing with it, and the small church enclosed against the sea, constantly in need in repair. And I know which place for me is *All Holy*.

Though these visions come to us through women, they do not belong to women exclusively. They offer insights essential to us all, containing clues to a spirituality that can reawaken our sense of our connection to all living things, to the life force within us and without us. If we experience our connection to this finite and changing earth deeply, then we must find the thought of its destruction or mutiliation intolerable. When we know this finite changing earth as our true home and accept our own inevitable death, then we must know as well that spirituality is the celebration of our immersion in all that is and is changing. Then we will also know that there is no cause or ideology more precious than life itself. Such visions might undergird our survival. With every bone in my body, I pray, with Alice Walker, "Surely the earth can be saved for us."[25]

NOTES

1. Jonathan Schell, *The Fate of the Earth* (New York: Avon Books, 1982), 106, 7.
2. Gordon Kaufman, "Nuclear Eschatology and the Study of Religion," *Journal of the American Academy of Religion* 51, no. 1 (1983), 13.
3. Robert Scheer, *With Enough Shovels: Reagan, Bush, and Nuclear War* (New York: Random House, 1982), 18–19.
4. Susan Griffin, *Woman and Nature: The Roaring Inside Her* (New York: Harper & Row, 1978), 219.
5. *The American Heritage Dictionary of the English Language*, ed. William Morris (New York: American Heritage Publishing Company and Houghton Mifflin Company, 1973), 493.
6. *The Collected Dialogues of Plato Including the Letters*, ed. Edith Hamilton and Huntington Cairns (New York: Pantheon Books, 1966), 562.
7. Griffin, *Woman and Nature*, 5.
8. Mary Daly, *Pure Lust: Elemental Feminist Philosophy* (Boston: Beacon Press, 1984), 37.
9. See "Educational Guidance in Human Love," Vatican Congregation for Catholic Education," promulgated November 1, 1983, in *Origins* 13, no. 27 (December 15, 1983): 450-461.
10. See Caroyln Merchant, *The Death of Nature: Women, Ecology, and the Scientific Revolution* (San Francisco, Harper & Row, 1983).
11. Elizabeth Kübler-Ross, "Lighting Candles in the Darkness," *WomanSpirit* 8, no. 31 (1982): 46.
12. Helen Caldicott with Nancy Herrington and Nahum Stiskin, *Nuclear Madness: What You Can Do!* (Brookline, Mass.: Autumn Publishers, 1978), 67.
13. Scheer, *With Enough Shovels*, 210.
14. Ibid., 3, 241.
15. Ibid., 47.
16. Ibid., xi.
17. Joe Cuomo, "Ronald Reagan and the Prophecies of Armagedon," tape of a radio program broadcast on WBAI, the Pacifica station in New York City.
18. This is the title of the first chapter of Schell's *The Fate of the Earth*.
19. Adrienne Rich, *Of Woman Born: Motherhood as Experience and Institution* (New York: W.W. Norton, 1976), 39.
20. Griffin, *Woman and Nature*, 3.
21. Ibid., 160–1.
22. Ibid., 226, 224.
23. Ibid. 226.
24. Carol P. Christ, *Diving Deep and Surfacing: Women Writers on Spiritual Quest*, 2d ed. (Boston: Beacon Press, 1986) 20–23.
25. Alice Walker, *Horses Make a Landscape More Beautiful* (New York: Harcourt Brace Jovanovich, 1984), 79.

Bibliography

Ackelsberg, Martha. "Spirituality, Community, and Politics: B'not Esh and the Feminist Reconstruction of Judaism," *Journal of Feminist Studies in Religion* 2, no. 2 (1986), 109-120.

Ackroyd, Peter R. "Goddesses, Women, and Jezebel." In *Images of Women in Antiquity*, edited by Averil Cameron and Amelie Kuhrt, 245-259. Detroit: Wayne State University Press, 1983.

Alexiou, Stylanios. *Minoan Civilization*. Translated by Cressida Ridley. Heraclion: Spyros Alexiou Sons, n.d.

Allen, Paula Gunn. *The Sacred Hoop: Recovering the Feminine in American Indian Traditions*. Boston: Beacon, 1986.

Anderson, Bernard W. *Understanding the Old Testament*, 2d ed. Englewood Cliffs, NJ: Prentice Hall, 1966.

Andrews, Lynn V. *Medicine Woman*. San Francisco: Harper & Row, 1981.

———. *Flight of the Seventh Moon: The Teaching of the Shields*. San Francisco: Harper & Row, 1984.

———. *Jaguar Woman: And the Wisdom of the Butterfly Tree*. San Francisco: Harper & Row, 1985.

———. *Star Woman: We Are Made from Stars and to Stars We Must Return*. New York: Warner, 1986.

Auel, Jean M. *The Clan of the Cave Bear*. New York: Bantam, 1980.

Barstow, Anne L. "The Uses of Archaeology for Women's History: James Mellaart's Work on the Neolithic Goddess at Çatal Hüyük." *Feminist Studies* 4, no. 3 (October 1978): 7-18.

———. "The Prehistoric Goddess." In *The Book of the Goddess*, edited by Carl Olson, 5-28. New York: Crossroad, 1983.

———. *Joan of Arc: Heretic, Mystic, and Shaman*. Lewiston, NY: Edwin Mellen, 1986.

Barnard, Mary. *Sappho: A New Translation*. Berkeley and Los Angeles: University of California Press, 1958.

Baum, Gregory. *Is the New Testament Anti-Semitic?* Glen Rock, NJ: Paulist, 1965.

Beauvoir, Simone de. *The Second Sex*. Translated by H. M. Parshleys. New York: Knopf, 1953.

Brown, Karen McCarthy. " 'Plenty Confidence in Myself': The Initiation of an American Woman Scholar into Haitian Vodou." *Journal of Feminist Studies in Religion* 3, no. 1 (Spring 1987), 67–76.

Buber, Martin. *I and Thou*. Translated by Walter Kaufman. New York: Scribners, 1978.

———. *The Prophetic Faith*. Translated by Carlyle Witton-Davies. New York: Harper & Row, 1960.

Budapest, Zsuzsanna E. *The Holy Book of Women's Mysteries*. Vols. 1 and 2. Los Angeles: The Susan B. Anthony Coven No. 1, 1979, 1980.

Burkert, Walter. *Greek Religion*. Translated by John Raffan. Cambridge, MA: Harvard University Press, 1985.

Caldicott, Helen, with Nancy Herrington and Nahum Stiskin. *Nuclear Madness: What You Can Do!* Brookline, MA: Autumn Publishers, 1978.

Cameron, Anne. *Daughters of Copper Woman*. Vancouver, British Columbia: Press Gang Publishers, 1981.

Cameron, Averil and Amelie Kuhrt, eds. *Images of Women in Antiquity*. Detroit: Wayne State University Press, 1983.

Chicago, Judy. *Through the Flower: My Struggle as a Woman Artist*. Revised and updated. Garden City, NY: Doubleday, 1982.

———. *The Dinner Party: A Symbol of Our Heritage*. Garden City, NY: Doubleday, 1979.

Christ, Carol P. *Diving Deep and Surfacing: Women Writers on Spiritual Quest*. 2d ed. Boston: Beacon, 1986.

———. "Toward a Paradigm Shift in the Academy and Religious Studies." In *The Impact of Feminist Research in the Academy*, edited by Christie Farnham. Bloomington, IN: Indiana University Press, 1987.

Christ, Carol P. and Judith Plaskow, eds. *WomanSpirit Rising: A Feminist Reader on Religion*. San Francisco: Harper & Row, 1979.

Christian, Barbara. *Black Feminist Criticism*. New York: Pergamon Press, 1985.

Crites, Stephen. "The Narrative Quality of Experience." *Journal of the American Academy of Religion* 39, no. 3 (1971): 291-311.

Dahlberg, Frances, ed. *Woman the Gatherer*. New Haven, CT: Yale University Press, 1981.

Daly, Mary. *Beyond God the Father: Toward a Philosophy of Women's Liberation*. Boston: Beacon, 1973.

———. *Gyn/Ecology: The Metaethics of Radical Feminism*. Boston: Beacon, 1978.

———. *Pure Lust: Elemental Feminist Philosophy*. Boston: Beacon, 1984.

Daum, Annette. "Blaming Jews for the Death of the Goddess." *Lilith* 7 (1980): 12-13.

Daum, Annette, and Judith Plaskow. "Feminists and Faith: A Discussion with Judith Plaskow and Annette Daum." *Lilith* 7 (1980): 14-17.

Dempsey, Thomas. *The Delphic Oracle: Its Early History, Influence, and Fall*. New York: Benjamin Bloom, 1972. Originally published in 1918.

Dinnerstein, Dorothy. *The Mermaid and the Minotaur: Sexual Arrangements and Human Malaise*. New York: Harper & Row, 1977.

Downing, Christine. *The Goddess: Mythological Representations of the Feminine*. New York: Crossroad, 1984.

Downing, Marymay. "Prehistoric Goddesses: The Cretan Challenge." *Journal of Feminist Studies in Religion* 1, no. 1 (Spring 1985): 5-22.

duBois, Page. "Sappho and Helen." In *Women in Antiquity: The Arethusa Papers*, edited by John Peradotto and J. P. Sullivan, 95-105. Albany, NY: State University of New York Press, 1984.

Ehrenreich, Barbara, and Dierdre English. *Witches, Nurses, and Midwives: A History of Women Healers*. 2d ed. Old Westbury, NY: The Feminist Press, 1973.

Eliade, Mircea. *A History of Religious Ideas*. Vols. 1 and 2. Translated by Willard R. Trask. Chicago: University of Chicago Press, 1978, 1982.

———. "Some Observations of European Witchcraft." *History of Religions*, 14, no. 3 (February 1975).

Evans-White, Hugh G., trans. *Hesiod: The Homeric Hymns and Homerica*. Cambridge, MA: Harvard University Press, 1914.

"Excerpts from the Vatican's Declaration Affirming the Prohibition on Women Priests," *New York Times* January 28, 1977, 8.

Fasteau, Marc Feigan. *The Male Machine*. New York: McGraw-Hill, 1974.

Foley, Helene P., ed. *Reflections of Women in Antiquity*. New York: Gordon and Breach, 1981.

Fontenrose, Joseph. *Python: A Study of the Delphic Myth and Its Origins*. Berkeley and Los Angeles: University of California Press, 1959.

Frazier, R. M., trans. *The Poems of Hesiod*. Norman, OK: University of Oklahoma Press, 1983.

Friedrich, Paul. *The Meaning of Aphrodite*. Chicago, IL: University of Chicago Press, 1978.

Geertz, Clifford. *The Interpretation of Cultures: Selected Essays*. New York: Basic Books, 1973.

Gimbutas, Marija. *The Goddesses and Gods of Old Europe, 6500-3500 B.C.: Myths, Legends, and Cult Images*. New and updated edition. Berkeley and Los Angeles: University of California Press, 1982. Originally published as *The Gods and Goddesses of Old Europe* in 1974.

———. "Vulvas, Breasts, and Buttocks of the Goddess Creatress: Commentary on the Origins of Art," *The Creative Woman Quarterly* 6, no. 4 (Fall 1983): 8-11.

———. "Women and Politics in Goddess-Oriented Old Europe." In *The Politics of Women's Spirituality*, ed. by Charlene Spretnak, 22-31. Garden City, NY: Anchor Books, 1982.

Gilligan, Carol. *In a Different Voice: Psychological Theory and Women's Development*. Cambridge, MA: Harvard University Press, 1982.

Goldenberg, Naomi R. *Changing of the Gods: Feminism and the End of Traditional Religions*. Boston: Beacon, 1979.

———. "Archetypal Theory and the Separation of Mind and Body: Reason Enough to Return to Freud?" *Journal of Feminist Studies in Religion* 7, no. 1 (1985), 55-72.

———. "Resurrecting the Body: An Agenda for Feminist Theory." In *Women and Men: Interdisciplinary Readings on Gender*, ed. by Greta Hofmann Nemiroff. Tononto: Fitzhenry & Whiteside, 1987.

———. "The Return of the Goddess—Psychological Reflections on the Shift from Theology to Thealogy." *Sciences Religieuses / Studies in Religion* (June 1987).

Grene, David and Richmond Lattimore, eds. *The Complete Greek Tragedies*. Vol. 1. Chicago: University of Chicago Press, 1959.

Griffin, Susan. *Woman and Nature: The Roaring Inside Her*. New York: Harper & Row, 1978.

Grigson, Geoffrey. *The Goddess of Love: The Birth, Triumph, Death, and Return of Aphrodite*. London: Constable, 1976.

Gross, Rita. "Menstruation and Childbirth as Ritual and Religious Experience in the Religion of the Australian Aborigines." *Journal of the American Academy of Religion* 45, no. 4 (1977): 1147-1181.

———. "Female God Language in a Jewish Context." In *Womanspirit Rising*, edited by Carol P. Christ and Judith Plaskow, 167-173. San Francisco: Harper & Row, 1979.

———. "Hindu Female Deities as a Resource for the Contemporary Rediscovery of the Goddess." *Journal of the American Academy of Religion* 46, no. 3 (1978): 269-291. Reprinted in shorter form as "The Second Coming of the Goddess." *Anima* 6, no. 1 (Fall 1979): 48-59.

Hamilton, Edith and Huntington Cairns, eds. *The Collected Dialogues of Plato*. New York: Bollingen Series LXXI, Pantheon, 1966.

Harrison, Jane Ellen. *Prolegomena to the Study of Greek Religion*. London: Merlin Press, 1962. Originally published in 1903.

———. *Epilogomena and Themis*. New Hyde Park, NY: University Books, 1962. Originally published as separate volumes in 1921 and 1912.

———. *Mythology*. New York: Harcourt Brace, 1963. Originally published in 1924.

Hawkes, Jacquetta. *Dawn of the Gods*. New York: Random House, 1968.

Harding, M. Esther. *Women's Mysteries: Ancient and Modern*. New York: Putnam, 1971. Originally published in 1935.

Heschel, Susannah, ed. *On Being a Jewish Feminist: A Reader*. New York: Schocken, 1983.

Iglehart, Hallie Austen. *Womanspirit: A Guide to Women's Wisdom*. San Francisco: Harper & Row, 1983.

Iglehart, Hallie Austen [Mountainwing] and Barbry MyOwn. "A Ritual Celebration." *WomanSpirit* 2, no. 5 (Fall 1975). Reprinted as "Ursa Maior: Menstrual Moon Celebration." In *Moon, Moon*, edited by Anne Kent Rush, 374-87. Berkeley: Moon Books and Random House, 1976.

An Inclusive Language Lectionary: Readings for Year A. Atlanta, New York, Philadelphia: The Cooperative Publishing Association, 1983.

James, E. O. *The Cult of the Mother Goddess: An Archaeological and Documentary Study*. New York: Frederick A. Prager, 1959.

———. *The Ancient Gods: The History and Diffusion of Religion in the Ancient Near East and the Eastern Mediterranean*. New York: Putnam, 1960.

Jung, Carl G. *Psychological Reflections: An Anthology of the Writings of C. G. Jung*. Edited by Jolande Jacobi. New York: Pantheon, 1953.

Kalven, Janet and Mary I. Buckley. *Women's Spirit Bonding*. New York: Pilgrim Press, 1984.

Kanta, Katherine G. *Eleusis: Myth, Mysteries, History, Museum*. Translated by W. W. Phelps. Athens: n.p., 1979.

Kaufman, Gordon. "Nuclear Eschatology and the Study of Religion," *Journal of American Academy of Religion* 51 no. 1 1983: 3-14.

Keller, Mara. "The Mysteries of Demeter and Persephone: Fertility & Birth, Sexuality & Marriage, Death & Rebirth." Paper presented at the 1985 meetings of the American Academy of Religion.

King, Helen. "Bound to Bleed: Artemis and Greek Women." In *Images of Women in Antiquity*, edited by Averil Cameron and Amelie Kuhrt, 109-127. Detroit: Wayne State University Press, 1983.

Kramer, Samuel Noah. *The Sumerians: Their History, Culture, and Character.* Chicago: University of Chicago Press, 1963.

Kramer, Samuel Noah, and Diane Wolkstein. *Inanna, Queen of Heaven and Earth: Her Stories and Hymns from Sumer.* New York: Harper & Row, 1983.

Kübler-Ross, Elizabeth. "Lighting Candles in the Darkness." *Woman-Spirit* 8, no. 31 (Spring 1982).

Janowitz, Naomi and Maggie Wenig. "Sabbath Prayers for Women." In *Womanspirit Rising*, edited by Carol P. Christ and Judith Plaskow, 174-178. San Francisco: Harper & Row, 1979.

Langer, Suzanne. *Feeling and Form.* New York: Scribner, 1953.

Lerner, Gerda. *The Creation of Patriarchy.* New York: Oxford University Press, 1986.

Levy, G. Rachel. *Religious Conceptions of the Stone Age: And Their Influence on European Thought.* New York: Harper & Row, 1963. Originally published as *The Gate of Horn.* London: Faber & Faber, 1948.

Litwoman, Jane. "Woman Identified Judaism." *WomanSpirit* 8, no. 29 (1981).

Lorde, Audre. *Sister Outsider: Essays and Speeches.* Trumansburg, NY: The Crossing Press, 1984.

McFague, Sallie. *Models of God: Theology for an Ecological, Nuclear Age.* Philadelphia: Fortress Press, 1987.

———. *Metaphorical Theology: Models of God in Religious Language.* Philadelphia: Fortress Press, 1982.

Mellaart, James. *Çatal Hüyük.* New York: McGraw-Hill, 1967.

———. *Earliest Civilizations of the Near East.* New York: McGraw-Hill, 1965.

Merchant, Carolyn. *The Death of Nature: Women, Ecology, and the Scientific Revolution.* San Francisco: Harper & Row, 1980.

Morton, Nelle. *The Journey Is Home.* Boston: Beacon, 1985.

Miles, Margaret R. *Image as Insight: Visual Understanding in Western Christianity and Secular Culture.* Boston: Beacon, 1985.

———. "The Virgin's One Bare Breast: Female Nudity and Religious Meaning in Tuscan Early Renaissance Culture." In *The Female Body in Western Culture*, edited by Susan Suleiman, 193-208. Cambridge: Harvard University Press, 1986.

Murray, Margaret. *The Witch-Cult in Western Europe: A Study in Anthropology.* Oxford: Clarendon Press, 1967. Originally published in 1921.

Mylonos, George. *Eleusis and the Eleusinian Mysteries.* Princeton: Princeton University Press, 1961.

Nelson, Mary. "Why Witches Were Women." In *Women: A Feminist Perspective*, edited by Jo Freeman. Palo Alto, CA: Mayfield Publishing Company, 1975.

Neumann, Erich. *The Great Mother: The History of an Archetype.* Translated by Ralph Manheim. Princeton: Princeton University Press, 1955.

Olson, Carl, ed. *The Book of the Goddess: Past and Present.* New York: Crossroad, 1983.

Pagels, Elaine. *The Gnostic Gospels.* New York: Random House, 1979.

———. "What Became of God the Mother? Conflicting Images of God in Early Christianity." In *Signs* 2, no. 2 (Winter 1976): 293-303.

Papathanassopoulos, Yorgos. *Neolithic and Cycladic Civilizations.* Athens: Melissa Publishing House, n.d.

Parke, H. W. and D. E. W. Wormell. *The Delphic Oracle.* Vol. 1. Oxford: Basil Blackwell, 1956.

Patai, Raphael. *The Hebrew Goddess.* New York: KTAV, 1967.

Peradotto, John and J. P. Sullivan, eds. *Women in the Ancient World: The Arethusa Papers.* Albany, NY: State University of New York Press, 1984.

Phillips, J. A. *Eve: The History of an Idea.* San Francisco: Harper & Row, 1984.

Plaskow, Judith. *Sex, Sin, and Grace: Women's Experience and the Theologies of Reinhold Niebuhr and Paul Tillich.* Washington, D.C.: The University Press of America, 1980.

———. "Christian Feminism and Anti-Judaism." *Cross Currents* 28 (1978): 306-309. Reprinted as "Blaming Jews for Inventing Patriarchy." *Lilith* 7 (1980), pp. 12-13.

———. "Language, God, and Liturgy." *Response* 44 (Spring 1983): 3-14.

———. "The Right Question Is Theological." In *On Being a Jewish Feminist,* edited by Susannah Heschel, 221-233. New York: Schocken, 1983.

———. "Standing Again at Sinai: Jewish Memory from a Feminist Perspective. *Tikkun,* 1, no. 2 (1986): 28-34.

Plaskow, Judith, and Joan Arnold Romero, eds. *Women and Religion.* Rev. ed. Missoula, MT: Scholars' Press, 1974.

Pomeroy, Sarah B. *Goddesses, Whores, Wives, and Slaves: Women in Classical Antiquity.* New York: Schocken, 1976.

———. "Selected Bibliography on Women in Classical Antiquity." In *Women in the Ancient World,* edited by John Peradotto and J. P. Sullivan. Albany, NY: State University of New York Press, 1984.

Preston, James, ed. *Mother Worship: Theme and Variations.* Chapel Hill, NC: University of North Carolina Press, 1982.

Rich, Adrienne. *Diving into the Wreck.* New York: Norton, 1973.

———. *Of Woman Born: Motherhood as Experience and Institution.* New York: Norton, 1976.

———. *The Dream of a Common Language: Poems, 1974-77.* New York: Norton, 1978.

Rohrlich, Ruby [Leavitt]. "Women in Transition: Crete and Sumer." In *Becoming Visible: Women in European History,* edited by Renate Bridenthal and Claudia Koonz, 36-59. Boston, MA: Houghton Mifflin, 1977.

———. "State Formation in Sumer and the Subjugation of Women." *Feminist Studies* 6, no. 1 (1980): 76-102.

Rubenstein, Richard. *After Auschwitz*. New York: Bobbs-Merrill, 1966.

Ruether, Rosemary Radford. *Liberation Theology*. New York: Paulist, 1972.

———. *Faith and Fratricide: The Theological Roots of Anti-Semitism*. New York: Seabury Press, 1974.

———. *New Woman/New Earth: Sexist Ideologies and Human Liberation*. New York: Seabury, 1975.

———. *Sexism and God-Talk: Toward a Feminist Theology*. Boston: Beacon, 1983.

———. *Woman-Church: Theology and Practice*. San Francisco: Harper & Row, 1985.

———. *Womanguides: Readings Toward a Feminine Theology*. Boston: Beacon, 1985.

Ruether, Rosemary Radford, ed. *Religion and Sexism: Images of Women in the Jewish and Christian Traditions*. New York: Simon & Schuster, 1974.

Saiving, Valerie. "The Human Situation: A Feminine View." *Journal of Religion* 40 (April 1960): 100-112. Reprinted in *Womanspirit Rising*, edited by Carol P. Christ and Judith Plaskow, 25-42. San Francisco: Harper & Row, 1979.

———. "Androcentrism in Religious Studies," *Journal of Religion* (April 1976): 177-96.

Sanday, Peggy Reeves. *Female Power and Male Dominance: On the Origins of Sexual Inequality*. Cambridge: Cambridge University Press, 1981.

Sargent, Thelma, trans. *The Homeric Hymns*. New York: Norton, 1973.

Saunders, James. *Torah and Canon*. Philadelphia, PA: Fortress Press, 1974.

Scheer, Robert. *With Enough Shovels: Reagan, Bush, and Nuclear War*. New York: Random House, 1982.

Schell, Jonathan. *The Fate of the Earth*. New York: Avon Books, 1982.

Scholem, Gershom. *Major Trends in Jewish Mysticism*. New York: Schocken, 1969.

Schüssler Fiorenza, Elisabeth. *In Memory of Her: A Feminist Theological Reconstruction of Christian Origins*. New York: Crossroad, 1983.

———. *Bread, Not Stone: The Challenge of Feminist Biblical Interpretation*. Boston: Beacon, 1985.

Scully, Vincent. *The Earth, the Temple, and the Gods: Greek Sacred Architecture*. Rev. ed. New Haven: Yale University Press, 1979.

Shange, Ntosake. *for colored girls who have considered suicide when the rainbow is enuf*. New York: Macmillan, 1976.

Smith, Morton. *Palestinian Parties and Politics which Shaped the Old Testament*. New York: Columbia University Press, 1971.

Spretnak, Charlene. *Lost Goddesses of Early Greece: A Collection of Prehellenic Myths*. Boston: Beacon, 1984. Originally published in 1978.

———. *The Politics of Women's Spirituality: Essays on the Rise of Spiritual Power Within the Feminist Movement*. New York: Doubleday, 1982.

Spretnak, Charlene, and Fritjof Capra. *Green Politics: The Global Promise*. New York: Dutton, 1984.

Starhawk. *The Spiral Dance: A Rebirth of the Ancient Religion of the Great*

Goddess. San Francisco: Harper & Row, 1979.
———. *Dreaming the Dark: Magic, Sex, and Politics*. Boston: Beacon, 1982.
Stele Steigers, Eve. "Sappho's Private World." In *Reflections of Women in Antiquity*, edited by Helen P. Foley, 45-61. New York: Gordon and Breach Science Publishers, 1981.
Stone, Merlin. *When God Was a Woman*. New York: Dial Press, 1976.
Teish, Luisah. *Jambalaya: The Natural Woman's Book of Personal Charms and Practical Rituals*. San Francisco: Harper & Row, 1985.
Teuval, Sabina J. *Sarah the Priestess: The First Matriarch of Genesis*. Athens, OH: Swallow Press, 1984.
Thistlewaite, Susan. *Metaphors for the Contemporary Church*. New York: Pilgrim Press, 1983.
———. "Opening the Mail that Did Not Tick." *Review of Books in Religion*. 12, no. 2 (May 1984): 6-8.
———. "Every Two Minutes: Battered Women and Feminist Interpretation." In *Feminist Interpretation of the Bible*, edited by Letty M. Russell, 96-107. Philadelphia: Westminster Press, 1985.
Tillich, Paul. *The Dynamics of Faith*. New York: Harper & Row, 1957.
Trible, Phyllis. *God and the Rhetoric of Sexuality*. Philadelphia: Fortress Press, 1978.
———. *Texts of Terror: Literary-Feminist Readings of Biblical Narratives*. Philadelphia: Fortress Press, 1984.
Umansky, Ellen. "(Re)Imaging the Divine." *Response* 41-42 (Fall-Winter 1982): 110-119.
———. "Creating a Jewish Feminist Theology: Possibilities and Problems." *Anima* 10, no. 2 (Spring 1984): 125-135.
Walker, Alice. *Horses Make a Landscape Look More Beautiful: Poems*. New York: Harcourt Brace Jovanovich, 1984.
———. *In Search of Our Mothers' Gardens: Womanist Prose*. New York: Harcourt Brace Jovanovich, 1983.
———. *The Color Purple*. New York: Harcourt Brace Jovanovich, 1982.
Warner, Marina. *Alone of All Her Sex: The Myth and Cult of the Virgin Mary*. New York: Knopf, 1976.
Weil, Simone. *The Iliad of the Poem of Force*. Translated by Mary McCarthy. Wallingford, PA: Pendle Hill, 1956.
Wiesel, Elie. *Night*. Translated by Stella Rodway. New York: Hill & Wang, 1960.
———. *The Town beyond the Wall*. Translated by Stephen Becker. New York: Avon Books, 1969.
———. *The Gates of the Forest*. Translated by Frances Frenaye. New York: Schocken, 1982.

Index